THE
LEEDS
BOOK
OF
DAYS

MARGARET DRINKALL

First published 2013

The History Press
The Mill, Brimscombe Port
Stroud, Gloucestershire, GL5 2QG
www.thehistorypress.co.uk

© Margaret Drinkall, 2013

The right of Margaret Drinkall to be identified as the Author
of this work has been asserted in accordance with the
Copyrights, Designs and Patents Act 1988.

British Library Cataloguing in Publication Data.
A catalogue record for this book is available from the British Library.

ISBN 978 0 7524 7962 0

Typesetting and origination by The History Press
Printed in India

January 1st

1870: On this date, the *Leeds Express* carried a report of an entertainment for the inmates of the Leeds workhouse and Industrial School, which was held on Thursday December 29th last. The report stated that: 'Through the kindness of Councillor and Mrs Whiting, the dining hall of the workhouse was filled with about 400 adults and 300 children. After a magnificent meal of roast beef and plum pudding, the son of Mr Whiting made his appearance in the guise of a veritable Father Christmas. Under his genial influence, three well imitated snow balls of immense size were transformed into baskets laden with toys for the children. This was a pleasing surprise to the young people of the workhouse and industrial school, every one of whom obtained a gift from so unexpected a source. The drum and fife band of the school performed a number of airs during the evening, which were very pleasing. Several members of the Leeds Board of Guardians including Mr Middleton (the chairman), Mr Ingram (the vice chair), Mr W.H. Conyers and others, were also present at the festivities. Mr Middleton gave thanks to Councillor and Mrs Whiting and to the master and matron of the workhouse, for their efforts in providing such a welcome treat'. (*Leeds Express*)

JANUARY 2ND

1872: The *Leeds Mercury* reported on an exhibition, by Mr Hardy Gillard, at the Leeds Music Hall. The show contained a panorama of the United States, on which the *Mercury* wrote, 'It differs greatly from similar entertainments as the object is of an educational character and the display is so well arranged and so new and faithful in details, that it is highly interesting as well as instructive. It opens the country from New York to the Golden Gate, taking the track of the Trans-Continental Railroad. In a series of carefully painted views, the spectator has placed before him a tolerably vivid view of the many topographical features of the country and of its industrial resources.' The report agrees with the descriptions furnished in such works as Mr Rae's *Westward by Rail* and the displays are 'supplemented, not only by a judicious lecture, but with a bird's eye view of the whole journey. The view itself measures 40ft by 8ft and supplies at a glance a splendid geographical representation of the country and of its railroads'. Mr Gillard stated that the performance would continue for the following two weeks before the panorama continued on at Wakefield. *(Leeds Mercury)*

JANUARY 3RD

1855: A short distance from Leeds Central Station, a serious accident occurred involving a Great Northern Railway train. A passenger carriage was thrown from a viaduct where it landed, 27ft below, onto a goods wagon. The accident was caused by some irregularities on the points, which threw the forward part of the train off the line. It was recorded that Robert Hall Esq., the Recorder of Doncaster and Deputy Recorder of Leeds, sustained serious injuries of the most extensive and dangerous nature. At the same time other passengers were injured, though, incredibly, not seriously. The carriage in which Mr Hall was seated was, unfortunately, the one which had been thrown over the viaduct. The carriage itself had been a complete wreck – the roof, sides, and ends being broken into splinters, and scattered in all directions, Mr Hall's injuries included a wound to the scalp, and severe bruising of the head. He also sustained fractures to the right arm, right thigh, left leg, and left forearm. The doctor who treated Mr Hall stated that 'he was lucky to have survived the accident'. At the York Assizes on July 21st, Mr Hall recovered £4,500 damages from the company. (*Leeds Times*)

JANUARY 4TH

1872: Printed in *Fraser's Magazine* was a criticism of a person at the Leeds parish church. An unnamed character, who regularly reported on his travels, stated that 'There is little time today to do more than hasten through crowded streets to see the outside of the parish church. I found the outer door open and penetrating into a vestry, where a very churlish person was turning over some music. A little door beyond him entered the church; and half a minute would have sufficed for him to open it and afford a glimpse of the interior. But the churlish person, in answer to a civil request, stated that it was not his business to show the church; and then went on turning over his music. On asked whether he was forbidden to show the church, he sulkily replied "yes". Of course there was nothing to do but retreat. If the statement was true, which I am bound to believe, the authorities of the parish church at Leeds may be esteemed as what some people call "a caution". Urging the authorities of the church to "deal" with this rogue summarily, in order that a better welcome is afforded to the traveller'. (*Fraser's Magazine*)

JANUARY 5TH

1870: It was reported in the *Leeds Mercury*, that the teachers of the Baptist Sunday School on York Road had invited the school's old scholars to tea: 'Upwards of 600 persons from the town and surrounding villages responded to the invitation. The schoolroom was specially decorated for the occasion, having in the centre a banner which stated in large characters:

A HEARTY WELCOME TO OLD SCHOLARS

After tea, half an hour was allowed for conversation and the shaking of hands, which was seen to be "long and continuous". Old faces that had not seen each other for fifteen, and in some cases upwards of twenty years, were brought together all around the room. There were even a few present who had been admitted as scholars the first morning the school was opened in 1843. After several speeches, Mr John Purchon, one of the founders of the school and one of the first superintendents, gave a few kind words of advice. He stated that "he was delighted to see some of his old pupils; and urged them always to remember the teachings of the school". This brought the meeting, one of the most interesting and longest to be remembered in the school room, to a close'. (*Leeds Mercury*)

JANUARY 6TH

1850: A man named Charles Culley and three young girls who had stolen for him, were brought into court. A custom house official stated that as he was walking down Duncan Street, he saw the three female prisoners standing in a court. One had a bundle under her arm, but on seeing him, dropped it and ran away, along with the other two girls. The bundle was found to contain eleven woollen mufflers which had been stolen. A detective found the girls in Culley's house on Hudson Street, and when the house was searched, other stolen goods were found. The oldest girl told him that the old man encouraged them to steal and to bring the goods to him in order to sell them on. One of the girls was only eight years of age yet, despite her young age, had been before the bench on seven different occasions and discharged because of her extreme youth. Her aunt, and a father of one of the other girls, told the court that the children were harboured in Culley's house and they could not be kept at home. The magistrate remarked that they were, no doubt, under the training of the old fellow and decided that the best thing to do was to send the whole of them to trial. (*Leeds Mercury*)

January 7th

1866: A fatal accident occurred at the building site of the new infirmary, Leeds, which was, at the time, in the process of being erected. Six men were engaged in turning two arches in the portion of the building known as the Angle Tower, which was situated at the south-west corner. Three labourers arrived at the top almost simultaneously, and threw their loads of bricks heavily on to one of the centrepieces – it unexpectedly gave way, and threw four of the men to the bottom, a distance of about 20ft. The four men were found to be so severely injured that they were transported, at once, to the old infirmary, where they were promptly attended to by the surgeon, Mr Dale. One of the men, Bartholomew McGrail, was found to have received an acute fracture to the skull and was in the most dangerous condition. Another man named Peter Dean, had an abrasion on his chest and a broken leg. The third injured party, William Greetham, had received a scalp wound and contusions to various parts of his body. The fourth man, John Jackson, was treated for minor injuries and was able to return home. (*Leeds Mercury*)

JANUARY 8TH

1854: The family of Mr Longbottom of Hunslet were involved in a most extraordinary and mysterious occurrence. It appears that Longbottom's son, Thomas, had married on the previous Christmas Day. On the night of January 7th, the newlywed couple retired to bed about eleven o'clock, apparently on most friendly terms. The next morning, about seven o'clock, looking out of his window Mr Longbottom saw his daughter-in-law laid on the stone landing outside of the house, in a state of insensibility and in her nightdress, evidently having fallen from the chamber window which had been open. A search then began for the son, who was ultimately found drowned in the River Aire; also in his nightdress. When the wife had recovered sufficiently to give evidence before the coroner's jury, she stated that she could not remember how the accident had happened; that her memory was a complete blank from retiring to rest on the Saturday night the 7th of January, to Thursday morning following, when consciousness returned. It was later reported that the father of the same young man committed suicide on the night of May 30th 1859, by throwing himself down the shaft of his own pit at Hunslet. (*Leeds Times*)

JANUARY 9TH

1860: A Mr Radcliffe, the medical officer of health, brought to the attention of the Leeds Board of Guardians the alarming state of the workhouse. He stated that each week the workhouse became more and more overcrowded, and, as a consequence, was in a very unhealthy state. He told the guardians that, at that present time, there were 104 inmates and two dead bodies in the house. Of these, thirty-forty inmates were ill and, because of the overcrowding, there were one or two deaths daily. He urgently impressed upon the board the completion of the new workhouse as quickly as possible. Mr Thompson, the chair to the guardians, confirmed the statement, after which several on the board expressed their regret that they had not known this before – as they had only that day made orders for more persons to be admitted. Mr Thompson stated that it was quite clear that no more persons could now be admitted to the old workhouse. He then read the report of the building committee to the other members of the board, which stated that it was fully expected for the new workhouse to be completed around spring of that year. (*Leeds Mercury*)

JANUARY 10TH

1814: It was on this day that Leeds heard about the death of Mr Joseph Linsley, who, for more than thirty-four years, had been the master of the Leeds workhouse. It was said that he 'fulfilled that important though often unthankful office with infinite credit to himself and advantage to the town'. The benevolent, yet economical, guardian of the poor was often visited by the philanthropic Mr Howard, who wrote as follows: 'The poor of Leeds are well fed, and taken care of; indeed they, and the people at large, are happy in having a worthy and very honest man for the master of the workhouse, a Mr Linsley, who was formerly a manufacturer in the town. His temper and disposition, as well as those of his wife, seem peculiarly adapted to their charge; mildness and attention to the complaints of the meanest, joined with the firmness of manner, gain the respect of the respect of those who are placed under their care. I am at the same time convinced, by his open manner in showing me the books, that he transacts the business of the town with rectitude and economy'. (*Leeds Mercury*)

JANUARY 11TH

1856 The mayor convened a preliminary meeting today, for a group of local gentlemen – who later became known as the Nightingale Fund – with the view to commemorate, with a testimonial, the devoted, patriotic and laudable services of Miss Florence Nightingale, in the Eastern War. The mayor took the chair of the meeting, which was held at the Town Hall, to decide what course of proceedings to adopt with regards to the character of the testimonial. It was finally agreed that a committee would be formed in order to establish the variety of testimonial the people of Leeds would like to send to Miss Nightingale – as well as public subscriptions to be open at banks, and other public places, for the people of the town. One of the Aldermen, Mr Gott, stated that, 'The public minds were full of the heroism of Miss Nightingale and that the citizens of Leeds would be anxious as to show their appreciation'. A discussion then took place as to whether a public meeting should be called, but it was agreed that no point would be served and that the committee would decide what form the testimonial should take. (*Leeds Express*)

JANUARY 12TH

1832: On the evening of this date, there was a performance by the celebrated Paganini at the Leeds Music Hall. A reporter from the *Leeds Mercury* attended the concert and described the evening. He stated that Paganini delighted his audience and it was later said that 'there was something unearthly about him... his face is on the whole agreeable, and his smile indicative of a great good nature'. The report stated that: 'We do not feel ourselves competent to speak of what may be termed as his miracles; we can admire his delightful harmonies, his cadences, his extraordinary dexterity, the more than musical sound of his fiddle. He can make it squeak and squall, and laugh and cry, and nearly speak. He can express mirth and sorrow, tragedy, comedy or farce. His performances were hailed with unbounded applause, but he declined to obey the cries of "encore".' Messrs Sykes & Son, who had brought the maestro Paganini's performance before the Leeds audiences, liberally donated £50 of the proceeds to the Leeds Poor Fund. At the end of the performance it was announced that the Great Signor himself, in a very magnificent gesture, had also gave twenty guineas to the same object. (*Leeds Mercury*)

January 13th

1825: It was reported that an explosion had occurred at Middleton Colliery, near Leeds, at about 7 o'clock in the morning on this date. A bang as loud as a cannon was heard for miles around. Nearly all of the men who were working in the area of the explosion were killed, apart from a lucky few who were taken to the infirmary at approximately 2 a.m., but they were unable to give an account of the explosion themselves. It was thought that foul air collected in a space where the men were working, causing it to catch fire and explode. Upon investigation it was suggested that some of the men who were killed had neglected to cover the naked flame of their lamps and more injury was claimed by something called 'black damp'. There were ten men in a distant part of the pit who, although they had felt the effects of the shock, received no further injury apart from being knocked down by the violence of the explosion. It is thought that the number of men to have been killed was twenty-four, including a young boy only five years of age. The newspaper urged that a subscription be started in the neighbourhood, in order to alleviate the distress of the families from their losses. (*Leeds Intelligencer*)

JANUARY 14TH

1844: A man named George Nicholls of Pottery Field – who was taken into custody the previous week charged with having married three wives – was brought into court on this morning. The three women, who at the time of their marriage to Nicholls had all been widows, were also in court. The first wife, then Miss Sarah Illingworth, married Nicholls at Manchester parish church in the year 1830. They lived together as man and wife for only three months, at the end of which she left him, suffering from three broken ribs, and did not reside with him again. His second wife, Miss Elizabeth Brown, he married at Leeds parish church in July 1837. He lived with her for a month before leaving her; she had suspected at the time that he had another wife. They agreed to live together again at Churwell near Leeds, but they were not together long before she had him bound over to keep the peace. The third wife, Miss Sarah Holroyd, Nicholls married on July 31st the year before. The two previous wives had made acquaintance with each other in the past, and, meeting him on Leeds Bridge, they gave him into custody before finding out that a third wife had been involved. He was sent for trial at the next assizes, where he was sentenced to be transported for seven years. (*Leeds Mercury*)

JANUARY 15TH

1844: The state of the local streets was discussed in today's *Leeds Mercury*, which reported that: 'Since the thaw of the present week, the deep covering of black mud rendered the streets all but impassable. The quantity of ash from the engine furnaces used in repairing the roads, harmonize with the clouds of smoke from the chimneys of the same furnaces. This pours into the loaded atmosphere making a trial for the lungs as well as the tempers of its inhabitants'. The reporter requested that 'something be done to make the roads more passable'. (*Leeds Mercury*)

———— • ◆ • ————

1873: During the destruction of some old buildings at Bramley, near Leeds, a curiosity in the shape of a 'witch's box' was found secreted on the top of an oaken beam in one of the buildings' roof. It was stated that the box was in a good state of preservation, neatly lined, and contained a rusty nail wrapped in a cotton wick and about half a dozen pins in an upright position, for the use of the witch. Behind the door of the house was nailed an old horse shoe, which was formerly considered to be a charm against witches. (*Leeds Express*)

JANUARY 16TH

1879: On this date, the *Leeds Mercury* gave an account of a new machine which was able to manufacture boots automatically. The reporter stated that: 'There was yesterday a practical exhibition at the works of Messrs Pearson and Co., Chadwick Street, Leeds, of an improved patent sole-sewing machine. The chief object of the patentee has been to simplify the machinery, and he has succeeded in reducing the number of pieces in some cases to the extent of 50%, whilst he claims at the same time to increase its effective and productive power'. A technical description of the machine was given, before continuing: 'The result is a machine, which because of its simplicity, is easily mastered and will attach soles to as many as 600 to 800 pairs of boots per day. The machine will do the work of several men and is worked by foot or steam power. It can be used to attach soles to the lightest shoe or to the thick shooting boot and we are assured that as a result the soles are in every respect as strong as hand sewn shoes. We can only say that the machine patented by Messrs Pearson and Co. can accomplish in a day what may take experienced workmen many weeks'. (*Leeds Mercury*)

JANUARY 17TH

1855: Elizabeth Snowden, an incorrigible young thief, was brought before the court, aged only eleven years, under the charge that on the previous weekend she had stolen a pair of women's boots from the shop of Mr Timothy Longbottom, at the Central Market in Leeds. The juvenile, whose head did not reach to the rails of the dock, was in custody the previous week charged with a felony. The bench, in order to avoid sending her to prison, kept her a day or two in a cell in the lock-up. On the same morning of her release she committed the theft of a pair of slippers from the same shop belonging to Mr Longbottom; when she foolishly returned back to the shop in the afternoon she was recognised, and a watch was kept on her. Mrs Longbottom stopped her as she left the shop and found the pair of boots hidden under her pinafore. She was given into custody once more and brought into the court. The magistrates told her that they could not deal with her so lightly on this occasion and sent her to the Wakefield House of Correction for three months. (*Leeds Mercury*)

JANUARY 18TH

1839: Joseph Elliott, a machine maker, in the employ of Messrs MacLean and March of Leeds, was brought before the magistrates and charged with assaulting his wife. The parties had only been married a few weeks, and yet it had been reported that frequent disagreements had occurred between them. The substance of the charge was that the defendant had struck his wife on several occasions, which she claimed were without any cause whatsoever. The defendant admitted the latest assault, but pleaded justification on the grounds of his wife's disobedience. He said that he had requested her to accompany him home from the public house, which she refused to do. He consequently knocked her down in the street, and he asked the magistrates 'what less any husband could have done?' The Bench assured him that his conduct was extremely disgraceful, and ordered him to find a surety of £20, and he was ordered to keep the peace for six months. The magistrates informed him that he was to be kept locked up until these arrangements could be arranged. (*Leeds Times*)

JANUARY 19TH

1678: On this night, a man named Leonard Scurr was murdered, along with his whole family. It seems that he was a colliery owner who had filled the office of Minister of Beeston Chapel during the time of Cromwell. Scurr had collected a considerable sum of money to take to London for the purpose of trade, a fact that soon became known to some of the neighbours. The previous night, two ruffians named Holroyd and Littlewood, with some other persons, entered his house at the hour of eleven o'clock and murdered Mr Scurr, his aged mother and a servant girl – who they beheaded at the instigation of a woman of the party. They then stripped the house and set fire to it.

The party then fled to Ireland where the woman was identified, whilst wearing some apparel belonging to the elderly Mrs Scurr. They were arrested and brought to take their trial at the Lammas Assize at York. Holroyd was hung in chains on Holbeck Moor before a crowd of 30,000 people. The woman was released and Littlewood was reprieved, in the hope that he would confess, but to the consternation of the police authorities, he disappeared. (Robinson, P., *Leeds Old and New*, Leeds, Wakefield, S.R. Publishers Ltd, 1972)

JANUARY 20TH

1840: At the Barracks Tavern, an inquest of a suicide was held concerning the body of Edward Heslop, who was twenty-three years of age. Heslop had been found suspended by the neck from a beam in the cellar of an unfinished house in Sheepscar Road. It appeared from the evidence of his uncle, Mr Edward Calvert of Prussia Street, Lady Lane, that the deceased had been a tanner and for many years had worked as a journeyman tanner in York. Mr Heslop left York and had travelled to Leeds, where he had been living with his uncle. Mr Calvert told the inquest that his nephew had told him his reasons for leaving York were 'because the woman with whom he had lodged, had bewitched him and told him that he would hang himself'. He had left his uncles house about 7 p.m. that night, seemingly in a good state of health. However, even though every enquiry had been made, no intelligence had been received of him until he was found as described above. The sum of 14s 3d was found in his pockets, together with an excellent silver watch. A verdict was given of suicide through temporary insanity. (*Northern Star*)

JANUARY 21ST

1826: During the industrial depression, the people of Leeds suffered hardships within the town. It was on this day, January 21st 1826, that an account of a generous donation to alleviate this hardship was recorded. In December of the previous year, in a letter to the editor of the *Leeds Independent*, a man had anonymously offered to donate £100. The previous week, two gentlemen had called upon the editor asking for the name of the generous donor, who was found to be William Hirst, a cloth manufacturer. Several gentlemen were sent about the town to report back on conditions, which 'they concurred in representing the sufferings of the poor as heart rending, and as calling for the most immediate interposition of benevolence. It gives us great pleasure to add, that they concur in two other things more agreeable, the readiness of everyone to afford relief according to his power, and the general disposition shewn on the part of the poor, not to avail themselves of the generosity offered, unless compelled by absolute necessity, but rather pointing out to visitors, neighbours who are greater sufferers than themselves. The reports having been received, from which it appeared that upwards of £1,000 had already been collected, farther measures were adopted for carrying into effect the immediate relief called for'. (*Leeds Independent*)

JANUARY 22ND

1865: A skating accident of a melancholy nature occurred on the evening of this date, resulting in the loss of two young lives. It was reported that the frost had been quite severe for the previous two or three days. Throughout the course of the day of the accident, a large number of people ventured upon the ice at Mr Coopers pond, in the grounds of Gledhow Hall. Early in the afternoon, the number had increased to about 130 people, but when dusk descended, only a small number remained. The ice had been thin in some places and even broken in some parts, but still most of the pond had been skated over. A young medical student, named Broughton, was skating on the ice and pushing a chair on which Miss Bulmer, the daughter of a surgeon of Leeds, was seated. Suddenly there was a loud crack and the ice gave way – the two of them were instantly deposited into the freezing water. Two gentlemen hastened to their assistance – unfortunately Miss Bulmer, along with one of her rescuers, a man named Mr Smith, died. Mr Broughton's life was saved, having being successfully rescued by his brother. (*Leeds Express*)

JANUARY 23RD

1643: Sir Thomas Fairfax, a Parliamentarian, stormed and seized the town of Leeds, which, at the time, was held for the King. An extract from Fairfax's diary states that: 'On Monday being 23rd January, I marched from Bradford with six troops of horse and three companies of dragoons and almost 1,000 musketeers and 2,000 clubmen...where we marched to Woodhouse Moor...I dispatched Sir William Savile with a written requirement for the town to be delivered to me for Parliament, to which Sir William disdainfully answered immediately and said he was not used to give answer to such frivolous demands'. Sir Thomas Fairfax, reportedly incensed by this remark, rode at the front of his troops, and the town of Leeds was stormed most furiously. Although not a vast number of men were killed that day, he wrote that, 'there was not above forty slain whereof ten or twelve on our side and the rest on theirs. Sergeant Major Beaumont, in his flight, endeavoured to cross the river and was lost by being drowned therein. Sir William Savile, their General in his flight also crossing the same river, hardly escaped the same fate'. (Robinson, P., *Leeds Old and New,* Leeds, Wakefield, S.R. Publishers Ltd, 1972)

JANUARY 24TH

1786: An extract from a letter from York was printed in *The Times*, which stated that: 'On Friday sennight, about six in the evening, as Thomas Wilson, a barber of Selby was returning from Leeds, a person on horseback overtook him about half a mile from Peckfield turnpike gate, upon which they entered into a conversation with each other for some time. When Wilson turned off the North Road to come to Selby, the person demanded his money. Wilson told him that he had none, and wanted to move forward, when the person took the thick end of a large whip and knocked him off his horse. Wilson, not liking such treatment, gave him what he had, which was only eighteen pence. Not satisfied with this, the robber dismounted and examined the outside of Wilson's breeches and waistcoat pockets, and a basket he had behind him. Finding nothing to his purpose, he took Wilson's hand whip, and with great imprecations at so small a booty, rode off towards Ferrybridge. He was described as a middle sized man, had straight hair, had on a brown coat, but no great coat, and rode a bay horse'. After being informed of the robbery, the police authorities proceeded to make enquiries regarding the crime. (*The Times*)

January 25th

1846: A caution was issued to persons throwing orange peel onto the causeway, in the *Leeds Mercury*. It seems that a Mr Fox had slipped on some peel and had broken his leg, resulting in such an acute compound fracture that it was rendered necessary for an amputation below the knee. The report read as follows: 'For some days his life was despaired of, but by skilful medical treatment, he is now considered to be quite out of danger. Although still confined to his room, it is expected that even under the most favourable circumstances, he will be unable to leave his house for several weeks to come. His sufferings for some time after the accident were very great and it is about two months since the accident occurred. This instance of the thoughtless practice of throwing orange peel on footpaths is a proof of what serious injuries may be caused by it. The penalties to which parties expose themselves, and the dangers to which they subject others, were made the subject of remarks by the Mayor last Saturday. He cautioned the inhabitants of the town to use more care when eating in the street and to dispose of such rubbish with more care'. (*Leeds Mercury*)

JANUARY 26TH

1875: An article on a fancy dress ball, which had been held at the Albert Hall in Leeds, was published today. Arrangements for the ball had been in progress for several weeks prior to 'the society event of the year'. Although, due to the exclusivity of the guest list – only the elite of social society – the number of people in attendance only reached 300. 'For once the somber evening costumes of gentlemen were exchanged for a grandeur which vied with accustomed gaiety of feminine fashion. The ladies themselves also gave a much wider range than usual in their tastes and fancy in attire. The costumes were made up of subjects that were historical, allegorical and dramatic. Gallant courtiers from the court of King Charles II were seen indulging in mild flirtation with a simple shepherdess. Mephistopheles was seen dancing with fair Ophelia and Mary Queen of Scots with a Spanish matador. There were representatives of French cook, a Hungarian Hussar, a Grecian woman as well as Hindu's, a Chinaman, courtly cavaliers mixed with jesters, kings and brigands. Most of the dresses were made by professional costumiers and the music for the ball was played by a band of the Queen's Royals'. (*Leeds Mercury*)

JANUARY 27TH

1831: On this day the Telegraph Coach, which ran between Leeds and Newcastle, met with a fatal end. The coach was descending the hill at Harewood Bank, at a swift pace, when the pole chain broke, and the vehicle overturned with a tremendous crash. It was reported that 'the coachman, Mr James Walls, was so much hurt that he died in a short time. Mr Trees of Scaro Mill, Ripley, was also so severely injured that he now lies at Mr Sturdy's at Harewood, in a state of suffering which precludes all hope of recovery. William Roughead, the guard, is also dangerously ill as his spine is incurably injured. Several of the other passengers have contusions, but not so seriously as to prevent them from proceeding with their journey in a post chaise. We fear that neglect was the cause of this catastrophe. The Telegraph is noted as a safe and steady conveyance, but on the present occasion the wheels were not locked and the descent of the hill was so rapid as to alarm the outside passengers. One of them is said to have leaped from the coach but we are told received no damage'. (*Leeds Intelligencer*)

JANUARY 28TH

1875: Today's newspapers carried the story of a theft of old newspapers from the Central Station at Leeds. Yesterday, a 12-year-old boy, James Jackson, was brought into court charged with stealing 312 papers, which had been returned unsold. PC Herbert saw the boy carrying on his head a bundle of newspapers and, following him, saw him take them to Mr Newby's fishmonger on Boar Lane, where he heard the prisoner offer the newspapers for sale. When questioned, the boy at first said that he had bought them legitimately, but then admitted that he had stolen them. A member of the railway police, Detective Officer Wokes of the Lancashire and Yorkshire Railway Company, said that he saw the prisoner take them from the ground near Smith's bookstall at the station, but not suspecting he was stealing them, did not apprehend him. The newspapers were returned from towns all over Yorkshire, which included Bradford, Huddersfield, Wakefield and Doncaster. 'During the last few weeks a large number of these old newspapers have been stolen from the above station, but the thieves have up to the present time, with this one exception, escaped detection. The magistrates remanded the boy until Friday in order that enquiries might be made into his previous character.' (*Leeds Mercury*)

JANUARY 29TH

1934: A bold scheme of rent rebates was announced by the housing section of the Leeds Corporation. This scheme was designed in an attempt to adjust the rents of municipal tenants. *The Observer* stated that: 'There is every prospect that the scheme that will be passed by the city council and the outcome will be watched by other local authorities. The Greenwood Act expressly empowers the charging of different rents to different tenants, and twenty-one towns had set aside part of their subsidy from which small abatements are allowed to families whose income falls short of a specific scale. Families in municipal housing can live rent and rate free if their total income falls below the following standard:

Man and wife	19s
Children under 10	4s
Children 10 – 13	5s 6d
Children 14 and over	8s

The first 5s of earnings is not to be taken into account. Few towns have even considered the possibility of grading rents on houses built before the 1930 Act. But if the Leeds experiment works well it will almost certainly be followed by others and a new phase in housing history will have begun'. (*The Observer*)

January 30th

1839: It was announced in the local newspapers about the great disappointment that had been felt in Leeds by the non arrival of the London letter bags. It was feared that some alarming accident had occurred on the railway to cause the delay – as it turned out the mischief was of another description. The mail guard of the London and Manchester Railway had sent the bags for the Manchester and Yorkshire area by a branch rail to Preston by mistake. It was in Preston that the error was discovered and the mail coach was delayed for a considerable time, in order to wait for the bags to be re-directed from Preston, before starting out to Yorkshire. After waiting for almost two hours, the mail coach was allowed to leave – without the letter bags – and the post office authorities had to forward them by the night mail coach, which normally arrived in Leeds at two o'clock in the morning. In this instance, owing to the immense weight of newspapers, they did not arrive until four o'clock. It has been reported that due to the many complaints the Post Office received about the delay, the guard was dismissed for his carelessness. (*Leeds Mercury*)

January 31st

1826: It was reported that the dead body of a Leeds man had been found at Newcastle, which had been sent from Leeds to a Mr Simpson of Edinburgh. The body was identified to be that of a Mr Thomas Daniels, who had been interred at St Johns churchyard. Mr Daniels' son immediately went to Newcastle, where he recognised the body of his deceased parent. The clerk of the telegraph office recognised Mr George Cox of Leeds, the son of a broker and a box maker, to be the gentleman who had delivered the package. He was consequently apprehended, though he pleaded that a stranger, who had lodged a short time at his father's house, was the real culprit. The man had employed him to make the box, and requested that he took it to the coach office. The label giving the address to which the package was to be sent was already attached to the box, and he swore that he did not know the contents of the box. Despite his protestations, he was found guilty of body stealing at the sessions and sentenced to six months imprisonment at York Castle. (Thornton, D., *Leeds: The Story of a City,* Ayr, Fort, 2002)

February 1st

1845: At the Leeds Court House, a butcher residing in the neighbourhood of St Ann's Street, Leeds was brought before the mayor, charged with wilfully wasting the Water Company's water. The running water was spotted by an Irishman named Doyle, who saw a stream of clear water flowing along a channel which he suspected had come from one of the taps of the Water Works Company. He followed the stream of water to a tap near to Mr Fisher's shop. There was a bucket under the tap, and when he enquired who the bucket belonged to Mr Fisher told him that it was his. Doyle remonstrated with him about letting the water run away and Fisher told him to mind his own business and that he paid for the water. Doyle repeated this information at the Water Office; he reiterated to one of the officers that Fisher had left the bucket under the water tap, whilst he had been busy serving a customer with a pound of meat. A neighbour – who lives near to the tap – corroborated the story, stating that it was not the first time that it had happened. The mayor concluded that a waste of water had taken place and fined Mr Fisher £1 and charged him costs of 10s. (*Leeds Times*)

FEBRUARY 2ND

1855: A letter was published in the *Leeds Mercury* from a Leeds soldier, Private J. Young, who was fighting at Sebastopol in the Crimea. He states that: 'We are well off for rations. We get two glasses of rum in the day and three when off duty at night. We are all issued with two flannel shirt, two pairs of drawers, two pairs of socks and a comforter. Ours is the nearest regiment to Sebastopol, being about half a mile from it. The Russians keep firing shot and shell at us day and night, but they do no damage. The French keep them very busy, and are always rapping away at them. They set part of the town on fire last night. When we are on sentry duty at night we can hear the Russians who are about fifty yards away from us, talking. There were a great many men died when we first came out here. We used to bury five or six a day with the cholera. You must excuse the writing for I have to use the palm of my hand as a desk'. These and other communications from the Crimean War were regularly printed in the *Leeds Mercury*, to keep readers up to date with the fighting in the Crimea. (*Leeds Mercury*)

FEBRUARY 3RD

1938: The decision not to employ married women within the corporation was taken in the town council chamber. The decision followed protests from women's groups, although the resolution excluded women whose husbands were incapacitated, or in approved cases, where their husbands were unable to support them, or where women had been deserted. The decision was not a popular one and the deputy Mayor, Mrs L. Hammond, disagreed with the decision. She stated that: 'I have been brought up to believe that I am mentally and physically equal to a man. I do not look on marriage as a career, but as a mutual agreement between two people. If the woman felt that she wanted to continue in employment after marriage, it was not for the council to say she ought to be banned. If the council carried that to its natural conclusion then woman members of that council ought not to be there, and there should be no women in Parliament or in any sphere of public life. One of the arguments was based on the outdated belief that a woman's place is in the home'. Despite the many protests from herself and other women the resolution was carried forward. (*Manchester Guardian*)

FEBRUARY 4TH

1857: 'The Life of John Bunyan', a lecture by the Revd W. Punshon, was delivered before the Young Men's Christian Society. The reporter stated that: 'Reverend Punshon has gained an excellent reputation for his lectures, which are very popular, and as a result not only was the Hall crowded but there was barely enough standing room at the back'. The reporter commented that: 'Perhaps there has never been so eloquent an oration delivered in the building. Such force and fervour, such judgement and fancy, such winged words, weighty matter and splendid manner, I never before witnessed. And this seemed to be the universal feeling on the platform, in the gallery and through the vast area, for not content with the usual demonstrations of applause, the great congregation once and again rose from their seats, and burst into a loud, prolonged and triumphant "hurrah".' Such was the enthusiasm from the audience that Revd Punshon when he concluded the lecture was treated to a standing ovation'. The report continued: 'It is understood that the Revd Gentleman has consented to repeat his lecture in the Stock Exchange Hall on the 18th February'. (*Leeds Express*)

FEBRUARY 5TH

1848: On this day there was a report of 'a disgusting exhibition' in Leeds, when an enterprising showman named Andrew Purchase brought to the town an exhibition regarding the recent hanging of the 'Mirfield Murderer', Patrick Reid. Reid had been found guilty of the murder of James Wraith, his wife Ann and servant Caroline Ellis – aged 21 years – and he was executed on January 8th 1848. Purchase claimed that the exhibition used the actual clothing of the dead man, which had been put on a full length waxen likeness of Reid. This was exhibited together with the fatal rope with which he was hanged. The *Leeds Mercury*, which was known to be against capital punishment, was appalled that 'thousands of persons of morbid sensibility flocked to the exhibition which resulted in blocked roads and causeways'. They also declaimed that, 'On the previous Tuesday, the hangman of Reid, a man named Nathaniel Howard had come express from York, to take part in the exhibition and he displayed to the people of Leeds the mode of managing his horrible profession. He deposed to large audiences the authenticity of Reid's clothing; and actually by experiments with the rope and the figure demonstrated the execution'. The report stated: 'Surely this must be the climax of everything revolting to the better feelings of humanity'. (*Leeds Mercury*)

February 6th

1856: The people of Leeds read about a stabbing of a woman of 'questionable character', by her paramour's jealous wife. It seems that information was given to the wife of Mr Thomas Spence, a chimney sweep of Wade Lane, Leeds, that her husband was 'making free' at a notorious house in Lands Lane. She immediately proceeded to the house of ill repute and, ignoring the housekeeper's demands that she leave, found her faithless husband and a young girl named Mary Moorhouse in a bed chamber. The constables were called to deal with the resulting fracas and Moorhouse, who had a wound in her forehead, claimed it had been inflicted by Mrs Spence who, she alleged, 'carried a knife'. Mrs Spence was arrested and brought into court and it was later disproved that she had inflicted the wound with a knife. The defendant said that in her agitation she had merely thrown a gin glass at the girl, which had cut her on the head. The Bench heard all the details very patiently before it decided to inflict a penalty of £4 on Mrs Spence, including costs, or two months imprisonment in default of payment. She was also ordered to keep the peace for six months. (*Leeds Express*)

FEBRUARY 7TH

1822: A publican named Thomas Hellewell, living at Bruntcliffe, was aroused by fire in the stack yard. It was reported that: 'One of the two stacks had been set on fire, and the other might have suffered the same, were it not for the efforts and assistance of his neighbours. Great attempts were made to prevent the fire reaching the mistral, wherein thirteen head of cattle were housed. The detection of the miscreant was accomplished by the most extraordinary circumstances. A slight fall of snow had just covered the ground and footsteps could clearly be seen around the stack yard, which was formed by some very remarkable shoes. The sole of one of the shoes had been curiously mended and the nails were very prominent. Hellewell pursued this track with singular activity and resolution and succeeded after a devious chase in capturing the arsonist at Beeston, with the very shoes on his feet, before eight o'clock the same morning. His name was John Vickers and the motive was proved to be revenge for a very trivial provocation'. Vickers was convicted at York and only because of his youth escaped the death sentence, which was later commuted to transportation for life. (*Leeds Intelligencer*)

FEBRUARY 8TH

1845: It was reported that a corner stone had been laid at the site of the Leeds Borough Gaol by the Mayor. An inscription plate was read out to the assembly, stating that: 'The gaol was erected by the council of the borough of Leeds in the reign of her Majesty Queen Victoria. The building was commenced on the 18th March 1844, and this corner stone was laid on 3rd February 1845 by Darnton Lupton Esq. Mayor of Leeds'. One of the architects, Mr Perkins, took a sealed glass bottle containing a copy of the inscription on vellum and copies of the *Leeds Mercury*, the *Leeds Intelligencer* and the *Leeds Times*. One of each of the current coins of the realm were added to the bottle, ranging from a sovereign to a half farthing, and the bottle was then deposited in the cavity of the tower foundation stone. Another large block of stone was placed on the laid stone and the two were cemented together. The Mayor then took a mallet and gave the stone three knocks saying at the same time, 'thus, thus and thus I lay the principle foundation stone of the New Gaol'. (*Leeds Mercury*)

FEBRUARY 9TH

1795: On this day the River Aire, which had been frozen for a considerable time, overflowed due to a rapid thaw, and swelled the river which inundated all the lower streets of the town. It was reported that: 'Incalculable mischief was done by this foaming torrent and immense blocks of frozen ice, which carried away cloth and tenter's from the fields, threw down walls, dyehouses and several dwelling houses in its path. The water also damaged the bridge across one of the arches by a boat which had been forced on its side, and at length broken to pieces by the vast accumulation of ice and water, which, if the vessel had not given way, would have soon overthrown the bridge itself, as was feared by the spectators of this destructive flood. Three men were drowned in Hunslet dam and their bodies floated down the river, alongside horses, carts, timber and furniture in rapid succession. Many of the roads of the town were laid so deep with water, as to stop the mail coaches for several days. Mr John Robinson lost his life in attempting to cross the road near his own house, and a boat laden with coal sunk with its crew in the Calder and several bridges were swept away'. (*Manchester Guardian*)

FEBRUARY 10TH

1840: On this day Leeds celebrated the Royal Wedding of Queen Victoria and Prince Albert in right Royal fashion. The town awoke at 6 a.m. to the sound of bells ringing out a merry peal. Everyone celebrated the wedding and even the inmates of the poorhouse were not forgotten. The guardians had provided a veritable feast of roast beef and plum pudding. The meal was washed down with good old English ale for the men, whilst the females were served with tea and rum. After the meal, the guardians gave the inmates a present of a huge bowl of punch, with which they drunk Her Majesty's health and that of her Royal Consort. Shops closed at noon and a general holiday spirit prevailed in the town. A large tea party was held in the schoolroom, 'the Vicar in the chair, who entertained the company with anecdotes of the most useful kind'. In the evening a group of gentlemen met at the Golden Lion Inn and partook of an excellent supper. Many appropriate toasts were given and among them was a toast to 'the anticipated Prince of Wales'. Before the party separated they sang the National Anthem and wished the happy couple 'long life and happiness'. *(Leeds Times)*

FEBRUARY 11TH

1867: At St George's Church, in the midst of the Divine Service, the water which powered the organ was turned off, which caused the organ to fail. As a result, the choir and congregation were forced to sing without the instrument, and it was reported that 'the want of such support from the organ was much felt'. The *Leeds Mercury* stated that: 'It seems that however convenient these water engines are, where the pressure of water cannot be obtained, it leads to the vexation of the organist and the choir, when such instruments fail. It therefore seems very desirable that either an arrangement should be made to blow the organ by means of the old bellows handle, when such deficiencies occur, or that the waterworks authorities should not turn off the supply for a repair on a Sunday without giving any notice, and thus cause inconvenience as was felt yesterday at St George's'. The reporter stated that this was not the first time that the proceedings had been interrupted in such a manner, as there were at least three different occasions on a Sunday of the previous year. (*Leeds Mercury*)

FEBRUARY 12TH

1831: After a bout of recent forgeries in Leeds, the *Leeds Intelligencer* stated that: 'We caution our friends and the public to be particularly careful, just now, in the examination of bank notes, which have been given for goods received and in particularly for those for £5. Forgeries have been discovered, in particular for the £5 notes belonging to Hague's, Cook and Co. of the Dewsbury Bank, Messrs Fentons and Co. of the Rochdale Bank, and also of the Bank of England. These notes had been offered at a house in Leeds in the course of the previous Wednesday. At the same time several counterfeit coins were also proffered in return for sales'. The newspaper commented that: 'It is obvious that the Northern Gang, of whom several members were recently sent to Wakefield House of Correction, is not yet entirely broken up. We have seen the spurious Rochdale note; it is exceedingly well executed in all its parts, and can only be detected by a practiced eye. The public's best safeguard is, an individual mark or memorandum made upon the note, so that every man shall be able to say positively from whom he receives any given note'. (*Leeds Intelligencer*)

FEBRUARY 13TH

1853: The 182 workmates of the Geldard Road and Churwell collieries were given a rare but welcome treat, it was announced in the papers. The treat, which was described as 'a good old English supper of roast beef, plum pudding and ale', was served at the Wesleyan Reformers schoolroom at Churwell and was enjoyed by every person present. After the meal, the Revd C.G. Smith of Carlton Rectory gave thanks to the Churwell Coal Company, who, only a fortnight previously, had generously raised each collier's wages by one day's pay per week. The reporter stated that: 'The remainder of the evening was spent in perfect harmony and good order being interspersed with sacred anthems, sung by a choir engaged for the occasions. Loyal toasts were offered to great cheering by the colliery owners, Mr A.H. Smith and W.E. Morris Esq. and Mr William Ward the manager.' Finally the evening drew to a close and the National Anthem was sung at ten o'clock, after which the company broke up. The following day, twenty eight of the poor and old men and widows of the neighbourhood were given 2lbs of beef pudding and bread and a quart of ale each. 'Thanks must be offered to the colliery proprietors for this welcome treat to its workers'. (*Leeds Mercury*)

FEBRUARY 14TH

1877: The fifteenth report of the Armley Gaol at Leeds, compiled by the governor, the chaplain, the Roman Catholic Minister and the surgeon, was given today. The governor, Mr C.A. Keene, stated that at present there were 276 males and 96 females confined in the prison and he said that 'the conduct of the prisoners was on the whole good, although necessary punishments had to be inflicted from time to time. That year there had only one case of flogging which had been ordered by the magistrates and carried out by the prison authorities'. He claimed that 'it is in the association of prisoners that opportunities are most readily found for the badly disposed to communicate with others like themselves. At such times the more corrupt and hardened exercise a pernicious influence on those less habituated to wrongdoing. Those whose sentences were of long duration regard association as a fruitful source of misconduct'. The surgeon reported that no deaths had occurred that year and that there had been six childbirths, although two of those were stillborn. He also said that the Inspector of Prisons had informed him that Armley 'was a clean and beautiful prison and an example to others'. (*Leeds Mercury*)

FEBRUARY 15TH

1858: An eclipse of the sun took place on this date and was recorded in the local press. The article stated that: 'The eclipse began at Leeds at exactly 12.38 p.m. and it terminated at 14.10 p.m., the darkest period being exactly at 1 p.m.'. A local meteorologist, Mr Hind, estimated that 'at the commencement of the eclipse at Leeds, and for three hours before, the heavens were so clouded that the sun could not be seen, and continued so up to one o'clock. At this time a sudden opening in the clouds revealed half a ring of light, as thin as the thinnest crescent of the new moon, but of a much whiter and stronger light. The figure of the sun bore a resemblance to the form of a half circle. For about thirty-five minutes the sun was almost constantly visible, and every minute made the crescent broader, and brought back its radiance. Very few of the anticipated effects were realised which had previously been predicted'. He states that: 'The physical aspect of nature underwent no observable changes, other than days of ordinary cloudiness, and birds and animals did not betray any of the unusual symptoms as predicted'. Many people from the town gathered in streets and open areas to watch the eclipse. (*Leeds Express*)

February 16th

1933: The *Manchester Guardian* announced that Leeds has the largest and most difficult slum problem of any English town outside London. The article stated that: 'It is the classic example of back-to-back housing of the worst sort. The nature of the city's problems was outlined by the Coalition Government Unhealthy Areas Committee of which Neville Chamberlain was chairman. The committee found that well over half of the housing in Leeds was back-to-back. Thirty-three thousand of these are the worst built in long continuous blocks, opening directly onto the street and need to be completely cleared. Many of them are built of brick with no damp course and are of the one room down and one room above variety. Added to these are the unsanitary nuisances often with the lavatories only three or four feet away from the door. The 1930 Act offers Leeds a way of beginning seriously to tackle the slum problem. A week ago the council announced a building programme of 2,000 houses under the Greenwood Act, and we feel that this is only the beginning'. The reporter went on to comment that the medical officer estimateed that there were over 100,000 houses to be demolished in Leeds. (*Manchester Guardian*)

FEBRUARY 17TH

1832: The firm of Messrs Stansfield and Co. decided to close their mill, due to great differences between the employers and workmen in the Worsted Power Loom Manufactory at Kirkstall. The decision had been made on the grounds that, 'the competition in trade is so close that they cannot afford to pay higher wages than are paid by other manufacturers in the same line'. The *Leeds Mercury* stated that: 'We should regret extremely the closing of this mill, which would withdraw at least £200 a week in the shape of wages out of circulation. It would also diminish the comfort of perhaps 400 families, some of whom it would reduce to destitution. This would be a great local calamity, and we wish sincerely that the parties would try once more, in the spirit of conciliation to avert it. We have the greater hopes of the success of a renewed negotiation, from knowing that hitherto, no persons have stood better with each other than the master and the workpeople of this mill. The difference between them is not very considerable which makes reconciliation more achievable'. The newspaper requested a mediator to intervene and settle the matter. (*Leeds Mercury*)

FEBRUARY 18TH

1877: The newspapers on this day carried a report about the death of a soldier at the Leeds Barracks. 'On Tuesday an inquest was held on the body of John Harper, a private in the Scots Grays regiment, who was at that time stationed in Leeds barracks. On the previous Sunday morning about 12.30 p.m. the attention of the sentry was attracted by hearing a man groan. On searching he found the deceased lying on the ground and a woman was seen looking over the wall, who asked him if he had seen a man fall over. The woman then disappeared and despite enquiries still has not been found. The deceased was drunk and the Barrack hospital sergeant was fetched and on examining him found a slight cut on the side of his head, but did not think the man was so seriously injured as to warrant his removal to the hospital. The deceased was then placed in the guardroom and at 10 a.m. he was found to be unconscious and removed to the hospital, where he died the same day. A post-mortem showed that his skull was fractured and the jury returned a verdict of accidental death, whilst censoring the military authorities for their inhumane behaviour to an injured man'. (*Leeds Times*)

1844: A letter was printed to the editor of the *Leeds Mercury* regarding a report about the ill-treatment of a parish apprentice. The letter, which was written by the husband of the alleged perpetrator, stated: 'GENTLEMEN: Seeing a paragraph in your paper about the alleged ill-treatment by my wife towards a town's apprentice of the name of Hannah Townsend, would leave you readers believing that Mrs France had acted extremely cruel. I take the liberty of stating that the apprentice's statement was a false and wicked invention; that the striking with a stick never took place. In fact the wound on her head was occasioned by an accident arising from her own carelessness. The marks on her face, neck and arms arose from her stooping before the kitchen fire and pulling on her a saucepan of boiling water. My wife attended to her wounds with the greatest care leaving only the red marks visible. I cannot conclude without saying that I wished to get rid of this girl because of her filthy habits and had offered the Overseers £10 to take her back to the workhouse, but this was refused. I have penned this letter in order to relieve Mrs France from this calumny which is a wicked invention'. WILLIAM FRANCE. (*Leeds Mercury*)

February 20th

1867: It was reported in the *Leeds Express* that the Cookridge Street Baths were opened, 'through the public spirit and enterprise of the Oriental and General Bath Company'. The article stated that: 'The interest taken in the opening of the baths was so strong, that throughout the day there was a constant procession of visitors. For their outlay of £13,000, the directors of the Bath Company have succeeded in placing before the people of Leeds a building that's bathing arrangements will scarcely be excelled in the kingdom. Since the partial opening of the swimming baths in the latter part of July of last year, considerably over 20,000 people have availed themselves already of the advantages that the building offers. Tomorrow the Turkish baths, along with the slipper, ladies, plunge and other baths are to also be opened. The Turkish baths alone is so spacious that it occupies a very large portion of the entire premises. The floors of the hot rooms and cooling rooms are paved with ornamental tiles, and the couches are in keeping with the oriental theme. Now that this aid to physical enjoyment and sanitary improvement has been successfully established, it will receive the patronage it truly deserves'. The reporter stated that the baths were open for every day apart from the Sabbath. (*Leeds Express*)

FEBRUARY 21ST

1850: The *Leeds Mercury* of this date contained a report on a case of 'Mummy Wheat which had been cultivated which was estimated to be over 2,000 years old'. The reporter described how the ear of wheat had come into the possession of Mr Stears of Leeds, following the opening of a tomb of an Egyptian priest. The ear of wheat was found in the hand of the mummy and had been sent to one of the most active members of the Royal Agricultural Society, Thomas Maggandie Esq. The article described how 'by his able management, the ear of wheat was cultivated and succeeded in raising quite a quantity of wheat. It is said to be entirely different class from wheat grown in this country, the ear being much larger and having two or three similar ears growing from the same stem. The great fear was of its being of such a very large size that it would not be suitable to this changeable climate, being by its weight liable to being broken down by the wind and showers'. Mr Stears was reported to be delighted by the news and requested that some of the wheat be sent to his home in Leeds. (*Leeds Mercury*)

FEBRUARY 22ND

1865: Large crowds gathered outside the Borough Gaol today between 8 a.m. and 9 a.m., on account of a woman called Eliza Stafford, who had been imprisoned for a month for the theft of some dripping. It was said to be the property of Mr Henry Chorley, her employer, who was a surgeon and magistrate, and in whose service she had been for a few weeks as cook. As a result of the approbation caused by his actions, Mr Chorley had been subject to an anonymous letter and 'Chorley's Dripping' been written on walls about the town. It had been known that on this date Eliza would be released and the intention was to hold a mass demonstration and a triumphant parade around the town. But the plan was overturned when it became apparent that the poor woman had left prison at 6.30 a.m. and caught the train to Scarborough, where her daughter lived. The announcement was made by the Chief Constable of Leeds, who was pelted with snowballs at the news. The matter had so enraged the population which 'fermented rage amongst the ignorant and credulous', that the troops were called out and a state of siege existed in the town. By 7 p.m. a crowd of 2,000 had collected in front of the Town Hall and police were subject to stone throwing. (*Leeds Mercury*)

FEBRUARY 23RD

1835: Leeds and the neighbourhood were visited by a tremendous gale and its effects were reported in the *Mercury*. It stated that the wind blew with so much violence that it was dangerous for people to walk abroad in the town. The cloth dressing premises of Mr Laycock of Sheepscar had been blown in by the storm and reduced to a mass of ruins. Two men had been killed and three others were reported as being severely injured. The press shop chimney of Messrs O'Williams, at Kirkstall, was also blown down and fell into the river. The dye-house chimney of Messrs York and Sheepshanks, West Street, was blown down, and it broke through the first floor of the upper room down to the ground floor; three persons were buried in the ruins. The engine chimney of Messrs Smith and Co., Bowman Lane, was also subject to the gale – it too was blown down. The chimney at the house of Mr Harland, of Osmondthorpe, fell and burst through the roof, and similar accident took place at the house of Dr Williamson, in Park Place. Even the Kendal coach, on its route out of Leeds, was blown over on its side near Wellington Bridge. At Hunslet, a young man by the name of Hay had his thigh broken by a gate being blown violently against him. (*Leeds Mercury*)

FEBRUARY 24TH

1748: An old manuscript was found at Leeds which records that on this day, a man called Thomas Grave was murdered by the Lord of the Manor of Leeds, Josiah Fearne. The victim had four wounds on his body and died from his injuries on March 2nd. Fearne was committed to York Castle and tried before Sir Thomas Burnett; he was hanged on March 25th 1749. Soon after Fearne had been arrested, he sent his solicitor to see the wife of his victim, Mrs Grave, to offer her £20 a year for the rest of her life if she would sign a petition to the judge in his favour. Fearne felt that this would amply recompense her for the injury he had done to her and her eight children. However, she refused to accept it, knowing that the money would not make up for the injustice of the crime. It is the first recorded case of a Lord of the Manor being sent to the gallows. It was known throughout the neighbourhood that Fearne's temper was 'extremely rigid to the poor and his dependents, that he was dreaded by all, and beloved by none'. He was buried at Clifton near York on 31st March. (Thornton, D., *Leeds: The Story of a City*, Ayr, Fort, 2002)

FEBRUARY 25TH

1810: Today's newspaper reported on the collapse of the spire of the church of St Nicholas in Leeds. It has been said that the spire was a danger for many years. The article describes how 'bell ringers within the spire were exposed to the greatest danger, but they were all fortunate enough to escape, with the exception of one which was caught in the ruins along with a boy of 14 years of age, who was in the steeple at the same time. They were however both immediately extricated, by the exertions of the other ringers. The man, Thomas Rodgers of Meadow Lane, was just slightly wounded but the boy, Henry James Whitaker, has since died'. The alarm, it appears, was given to the ringers by the falling of a large piece of stone onto the fifth bell, which prevented its swinging. At this point other pieces of stone came from the interior of the spire and the bell ringers immediately ran out. The report continued, 'A moment did not elapse before the bells, beams and the upper floors fell to the bottom of the tower with a very loud crash. The escape of all the survivors would not have been possible had not the belfry been upon the ground floor'. (*Leeds Intelligencer*)

FEBRUARY 26TH

1872: In today's newspaper a report about the death of a woman, Eliza Willey of Meadow Lane, through self-poisoning, was heard by the Leeds coroner. At the resumed inquest, which had been adjourned in order that the surgeon, Mr Scattergood, was able to complete an analysis of the stomach contents, he told the court that during the post-mortem he had found strychnine in the deceased woman's stomach. This had been combined together with Prussian blue and starch, ingredients used in the manufacture of Battle's Vermin Killer. He gave his opinion that he had no doubt that this was the cause of the woman's death. The report stated that: 'For the last six months the woman, Eliza Willey, had been in a depressed condition about religion, and the evidence indicates that under an attack of melancholia, she had procured a packet of the vermin killer and had taken it when no one was in the room with her. The paper in which the powder was wrapped was not found, and there was no direct evidence to show where or how it had been obtained'. The jury were advised by the coroner to return a verdict that the deceased had poisoned herself with strychnine whilst temporarily insane. (*LeedMercury*)

FEBRUARY 27TH

1841: It was reported on this day that there was a case of 'Desecration of the Sabbath'. A reporter wrote that a policeman, who had been on duty in plain clothes on a Sunday morning, had seen a crowd of people gathered in a field at the back of the Catholic chapel on York Road, about 10.30 a.m. On proceeding to the field behind the church, he witnessed two men, John Allerton, a tailor, and Thomas Waggitt, an engineman, stripped to the waist and engaged in fighting each other in what was described as 'a pitched battle'. He took them both into custody, along with some of the witnesses who were present at the fight. The witnesses made their statements and the two men were charged. The prisoners were brought into the court and, although they did not deny the charge, both put the blame for the fight on the other. Witnesses stated that the fight had not been premeditated, and seeing the two men begin to fight, they, and others, had gathered to watch. The magistrates ordered that both men should be fined sureties of £10 each and promise to keep the peace for six months. The men and the witnesses were censored for indulging in such activities on the Lord's Day. (*Northern Star*)

FEBRUARY 28TH

1866: An owner of a traction engine was summoned by the police, before the West Riding Justices at Leeds, for having only one man in position on the engine whilst passing through Hunslet on February 16th. Mr Riley Briggs appeared with his solicitor, Mr Granger, before the court and told the magistrates that, whilst his client admitted the offence for which he was technically liable, three men had been sent to accompany the engine, but two of them neglected to turn up. He added that Mr Briggs regretted what had occurred and he assured them that he would do all in his power to ensure it did not happen again. Mr Briggs informed the court that the two men had since been dismissed for failing in their duty. At the end of the case one of the magistrates warned him that the law must be carried out to the letter and he must always ensure that there were at least three men in attendance on the engine. Another magistrate pointed out that it had been the defendant's servants who had actually been to blame. As a result, Mr Briggs was fined 20s and costs. (*Leeds Mercury*)

MARCH 1st

1879: A rather unique cause of death was heard at the Town Hall on this date, before the magistrate Mr Malcolm, concerning the death of Margaret Rose, wife of bricklayer Thomas Rose. Alice McGowan aged 18, the sister of the deceased woman, gave evidence at the inquest that her sister had been so neglected by her husband that she had died. A relieving officer had been told to visit the woman and to supply beef, sago, tea, and port wine, which he did. He interviewed the husband, who told him that he had only earned a few shillings the week before. Alice McGowan had told him that her sister's husband took food to the house occasionally, but he always took it away again. The surgeon stated that the woman had consumption but he had carried out the post-mortem and found that, although the lungs were deceased, the bowels were empty. He said that the husband was 'very queer against his wife and her sister'. Rose was sent to prison for four months for the neglect of his wife, but the surgeon said that consumption had caused the death and that it was just a matter of time. The jury brought in the verdict that death was from natural causes. (*Leeds Daily News*)

MARCH 2ND

1853: Newspapers announced a meeting which had been held last night regarding the establishment of 'a new and much needed charitable institution for the West Riding' – a hospital for women and children. The proposal was to establish a hospital for the treatment of the diseases that particularly affect women and children, and to treat them at the earliest opportunity. The idea of a hospital had initially been mentioned in October last and a preliminary meeting had been held on February 14th 1853, where subscriptions of £657 had been pledged. The proposal was approved of 'by those whose opinions were held in the highest respect throughout the district'. Indeed, the meeting included Dr Hook, the vicar of Leeds, the Mayor, Mr J.H. Shaw and eleven men of the title of Esquire. It was also stated that the 'proposal has been honoured with the patronage of most of the nobility, the leading clergy and many of the gentry connected with the country'. It was resolved that a meeting of the principle subscribers was to be called, and suitable premises in a convenient location be found on reasonable terms. It was intended that the hospital will treat 'respectable females who through no fault of their own were suffering from painful and tedious complaints'. (*Leeds Mercury*)

MARCH 3RD

1926: It was announced at a meeting of the town council that plans had been approved for a big street improvement scheme which, it was estimated, would cost over £500,000. The *Guardian* reported that 'the scheme will completely change the aspect of Leeds from Victoria Square to Vicar Lane. The plans, which have been designed by Sir Reginald Blomfield, have been agreed by the town council in order to provide for a new road to be built which will be nearly 1,000 yards long and 80 feet wide. The area affected is close to the centre of the city. It is intended that palatial buildings of sand-faced brick with Portland stone dressing are intended to line the route and will be erected for both shops and offices. The existing properties along the line of the route will have to be demolished, and this will be done in small sections, the work extending over several years. Incidentally the scheme will establish a fine approach to, and an outlet from, the city for road transport to the north. One of the councillors told our reporter that the new road will establish Leeds as one of the forward thinking cities of the Yorkshire area'. (*Guardian*)

MARCH 4TH

1867: On this day, crowds of people in the streets of Leeds were amazed to see a locomotive and tender perform several journeys between the old terminus in Marsh Lane and the new station in Wellington Street. The local newspaper recorded that: 'Railways through large towns might be a common enough sight by now, but a locomotive steaming across some of the principal streets in Leeds was so entirely novel, that the spectacle caused no small amount of amazement. Passers-by in the leading thoroughfares gazed on it wonderment and admiration, and trades people hastened to the doors of their business premises. The moving locomotive was best seen from a vantage point on Briggate where many people assembled. As it crossed the girder bridge at the foot of that busy thoroughfare, the passengers inside the locomotive gave a hearty cheer to the crowd. As the sound died away those who had heard it became fully alive to the fact that the new station in Wellington Street was rapidly approaching completion, and that in reality the enormous traffic of a giant company would, ere long, be carried across the street and amongst the house tops'. The new station was opened to the public in 1869. (*Leeds Mercury*)

MARCH 5TH

1846: Today the costs of transporting Scotch and Irish paupers back to their place of birth were listed in the local newspaper. These paupers were initially taken from Leeds Workhouse to the main depot at Huddersfield and then to their destination, in order to prevent them becoming chargeable to the parishes of the West Riding. The *Leeds Times* listed all the costs, which include:

- To the clerk of the justices for examination 2s; for three orders of removal 2s
- To the constable for conveying paupers to Huddersfield, one pauper 9d, for every additional pauper above 12 years 3d, under 12 years, 2d per mile
- An allowance of 1½lbs of bread per day to each person above the age of 12 years, for subsistence on the journey and 1lb bread for each child under 12 years
- To the conductor for his time and trouble, the sum of 10s a day; maintenance 6s a day; travelling 2d a mile
- To the agent at Liverpool, for his time and trouble in seeing such poor persons on board vessels, and board and lodgings when required 1s 6d

(*Leeds Times*)

MARCH 6TH

1552: The first endowment of the Leeds Free Grammar school was made on this day, in the will of Sir William Sheafield, a priest. The endowment 'by which he vested in Sir John Neville, knight and sixteen others, as co-feoffees (co-possessors) certain copyhold lands, situated near Sheepscar Bridge: "for finding sustenance and living of one honest, substantial and learned man to be a schoole maister, to teach and instruct freely for ever, all such yonge scholars, youths, and children, as shall come and resort to him from time to time, to be taught, instructed and informed in such a school-house, as shall be founded, erected and builded by the paryshioners of the said town and parish of Leeds; to the clear yearly value of £10 for ever, within four years after his decease, then the feoffees should stand seized to the use of the poor inhabitants of Leeds. The feoffees and their heirs for ever, should have the nomination, election and appointment of the said school maister; and give them power to put him out for reasonable cause at their discretion"'. (Feather, J.W., *Leeds: The Heart of Yorkshire*, Leeds, Basil Jackson Publications, 1967)

MARCH 7TH

1831: On this day, the *Leeds Mercury* reported that the funeral of Sergeant Richard Norton, a paymaster's clerk for the 10th Hussars, which was due to take place yesterday, had been called off. Sargeant Norton had hanged himself in a fit of insanity in one of the bedrooms of the Horse and Trumpet Inn, Briggate, Leeds, the previous week. The funeral was appointed to take place in Quarry Hill churchyard and was accompanied with the usual military honours and attended by a great concourse of people. The invited guests flocked to the place of internment; however, upon arrival the Revd Wardle, who was due to officiate at the funeral, refused to read the burial service over the body because the man had committed suicide. As a consequence of this Revd Wardle was subjected to a great deal of abuse from friends and family of the deceased man. The body was left overnight in the chapel of rest and the following day Revd Wardle found that an immense crowd of over 5,000 people had gathered, including a party of 3rd Dragoons. Reverend Wardle, fearing the excitement of the multitude of people, performed the service and the crowd dispersed. (*Leeds Mercury*)

MARCH 8TH

1873: On this evening, there was a meeting of the Leeds Female Servants Home Society in the Grand Jury Room at Leeds Town Hall. The chairman, Alderman Oxley, stated that although the institution continued to do good work among those for whom it was intended, there had been a slight decrease in the number of inmates during the past year. This decrease might have risen from some unemployed servants preferring the entire freedom of common lodging houses. However, he suggested that is was more than probable that the real reason might be that the demand for domestic servants exceeded those who were available. He stated that most ladies know the difficulties of finding good servants, to which there were shouts of 'hear, hear'. He continued that 'there was no reason why healthy young women with good character should be without situations in respectable families. For those who needed a period of rest to recruit their strength, or for those who had no home when out of work the Home provided comfort, a healthy moral atmosphere and safety from temptation (hear, hear and applause). The Home was calculated to do more good than it had already established'. (*Leeds Express*)

MARCH 9TH

1856: At the courthouse today four women were brought before the bench summoned by Mr Thomas Roberts, the agent for Messr Peter Williams Esq., cloth manufacturer, for leaving their work in an unfinished state. It seems that the women had all taken out warps and on Monday they left and had not returned to work. There was a combination [trade union] among the women and seventeen of them had abruptly left Williams' employ as a protest against pay. Mr Roberts told the Bench that he only wished the women could be compelled to finish the work they had started, and then they could go where they pleased. The defendants stated that they were not paid sufficient for their work. The magistrate asked how much they earned and Mr Roberts told them 9s to 12s a week. The whole of the seventeen women who were in court raised an outcry at this, one of them telling the bench that she had earned 6s 8d in a fortnight and that involved working ten hours a day. The magistrate agreed that 3s 4d a week wasn't much for a week's pay, however he pointed out the women had contracted to complete the work and it was agreed that they would fulfil their contract. (*Leeds Mercury*)

MARCH 10TH

1863: In Leeds there was a celebration of the marriage of the Prince of Wales and Princess Alexandra on this day. Among the wedding gifts was a diamond bracelet given by the ladies of Leeds and valued at 500 guineas. The *Leeds Times* reported that: 'The day started with a procession of the mayor of the corporation, magistrates, the volunteers, etc., through the public streets to Woodhouse Moor, where there was a display from the local militia. This was followed in the evening by a dinner and ball in the Victoria Hall; the rejoicings being wound up with an illumination of the Town Hall, and other places. The principal façade of the Town Hall was lit up in a truly gorgeous manner. There was also a display of fireworks on Woodhouse Moor. A profuse display of flags, banners, and designs of every description, and decorations in every style of elaboration, were prepared in all the principal thoroughfares, producing a gay and brilliant effect. In fact, not since the visit of Her Majesty to Leeds had the town spontaneously given itself up to festivity as it did so universally this day, and the same may be said of every large town in the kingdom.' (*Leeds Times*)

MARCH 11TH

1878: Newspapers reported that the programme for the evening entertainment sessions at St James Hall on York Street continued to attract large audiences of working class people. A reporter noted that 'it was gratifying to see that the hall was crowded and before an hour had elapsed, not a single seat was empty. Last night an excellent vocal concert was given by Messrs Radcliffe, Bingham and Williams, which concluded to rousing cheers. This was followed by some comedy songs and a recitation by Mr Thomas Marshall. The audience were then treated to another concert by the members of the Leeds Private Vocal Society, which were conducted by Mr E.O. Dykes. There was a very large and most appreciative audience, and the singing throughout were received with the most heartiest of applause'. The reporter concluded that 'it is a matter for congratulations that the committee of management for the Hall is able to offer entertainment of such a high order as that given last evening at the almost nominal price of a penny. We are told that a further six evening concerts are planned and if they continue to be successful that more are designed to follow'. (*Leeds Express*)

MARCH 12TH

1870: The *Leeds Mercury* held an account of the death of an unknown woman who had died in the police cells in Leeds. The *Mercury* writes: 'The Leeds coroner held an inquest on Thursday on the body of a woman unknown of the age of around 35 years. On Tuesday morning around 4 a.m. the deceased was found by PC George Kendall, in a yard in Marsh Lane, in a state of insensibility. The officer concluded that she was drunk, and he found there was a bruise on the side of her face and more along her arms and legs. He had removed her to the Duke Street police station, where she died at 4 p.m. on the same day, having remained insensible from the time she was found. Mr Bramley the surgeon was called in before she died, but was unable to assist the poor woman. He was later asked by the coroner to complete a post-mortem on the body. He found that death had been caused by the rupture of a blood vessel on the brain, which produced concussion. He concluded that this could have been caused by a fall or a violent blow to the head. Guided by his expression of opinion the jury returned an open verdict'. (*Leeds Mercury*)

MARCH 13TH

1861: A case was brought before the magistrates of shocking cruelty from parents towards their children. The father, Alfred Robinson, who lived with his wife in Barrack Street, Buslingthorpe Lane, had recently been dismissed from the local police force for drunkenness. They were charged after Mr English, the Chief Constable, had received information that they had rubbed the face of one of their children in its own excrement. The neighbours reported that the children were so deprived of food that they had gone to swill bins to satisfy their hunger. One of the children, a boy aged about seven, was brought into the court, where he appeared to be incredibly emaciated and his back was covered in bruises. One of the magistrates, Mr Chorley, had made a statement saying he had visited the house and found the children in an appalling state and evidently starving. As a result of this he had sent the children into the workhouse, where they were being cared for. Because Mr Chorley was not on the magistrates' bench that morning, the case was adjourned. The following week the parents were sentenced to six months imprisonment with hard labour and were censored by the magistrates for their inhuman behaviour. (*Leeds Times*)

MARCH 14TH

1840: Today's newspapers recorded 'an amazing fall of trees' which had occurred one night about three weeks prior in a wood situated on the River Aire. It seems that the wood was situated a little below Calverley Bridge, and was know by the locals as Swaine Wood. In consequence of the late, very heavy and continuous rains which had purveyed the area, a portion of the ground had given way and a number of trees had slid down the hill. The passage of the trees was only impeded in its progress at the bottom by larger trees, which were too deeply rooted to give way. The resulting mass of earth and wood had entirely covered a wall and partially stopped the course of the river, which no doubt would have been completely diverted had it not been for the large trees. Gamekeepers, who had been watching for poachers near the place at the time, were completely astounded and ran off, thinking that it was an earthquake. A group of workers were sent to the area in order to remove the blockage and it was reported that the noise, occasioned by the disruption, had been heard a considerable distance away. (*Leeds Mercury*)

MARCH 15TH

1850: A report in the *Leeds Times* stated that The Equestrian Company belonging to Mr W. Crookes had been performing in Leeds to large audiences during the past three weeks. It was reported that 'as an entertainment of its kind, it is much superior to any that has for a considerable period visited Leeds. The performance of the horses is one of considerable extent and great beauty; the feats of horsemanship and vaulting are of a most surprising and often very daring kind, and all the spectacles are got up with gorgeous effect. The horses were groomed to perfection and acted in formation with perfect ease and supreme organisation'. It was noted that large and respectable audiences assembled nightly to witness the performances. The reporter stated that, 'only last week was patronized by the Earl of Harewood and that of Thursday night last by the officers and men of the 81st Regiment, who showed great interest in the expert horsemanship. There were also many ladies in the audiences who seem to be very gratified at the superb performances'. The report sadly concluded that, 'we have been informed that the Equestrian Company will come to a close at the end of next week and urge all those who have not seen it to make no delay in securing tickets'. (*Leeds Times*)

MARCH 16TH

1866: There had been several rumours in circulation for some time in the town of an expected outbreak of Fenians in Leeds on St Patrick's Day, gossip of which was heard on every corner. As a result of these rumours the Mayor stated that he had been given information of pike making and secret drilling being carried out in the town by the supporters of Fenianism, and that several known Fenians were in constant communication with the friends of the movement in Ireland. A meeting of the magistrates of the borough was quickly assembled to consider the subject. They decided to adopt precautionary measures, in order that 'the civil power might be in a position to act with vigour should the necessity arise'. The meeting resolved 'to augment the existing police force by another forty from the West Riding constabulary, and fifty of the resident pensioners would also be taken on temporarily as night watchmen. A large number of the members of the Volunteer Corps of the town, together with 100 tradesmen, were also sworn in as special constables. Perhaps as a result of this, up to the time of going to press, the town remained quiet'. (*Leeds Mercury*)

MARCH 17TH

1880: There was an announcement of the first social gathering of Leeds letter carriers, which had been held on a previous evening at St James Hall. At the invitation of the Mayor, 120 persons, including postmen and their wives and families, sat down to a sumptuous tea of sandwiches and cold cuts. Subsequently, a number of suitable addresses were delivered by the Mayor and Revd R.A. Sharples, which praised the postal authorities and their workers for the service they received in Leeds. The addresses were then followed by songs given by the Arion Quartet, the members of which gave their services gratuitously. It was noted that 'a pleasing feature of the evenings proceedings was the distribution to each postman, the present of a letter, signed by the Mayoress on behalf of a number of local ladies' groups, in which sincere wishes were expressed for the welfare of the postmen themselves, their wives and families, and in which they were asked to accept a copy of the New Testament, which accompanied each letter'. The evening ended with a rousing rendition of the National Anthem and the company dispersed. (*Leeds Mercury*)

MARCH 18TH

1848: About a quarter to ten on this night, a serious and fatal accident occurred at the circus of Mr W. Darby, alias Pablo Fanque, of King Charles Croft, Leeds. It was the benefit night for Mr W.F. Wallett, the clown, and the circus had built a temporary wooden structure for the performance, which was crowded with people. The pit, which contained more than 600 persons, fell with a tremendous crash, precipitating a great number of people into the gallery adjoining the front of the pit, but on a lower level. A great many others fell into the lobby, and some out at one side. The weight of the falling timber, and the people together, had burst out a portion of the side of the circus nearest to Land Lane. Mrs Darby and Mrs Wallett were both in the lobby at the time of the occurrence. They were both knocked down by falling timber; two heavy planks fell upon the back part of the head and neck of Mrs Darby, and killed her on the spot. Mrs Wallett, and many other persons, received bruises and contusions, but unbelievably Mrs Derby was the only fatality. The unfortunate woman, who was aged forty-seven, was later interred at the Woodhouse cemetery. (*Northern Star*)

MARCH 19TH

1859: The *Leeds Mercury* reported that a correspondent had drawn their attention 'to the insecure and dirty condition of Carlton Hill, Woodhouse Lane, which is a much frequented thoroughfare by the inhabitants of Little London'. The reporter stated that: 'The neighbourhood at this season of the year is continually ankle deep in mud and very nearly impassable. A portion of the footpath, because it has not being flagged, in rainy weather is washed into the road. Numerous pedestrians, driven thence, have frequently found themselves floundering in an open ditch on the other side of the road. But the evil most loudly complained of, is the havoc created by the troop of Cavalry who are quartered in the barracks, who make it their route to and from Woodhouse Moor where they hold training. They ride three and four abreast, cutting up roads and paths in all directions, and creating these dangerous conditions'. He concluded 'this results in an indication that the "progress of the military" is only seen by the ruin and destruction they have left behind them. It is hoped that the road might be flagged as soon as possible in order that pedestrian traffic might be made safer and less accidents might be witnessed'. (*Leeds Mercury*)

MARCH 20TH

1847: Today's *Leeds Times* carried a report about the selling of unwholesome meat in the market of the town. Thomas Ackroyd, described as 'a middle aged man', was brought before the magistrates on the previous Monday, charged with having in his possession the unwholesome carcass of a pig, which he was intending to sell for human consumption. The meat was seized by Mr Massey, the Market Health Inspector, on Saturday at Ackroyd's house. It appeared that the pig had belonged to a man residing at the Bank and, hearing of its death, Ackroyd went to this person's house to beg for the carcass. He was given the carcass on the condition that he took it to a soap house to render it down for soap. Instead of complying with this request, he took the pig home and dressed and salted it, ready for use, and it was in this state when it was seized by Mr Massey. A jury of butchers unanimously condemned the meat, and censored Mr Ackroyd for his behaviour. The man that formerly possessed the pig stated that it had died during the night without having manifested any previous illness. Ackroyd declared that the meat was perfectly good, and expressed a wish that he had more of it. The magistrates 'with better taste' ordered the meat to be destroyed and Ackroyd was fined 10s and costs. (*Leeds Times*)

MARCH 21ST

1873: A Sanitary Board prosecution took place today at the Leeds Borough police court, when Thomas Neeson, who lived in Pollard Yard situated at the bottom of Union Street, was fined. It was reported that he had been summoned for 'having his dwelling house so dirty and unwholesome as to be prejudicial to health of other residents'. The defendant, who was described as a labourer, was employed with the Highways Department of the Leeds Corporation. It was reported by Inspector Newsome that he persisted in keeping his house in such a filthy state, despite the fact that many members of his family and neighbours had the fever from the unwholesome condition of the place. The Inspector also laid information about two other people, Martin Whalin of Galway Street, York Street, and John McHale of Plane Street, also of York Street, Leeds, who had been accused of overcrowding their lodging houses. Both men had been visited and complaints had been received about the unsanitary conditions. He reported that when he visited, several beds were in each bedroom, which had been occupied by persons of either sex. All three men were fined 20s and costs. (*Leeds Mercury*)

MARCH 22ND

1885: For some time past, Dr Goldie, the Medical Officer of Health, had been urging upon the Sanitary Committee the desirability of providing a sanatorium for Leeds. At the meeting the day before he told them that such a building could provide an advantage in cases in which infectious diseases break out. Instead of patients with fever being taken to hospital, where other inmates could also contract the disease, they could be sent to the sanatorium, where they could be kept segregated from other patients. Whilst they were being treated safely, arrangements could then be made to have their homes, bedding and clothing thoroughly disinfected and cleaned. Dr Goldie urged the Committee to understand that 'by such means, the spread of infectious diseases would in all probability be prevented from spreading much more than it is at present'. He felt that if the proposition was put to the people of Leeds, a subscription could be started and the building could be opened and put into use very quickly. The chair of the Sanitary Committee, Mr Ward, agreed that such a building would be beneficial to Leeds. The Committee resolved to appoint a sub-committee to investigate the matter and they were to report back at the next monthly meeting. (*Leeds Mercury*)

MARCH 23RD

1883: It was reported today that yesterday afternoon a very serious accident was prevented by the quick thinking and swift action of two young men. About 2 p.m. a horse that had been waiting in between the shafts of an empty lorry in Albion Street, was alarmed by a loud noise and set off at a smart pace. The panicking horse and wagon, with another horse tied behind it, swung round the corner into Bond Street and proceeded to charge up the street. Thankfully, the street was unusually clear of wheeled traffic or there might have been very serious consequences. Fortunately, the people in the street were made aware of the charging wagon and horses, and several people tried to catch the horse unsuccessfully. Finally, the animal's head was caught by Mr Thomas Lister, an assistant to Messrs Pierce and Co., jewellers of Commercial Street, who had ran alongside the horse, at considerable risk to himself, for a few yards. Despite the slippery condition of the road, he managed to bring the horse to a halt with the assistance of another passer-by. The newspaper cautioned 'the incident should convey a warning to the drivers of such vehicles to ensure that their horses are tethered safely'. (*Leeds Express*)

MARCH 24TH

1938: It was announced today that Leeds will be one of the first cities to have an air-raid precaution scheme. The scheme had been adopted by the town council in their meeting and submitted to the Home Office ARP department eighteen months ago. The mayor stated that: 'Every department of the Leeds Corporation has its duties clearly defined and coordinated with the Town Clerk, Mr Thomas Thornton'. However, he also stated that: 'it has to be said that recruitment figures for the ARP services at this time are not good. In a city like Leeds with a population of nearly 500,000 people, at least 3,500 air wardens will be needed to man 450 posts. Although 1,000 of these have already been enrolled through the police department who has been recruiting for over a year, and the city engineer has been surveying for shelters in two of the city's new building schemes'. The mayor concluded that, 'finally the city has organised an ARP display on April 9th to hold mock air raids, in which anti-aircraft guns, searchlights and aeroplanes will take part and the different services will come into action'. He concluded that he hoped that more recruits would come forward after observing such displays. (*The Observer*)

MARCH 25TH

1912: Newspapers carried reports that the people of Leeds were suffering heavily from the coal strike. A careful estimate had been made in the Lord Mayor's office, where it was found that 25,000 men had been thrown out of work and as a consequence 'thousands of families are in want of food and fuel'. It was estimated that there were 8,000 miners in the Leeds district, who made the nucleus of the great body of workless men. The newspaper reported that: 'Within the last week or so additions to this number have been made almost daily by the closing down of the iron and steel works, which form an important part of the city's industry. It is said that the numbers of unemployed men in these industries total between 16,000 and 17,000 persons. Other industries have also had to close or reduce the hours of working because of the strike. The Lord Mayor has opened a fund to help some of these distressed families and the amount subscribed up to last night was £3,000. It is proposed to give relief in money at the rate of 2s 6d for adults and 1s 6d for each child. The Education Committee is providing meals for school children and the Distress Committee will make provision for mothers and under school age children'. (*The Observer*)

MARCH 26TH

1662: On this day, the Corporation records show that: 'Having Received great Testimony and satisfaction of the abilitye and fitness of Thomas Gorst in the Art, Trade or Mistery of a Cooke, it was ordered that the said Thomas Gorst should from thenceforth be reputed and taken to be the sole and only cooke to the present, or hereafter Maior and Alderman of the said Burrough' and that he should 'from tyme to tyme, upon any publique occasion, dresse or order to be dressed, the severall dishes appointed for any such meeting or solemnitye'. The authorities took great pride in demonstrating their excellence of the Mayor's cook. However, there is a complaint recorded from later in the same year which states that: 'Many Masters of families and Parents of Children, doe give liberty to their Servants and others to profane the Sabbath, by theire open playing in the streets, sitting in the publique places, to the great dishonour of God in poynte of divine Worshippe in Scandall to Christian profession, and to the bad example of the younger sorte in poynte of Education'. (Robinson, P., *Leeds Old and New*, Leeds, S.R. Publishers Ltd, 1972)

MARCH 27TH

1861: Today's *Leeds Mercury* reported on the formal opening of the new Leeds Workhouse at Burmantofts, although it recorded that the workhouse has been unofficially occupied for several weeks. The report stated that, 'the workhouse will accommodate 810 inmates and it is estimated that the costs will exceeded £31,000'. The architects of the new workhouse were Messrs Perkins and Backhouse of Leeds. The workhouse was described as 'being in the Elizabethan style of architecture, and had been designed to harmonize with the Industrial School. It ranges in a line with that same edifice and the façade is of a great extent and beauty. The chapel which is attached to the workhouse is very neat and picturesque, in the Byzantine style. It is cruciform in shape and is surmounted by a tower and spire on the south and a circular tower on the north. In the rear is a detached infirmary and is midway between the workhouse and the industrial school'. The formal proceedings started at 10.30 a.m. when a special service was heard in the chapel before town councillors and the mayor. At the conclusion of the service these officials inspected the workhouse, admiring the layout of the wards, the dining room and the hospital. (*Leeds Mercury*)

MARCH 28TH

1867: A disastrous explosion, which arose from an accumulation of gas, occurred at a provision dealer's and draper's shop at the corner of Scott Street and Woodhouse Street, Leeds. The premises consisted of a shop with two large windows and a small living room at the side, with sleeping apartments on the second storey. The residents were the proprietor, Mr John Howell, his wife, two children – aged respectively a year and a half, and seven years – and his niece, Sarah Howell, a young woman about seventeen years of age. At the time of the explosion Mrs Howell was in the shop, attending to a customer named Maria Marshall. The report states that: 'The niece, it would seem, observing a strong smell of gas, incautiously took a lighted candle partly into the cellar underneath the back room to ascertain where the leakage arose. A dense volume of gas had accumulated in the space underneath the flooring of the shop and in the cellar, and the introduction of the candle into its midst caused a terrific explosion, which alarmed the whole of the inhabitants of the locality. The windows and door of the shop were completely demolished, but thankfully all were rescued from the mass of debris of bricks, mortar, timber, and grocery and drapery goods'. (*Leeds Mercury*)

MARCH 29TH

1916: Today the Number 6, Platoon B Company of the Leeds Pals had their first night in the trenches. Lieutenant S. Morris Bickersteth kept a diary where he recorded: 'The only thing that bothers me is the rats and they are legion and here the trenches are simply alive with them at night, but I believe the whole line is the same. We started marching off from the village where we had spent the night at 7 a.m. this morning. After we had gone half a mile or more, we were met by guides from the regiment who we were relieving. We got to a village about 1,000 yards from the front line to where there was hardly a house left standing. We soon arrived at the head of a communication trench and we all silently filed in. The trench was in fairly good condition, but it soon started to snow and the trench soon became slushy. We took over from the Irish Territorial Regiment who have been here since October last and were now going to a rest billet for a change. There is practically no chance of sleep except between the hours of 2 a.m. to 4 a.m.'. (Milner, L., *Leeds Pals,* Leeds, Pen and Sword Books Ltd, 1998)

MARCH 30TH

1847: An amusing report of a sheriff who had been outwitted by a girl was said to be the talk of the town. The unnamed sheriff, who had previously been celebrated for his sharpness in his dealings, was called, in the exercise of his duty, to take possession of the household goods of a certain party who had become bankrupt. Armed with his letter of authority, he proceeded to the property and, no doubt under some sympathy to the plight of the householder, went to the back door. Knocking softly, the door was answered by a young woman, who, when he informed her of his mission, stated that she would prefer him to come to the front door, instead of being admitted through the kitchen, which would lead him to be under the scrutiny of the servants. No sooner had he done so than he realised how he had been duped. The young woman locking and bolting both front and back door, then continued her conversation with the sheriff from the first floor of the building, to where he was left standing in the garden. The local newspaper reported that 'the scene and dialogue was less Romeo and Juliet than Catherine and Petruchio'. (*Leeds Mercury*)

MARCH 31ST

1888: In today's papers there was an announcement of an outbreak of smallpox in Leeds. The *Leeds Mercury* recorded: 'During the present month there has been seven cases of patients recorded of having contracted smallpox. Upon notification of the cases to the Medical Officer of Health, he ordered all of them to be admitted to the hospital. These include two children of tramps, who were conveyed from a lodging house in Marsh Lane on Saturday night last. It is understood that the parents of the children have recently come into the town from Sheffield. Another woman suffering from the disease was also removed from a house on Salem Place and we understand that she came from Normanton. In order to contain the disease, the Medical Officer also ordered the relative of those afflicted to have also been removed to the sanatorium on York Road. He said that as soon as it could be arranged, the houses which had been occupied by them will have been stripped of all wallpapers, disinfected and cleansed'. It was hoped that by such methods the infection and contagion of the disease would be kept to a minimum and would have reduced the spread of the disease to any more patients. (*Leeds Mercury*)

APRIL 1ST

1851: The *Leeds Mercury* praised the town's exhibits in the Great Exhibition in London with a sense of great pride. The article stated that: 'Among the various specimens of manufacture which our town is contributing to the exhibition, we have been much pleased with the inspection of two locomotive engines. These have been manufactured by Messrs Kitson, Thompson and Hewitson of Leeds, and the workmanship will not leave us behind any other district in point of excellence'. The engines were described as being much smaller than the usual class of engines, and their 'peculiarity' consisted with their construction to carry a supply of coke and water for the journey without having a tender attached. The report continued: 'One of them struck us as Lilliputian in its dimensions. It has cylinders nine inches in diameter, is carried upon four wheels, and is intended for working light trains, with a very small consumption of fuel. The second is a little larger in its dimensions having 11 cylinders and is carried upon six wheels'. The Great Exhibition was a world fair of culture and industry which lasted from May 1st to October 15th of this year in Hyde Park, London. (*Leeds Mercury*)

APRIL 2ND

1870: At this day's assizes, two Irishmen were acquitted for the manslaughter of John Murgatroyd in a beerhouse in Kirkgate, Leeds, on December 27th 1869. Described as 'a brutal affair' it seems that during the day a plasterer named Murgatroyd, who came from Bradford, accompanied by a fellow workman, came to Leeds in search of employment. They entered the Broughams Arms, where, because he refused to contribute to a performing fiddler, Murgatroyd was attacked by the two men named Francis Tighe and Thomas Docherty. Despite the attack being over quite quickly, the ferocity with which it was conducted meant that Murgatroyd was taken up quite dead. The two men were tried in Leeds before the magistrates and were found guilty of wilful murder. The bench commented that 'there was a need to stamp out such violence in the town' and they were committed to take their trail at the next assizes. During the trial, the learned Judge intimated to the jury that there was not enough evidence to bring the charge home against them. The jury returned a verdict according to his wishes and the two men were both acquitted. (*Leeds Express*)

APRIL 3RD

1852: Some workmen in the employ of Messrs Longley, of Wortley, near Leeds, were digging for clay for the purpose of making bricks, when they discovered at the depth of 10ft, a number of bones. The remains were found in dark blue sedimentary clay consisting of a texture which almost approached mud. Mr Denny of the Leeds Philosophical Society examined the bones and found them to be the remains of the great Northern Hippopotamus (*Hippopotamus Major*). He secured them for the Society's Museum, and stated that, 'they are unquestionably the most valuable series of British Hippopotami remains in the kingdom'. He also stated that amongst the bones exhumed were several others belonging to the Elephant (*Elephas Primigenius*) and the Urus (*Bos Primigenius*). Mr Denny also said that the remains of the Hippopotamus indicated the quadrupeds to have been of different ages, two of them had been adult individuals – one considerably larger than the other – and the other was a young animal. From the situation in which they were found, he said that, 'it is highly probable that the animals had lived and died in the immediate vicinity. As a consequence of their death the animals had subsequently drifted, together with remains of fragments of trees, to the bottom or lower part of a swamp'. (*Leeds Mercury*)

APRIL 4TH

1877: At Leeds Town Hall, a bad case of neglect was heard relating to the body of John Henry Hughes, the four-day-old son of Henry Hughes – who lived in a house that overlooked Hills Yard, Meadow Lane. The surgeon Mr Hollingsworth, who made the post-mortem examination of the child, stated that the child had died from inflammation of the bowels, leading to mortification and an effusion of blood on the brain. He stated that during the last illness of the child, it must have been apparent to the parents for at least two days before its death that the child needed medical aid, yet they did not seek it. The foreman of the jury asked that the parents be censured for their lack of care, but the coroner remarked that there was a high mortality rate amongst children in Leeds and particularly with babies of just a few days old. He said that 'parents ought to know that when their child was neglected, that they ran the risk of not only being censured by a jury, but of punishment of a more serious nature' and he cautioned Mr and Mrs Hughes to take more care of their children in the future. (*Leeds Times*)

APRIL 5TH

1851: It was announced that two former slaves, William and Ellen Croft, who had given their account of their escape from slavery at the Woodhouse Mechanics Institute, had been included in the Leeds census. The couple were staying at the home of Mr Wilson Armistead who, on March 30th, as householder, would have been required to complete a census return on their behalf. The form had to give the name, rank, profession and place of nativity of every person in the house that night. These two individuals were accordingly entered by Mr Armistead under the designation of '*Fugitives from Slavery in America, the land of their nativity*'. The newspaper reporter castigated America stating: 'What a disgrace to a professedly free and Christian country as America that such an acknowledgement should have to be made. It should be published that America's own born citizens are driven to seek refuge in a foreign clime, from the man stealer and the horrors of slavery'. The fugitives, who arrived about four months earlier in Liverpool, told the reporter that the first time they felt really free was when they set foot on English soil. Ellen was described as 'a gentle, refined looking young creature' and William 'holds manly and dignified deportment'. (*Leeds Mercury*)

APRIL 6TH

1911: It was reported today that the Leeds City Council passed a resolution urging the government to give facilities for the Women's Enfranchisement Bill, which had been introduced in Parliament by Sir George Kemp MP. The council voted by a large majority to approve that the franchise should be extended to women householders. Mr A. Willey, the only member to vote against the resolution, stated that 'he knew no member of the council who were over 60 and married, who would dare to go home and admit to their wives that they had voted against the resolution'. He said that in his opinion 'women voters in municipal elections caused great confusion and were a big nuisance. Many tyres of motor cars were worn out taking them to the poll and when they got there they didn't know what to do. In nine cases out of ten they probably made a mess of it and voted for the wrong man'. Referring to the suffragists who had stayed out all night rather than be involved in the census, Mr Willey remarked that 'he was married to a lady who had rather strong inclinations to the vote and he said that he might feel disposed to stay out himself all night after his speech had been reported'. (*The Observer*)

APRIL 7TH

1897: A meeting was held today by the City Council where the Mayor, Sir James Kitson MP, moved that the adoption of an address be presented to the Queen, on the occasion of her Diamond Jubilee. He outlined various means by which the celebrations would be commemorated at Leeds. He told the council that it had been suggested there should be a special procession on Monday June 21st to celebrate the Jubilee. The procession would include soldiers, volunteers, members of friendly societies, and other notable groups of the town. He suggested that there should be emblems illustrating the progress of trade during Queen Victoria's reign, and he hoped that the children and aged people would not be forgotten. Local rejoicing of all sorts could take place in the districts on the following day, and he, as Mayor, would be glad to provide an entertainment in Roundhay Park. Another of the town councillors stated that it was well known that the many Prime Ministers from the colonies had also been invited to visit various cities in England for the celebrations, and he suggested that some of them should be invited to visit Leeds. The Mayor agreed, saying that he would be pleased to entertain the premiers at a banquet at the Town Hall. (*Leeds Mercury*)

APRIL 8TH

1870: This day marked the second week of the spring assizes, which were being held at the Leeds Town Hall. The previous week, a man named Henry Madden was placed on trial for assaulting and robbing Daniel Hawksworth. He had been defended by Mr Gully, who said that he had a witness to prove that this was a clear case of mistaken identity. When the witness, Henry Jackson, was called into the court, however, he did not answer his name, and in his absence the prisoner was convicted and sent to prison. A few days later Mr Gully attended before the learned Commissioner, Mr Forsyth QC, who had tried the case and explained that the witness, Jackson, had been in the building during the trial, but did not hear his name being called. He only realised too late that Mr Madden had already been sentenced for the crime. He immediately informed some of the court authorities, but as the man had already been sentenced, there was little they could do. Jackson had since made a formal statement bearing upon the innocence of the prisoner, and a representation of the circumstances had been sent to the Home Secretary. It was later announced that Her Majesty's free pardon had been received by Mr Keene, the governor of Armley Gaol, and Madden was now a free man. (*Leeds Mercury*)

APRIL 9TH

1841: In the West Riding sessions, before the magistrate Lord Wharncliffe, the court heard of a case where a man named Sutcliffe had been summoned for not registering his child's birth. Sutcliffe's solicitor, Mr Baines, moved to quash an indictment which had been found against Sutcliffe for refusing to give the necessary information for the registration of the birth of his child. Mr Baines stated that 'he appeared on behalf of the Registrar General, who had brought the charge in order to vindicate the law and to show that parties could not disobey it with impunity'. The defendant, Sutcliffe, had clearly been guilty of the offence for which he had been summoned under the Act of Parliament, but he now consented to give the information that had been required of him. He had also, at the same time, expressed his very sincere contrition for the error into which he had fallen, through a misunderstanding of the law. The Registrar General had instructed Mr Baines to state that he was willing to hope that enough had been done for the purpose of justice, and Mr Baines asked for a motion to quash the indictment. The bench assented to the motion and the indictment was dealt with accordingly. (*Leeds Times*)

APRIL 10TH

1863: Mr S. Lawson, who for many years had taken a prominent part in the administration of the poor-law in the Leeds Township, was presented last night with his portrait by his friends on the board of guardians. It was intended that as recognition of his long services to the workhouse, the portrait would find a suitable home. The presentation was made by the local MP and chair of the board, Mr G.S. Beecroft Esq., at the White Horse Hotel. To shouts of acclaim and to great merriment, Mr Lawson, in reply to the question about what he would do with the portrait, observed with his usual wit that 'Mrs. Lawson said she had had sixty-two years of so much anxious care with the original, that she had expressed a wish not to have the copy in her own home'. As a result of this he therefore offered to hand it over to the Guardians of the Leeds workhouse, who he begged 'might dispose of it as they thought proper'. To much laughter at his comments it was agreed that, as a distinction towards his long service, the portrait would be placed in a proper place of honour in the Guardian's Board Room, on South Parade. (*Leeds Mercury*)

APRIL 11TH

1866: A sad accident occurred on this date at Beeston Royds, near Leeds, in which two men were killed and another one seriously injured. A party of workmen were engaged in deepening a well; two of them being employed on a platform 16 yards below the surface. It was conjectured that one of these two, in lighting his pipe after he had eaten his dinner, set fire to a quantity of gas, which had accumulated in the lower portion of the well. An explosion took place of such violence that the sides of the well were torn down and the unfortunate men in it were buried alive, while another of their comrades at the top received severe injuries from the stones of the well. Strenuous efforts were made to rescue the buried men, one of whom was heard groaning for more than twenty minutes after the explosion had taken place. Unfortunately, rescuers were unable to reach the men for a further three hours. By the time they dug out to a depth where the men had been injured, they were both found to be dead. The names of the two men were Hargreaves and Goodall, and the third man, called Bright, was quickly removed to the Leeds Infirmary where he was said to be slowly recovering. (*Leeds Express*)

APRIL 12TH

1853: Today it was announced that the Leeds Archers had held their first field day for the season, and celebrated the event by dining together at the Archers Hall, which had recently been erected upon their ground. The weather was reported to be 'very dull and gloomy, with occasional showers, which persisted throughout the competition to shoot 100 yards'. The reporter stated that the 'rain had the effect of preventing many from attending, more especially the brightest ornaments of an archery field, the fair sex who generally take a very great interest in this fine old English pastime'. As was usual in this annual event, three archers were selected from those in attendance and they were put through their trials. Gradually the weather began to improve and by the time the prize-giving was over, the sun was trying to shine. After the competitions the archers and their guests sat down to an excellent dinner in the hall, under the presidency of Captain Bell, and spent a very pleasant evening into the late hours. It was reported that the society 'is at the moment in a very prosperous condition and is likely to become one of the most influential archery clubs in the kingdom'. (*Leeds Mercury*)

APRIL 13TH

1840: A report was written in the newspapers about a balloon ascent from the yard of the White Cloth Hall in Leeds, which was said to be 'a most magnificent ascent which had ever been witnessed before'. The inflation of the balloon was completed by five o'clock, the car was then attached and four people climbed into it. The group of people included Mr Russum, the owner of the balloon, Mr Thomas Newsome, a reporter for the *Leeds Mercury*, and two other well respected men of the town. They took their seats at half past five, the cords were loosened and the immense machine rose majestically into the air, amidst the cheering of the spectators. A parachute containing a cat was dropped near Messrs Ives and Atkinson's mill, which alighted on top of a house in the Bank, 'where puss was hospitably received'. The reporter described the sensation of being in the air, which he compared to being merely that of a cool breeze. He wrote that, 'no absolute cold was experienced; indeed the air was so calm that the balloon was stationary for upwards of five minutes'. At twenty past six, Mr Russum prepared for the descent, which he accomplished in a field at Monk Fryston, near Selby, and the day was deemed a complete success. (*Leeds Mercury*)

APRIL 14TH

1844: It was announced that the Leeds Mechanic's Institute and Literary Society were now offering classes for discussion and instruction in the German language. The *Leeds Mercury* announced that it welcomed these classes 'as local firms in the town are becoming increasingly involved in German manufacture; it is thought to be very useful for better working relations'. The editor stated: 'We are glad to learn that this Institute is still increasing in usefulness and adding to its many attractions. The class on German discussion meets one evening a week, and already contains upwards of twenty members. The subjects discussed are of a general nature and the greatest care is taken to exclude those which are of a political or sectarian nature. The class is managed by members only, guided by the rules drawn up by the Committee of the Institution. The German language class is conducted with great energy and zeal by Monsieur Lafarge and numbers fifteen pupils. This class must prove of great value to a town like Leeds, which has so much intercourse with Germany'. The classes, which were to be held twice weekly, were expected to last for two hours starting at 6 p.m. and there were prizes awarded to the best student. (*Northern Star*)

APRIL 15TH

1841: A week before it had been announced that the North Midland Railway were operating an excursion to Derby on this date, and the fare to each passenger would be *6s*. A *Leeds Mercury* reporter was included, who gave his account of the day. He said that an immense number of spectators came to see the train off at 6.30 a.m., although it was 6.53 a.m. before the train departed. The train, which consisted of twenty-seven carriages, had two engines to speed its journey, which was described at length. He reported that 'the train reached Barnsley where it stopped for 8 minutes to take on water, at Masbrough it stopped for 15 minutes and Chesterfield for 5minutes. All along the route, the train was greeted with cheers from crowds who gathered to watch the train and passengers go by. It finally pulled into Derby, after travelling a distance of 72¾ miles, which had taken three hours and seventeen minutes, and once again the station was crowded. The train left Derby to begin its return journey at 18.07 p.m. and reached Leeds at 21.22 p.m., where it was estimated that the train had completed the journey at the rate of twenty-four miles per hour'. (*Leeds Mercury*)

APRIL 16TH

1825: An application was made for a sum of money for the erection of a new bridge at Leeds, over the River Aire, from School Close to Water Lane. The town council was told that the bridge that crossed the river at the moment was the only one over the river, and had become inadequate for the increased traffic on it. The existing bridge had been widened in 1730, 1760 and 1795 and to widen it again would cost £20,000; it was thought that still it would not suffice. One of the councillors suggested that a new bridge a few hundred yards to the west of the present one would cost much less, estimating it as being something in the region of £17,000. Such was the need for a new bridge that he had already had subscriptions pledged up to an amount of £9,000. He complained that on market day, 3,000 foot passengers, 132 horses, 203 carts and wagons, and 24 coaches had passed over the bridge. One of the town councillors stated that the bridge was in so dangerous a state that he never had passed over it without giving thanks to God for his deliverance. The application was granted on the understanding that the town of Leeds would be responsible for keeping the approaches to the bridge in good repair. (*Leeds Mercury*)

April 17th

1865: It was on this day that a lost child was returned back to the safety of its mother's arms. It seems that a girl, named Ellen Murray, lived with her aunt, a Mrs Conner, in Leeds. On Tuesday April 11th, she had gone out with her aunt's baby and returned without it. At first she stated that the child had been stolen by a woman, who decoyed her to a public house in St Peter's Square. On the following day she said that the child had fallen from her arms into the River Aire, and was drowned, but she contradicted this almost immediately afterwards. In the early morning the police were informed that Caroline Walton, the wife of a cabman, had a child in her house answering the description of the one lost, and on proceeding to the house, the woman confessed at once to the theft. She stated that, a few weeks previous, she had lost her own child during childbirth. Fearing her husband – who was in the habit of ill-treating her – would be angry, she kept the death secret from him. When she met Ellen Murray carrying her aunt's child, she took the baby in the manner described by the girl, in order to replace the one she had lost. The child was returned immediately to its mother, who, it need hardly be said, was overjoyed at its recovery. (*Leeds Express*)

APRIL 18TH

1872: The *Leeds Mercury* contained some advice from 'An Old Maid to Young Women'. The article described how married women should look after their husbands. The 'Old Maid' wrote: 'You should be prepared to manage a home properly and many marriages are spoiled by the wife's inability or indisposition to do that. If I were a young man looking for a wife, I'd search for one who had skill in the household line, was possessed of a good temper, and a grain of common sense. I wouldn't range the country in search of a fine face and figure. I once knew a decent man who was driven to drink by an untidy home. He used to return from work, sometimes wet and weary, to no fire, to dirty children, and to no end of confusion. When this happened on a Saturday, which was frequently the case and there was the mop bowl here, and the chairs piled up there, dust and dirt on the hand; a hungry child screaming in the cradle; and a jaded and somewhat testy wife on her knees cleaning the floor – he went to the alehouse. There he would sulkily remain, until it was likely that the chaos was reduced to order'. (*Leeds Mercury*)

APRIL 19TH

1873: A complaint was printed in the *Leeds Mercury* from a Leeds resident about a buzzer which called local men to work in the region of Clarendon Road. The report stated that: 'The Leeds Stipendiary Magistrate (Mr Bruce) stated on the bench today, that he had received a letter from a person signing himself as James Henderson of Clarendon Road in which the writer complained of a great annoyance to which he was subjected in consequence of a buzzer being used in his neighbourhood. The letter states: "As a ratepayer and resident, I shall feel obliged if you will publicly answer why I am yet compelled to submit to the nuisance of the buzzer, which awoke me yesterday morning and this morning before six o'clock. Has the Town Council given permission for it, or is it a persistent violation of the law?" Mr Bruce stated his sympathy with the letter writer in having to endure such a nuisance, but said that the letter had been sent to the wrong person. He told the members of the court that it should have been sent to the council or the police. He said "If there was a nuisance arising from these buzzers, this gentleman, like others, has his remedy".' It is not recorded whether the matter was taken up and dealt with. (*Leeds Mercury*)

APRIL 20TH

1873: A joiner and cabinet maker called Mr James A. Britton, of Farnley, was brought into court this morning, charged with deserting his wife. Mr Robinson, the relieving officer, told the court that this was not the only time he had left his wife and children and that he had done the same thing nine years previously. Censoring him for his inhuman behaviour, the magistrate, Mr Bruce, then sentenced the prisoner to three months imprisonment. After the case had been heard, a young woman named Sarah Kennedy stepped into the witness box just as the previous prisoner was removed, where she proceeded to tell the magistrate that she had been married to Britton, a week ago at Rothwell Church. When Mr Bruce asked her if she knew that Britton was already married, she confessed to him that she did, but that she also knew he did not live with his wife. She said that although she had been married to him, she had not lived with him, but went to live at her own residence. She admitted to being with child by Britton. The case was adjourned for a week in order for further enquiries to be made. The following week Britton was brought back into court and ordered to take his trial at the next assizes for bigamy. (*Leeds Mercury*)

APRIL 21ST

1846: It was announced in today's newspaper that a report had been presented to the Leeds Town Council, from the committee appointed, to consider the appointment of a Fire Brigade in Leeds. According to the report, a sum of £1,604 and no greater, would be necessary to carry into effect the object contemplated. 'It is proposed to place fire plugs [hydrants] in the streets, at a distance of forty to eighty yards apart and it is reported that there will be 300 of these safety plugs in different parts of the town. These plugs will be worked from eight different fire stations, each station to be occupied by one of the day police. The mayor announced that the Water Company has liberally proposed to supply the water required for the plugs gratuitously.' The reporter continued that: 'We should suppose that a scheme which contemplates the protection of the lives and properties of upwards of 100,000 persons, will not have to encounter any formidable opposition. The savings in diminished premiums of insurance by the ratepayers, will far exceed the whole annual cost of the establishment'. The report concluded that 'it is to be hoped that the erection of these plugs will be undertaken as soon as possible in order to deal with the many fires that Leeds has been prone too lately.' (*Leeds Times*)

APRIL 22ND

1839: A robbery was reported of a black leather portmanteau from the Rose and Crown Inn, Leeds, under the following circumstances. The mail from Manchester arrived at about three o'clock in the morning and the servants were called up by the housekeeper on its arrival. An American gentleman, who had been a passenger in the coach, went into the commercial room of the inn, taking with him his luggage comprising of the portmanteau and a carpet bag. After a light supper, he took his money from the portmanteau and left it with a hat case in the traveller's room, with orders that they should be conveyed to his bedroom in the morning. On the following morning, the landlord found that on opening the commercial room the portmanteau and hat case were nowhere to be found. The portmanteau had contained, beside an excellent wardrobe, a writing portfolio, four memorandum books, a box of samples, pocket handkerchiefs and a number of letters and papers of value only to the owner. Information was immediately given to the police but, despite their best efforts, they were not able to find the thieves immediately. A plea was issued urging anyone with any information to report it to the Town Hall, or the landlord of the Rose and Crown. (*Leeds Mercury*)

APRIL 23RD

1855: The *Leeds Mercury* on this date quotes the case of two Leeds girls who had been decoyed to Liverpool. It seems that the two girls, Mary Thompson and Eliza Blackburn, both aged sixteen, were brought up in the Liverpool court on Monday. The police arrested them on suspicion of being 'wrong characters' as they had on silk dresses and silk stockings, but no bonnets. On being questioned, they said they were dressmakers who had been engaged by Mrs Potter of Leeds, who kept a 'gay house', to go to Liverpool where 'they would have horses to ride and go daily to the theatre'. A man met them at Liverpool and took them to the infamous Madame Annie's house, telling her that they were 'two fresh girls'. They ran off on Thursday and were on their way home when they were apprehended. A subscription was raised for them and they were sent home to Leeds. The *Mercury* commented that, 'Madame Annie made a tour recently, visiting Leeds, Huddersfield and other towns, where she set her infamous agents to work'. Blackburn and Thompson were decoyed by 'the despicable Mrs Poole who has a house in High Street, Leeds'. The reporter states that: 'When the girls returned from Liverpool in their tawdry finery they were returned back to their parents who were respectable working people'. (*Leeds Mercury*)

APRIL 24TH

1843: Three boys, inmates of the workhouse, were brought before the magistrates charged with stealing shower bath plugs. One of the boys was deaf and dumb and had been employed in the shoemakers shop at the workhouse. After finishing work on Friday he put up the shutters and went to the shop of Mr Whittaker, where he sold him two plugs. The following day he arrived at Mr Whittaker's with three more plugs. By now the shopkeeper was suspicious and sent for Inspector Childs, who took the boy into custody. The other two boys' names were given during the questioning of the culprit, but they both claimed that at the time of the crime they were in the gaol on charges of vagrancy. Nevertheless, it was agreed by the magistrates and the police that all three of them would be tried together, to try to ascertain whether the theft had been a joint transaction. The reporter stated that: 'Although participation in the theft was not proved against the latter two boys, it was proved that along with the culprit, they were three of the most unruly and rebellious inmates and as a consequence, the bench sentenced them all to twenty-one days hard labour in the Wakefield House of Correction'. (*Leeds Mercury*)

APRIL 25TH

1840: A ball was held at the Assembly Rooms to honour the 21st birthday of Her Majesty the Queen. The number attending the party were reported as not being very numerous, but included 'the very select and fashionable people of the town. These including the majority of officers of the 4th Dragoon Guards, now stationed at the barracks, and other local, military and commercial gentlemen and their wives'. The dancing commenced about 9.30 p.m. and was reported to be 'extremely spirited, the parties having ample scope for waltzing, quadrille etc. to the enlivening strains of Horabin's celebrated band. The costumes of the men and the dresses of the ladies swirled around in all the colours of the rainbow. The full military band of the 4th Dragoons was also in attendance and charmed the company in the evening by playing many favourite airs. Great credit was due to the Stewards of the Assembly Hall for the superintendence of the entertainment, which afforded all parties to meet and celebrate the commemoration of Her Majesty's birthday'. It was agreed that the event was a great success and dancing continued until midnight, when, after a loyal toast to Her Majesty's health, the National Anthem was sung and the company departed. (*Leeds Mercury*)

APRIL 26TH

1859: This evening the people of Leeds were treated to one of the most spectacular natural displays that had been seen for many years. The *Leeds Mercury* dispatched one of its reporters to transcribe this wonderful event. The report reads: 'This evening there was one of the most brilliant displays of this electrical phenomenon which has presented itself for many years in this neighbourhood. The weather in Leeds had been cold but clear throughout the day, becoming more frosty around 4 p.m. At twilight the horizon in the north presented the usual indications attendant on the Aurora Borealis. About half past eight, the whole of the northern hemisphere was suffused with a deep rose colour, like the reflection of some extensive fire. This, after floating tremulously in the heavens for some time, gradually died away, and was succeeded by the streams of light shooting upwards from a dark segment resting on the horizon, which are ordinarily found connected with this singular and beautiful phenomenon'. Many people of the town came out in the streets to observe this phenomenon, which, it has been agreed, was the most spectacular in living memory. (*Leeds Mercury*)

APRIL 27TH

1954: Last night it was reported that Queen Elizabeth the Queen Mother, was the chief guest at a civic dinner given at the Town Hall in Leeds, on the occasion of the Jubilee celebrations of the University. She was accompanied by the Chancellor of the University, the Princess Royal, the Lord Mayor and the Pro-Chancellor of the University. Among the 300 specially invited guests were many delegates from other universities in Great Britain and overseas, members of Leeds University Council, Lord and Lady Scarborough, and the Duchess of Devonshire. Proposing a toast to the city of Leeds, the Princess Royal said that, 'she liked to think that throughout Great Britain and the Commonwealth there could be no University city in which the relationship between the city authorities and the council and senate of the University was more cordial and more comfortable'. The Lord Mayor replied to the toast, saying that 'it was his pleasure in welcoming such Royal visitors to Leeds and he hoped that Leeds University will long remain the beacon of light for adult education throughout the whole of the Yorkshire area'. (*Manchester Guardian*).

APRIL 28TH

1883: A letter was sent to the Leeds Town Council today from the Leeds Butchers' Association. It called attention to the fact that there was a recent Government enquiry about an application of the corporation to borrow £100,000 to open a new cattle market and abattoir on Copley Hill. The butchers seriously objected to the site, on the grounds that it was most unsuitable and inconvenient, stating that if the site was selected the money would be wasted and the cattle trade of the town ruined. The Butchers' Association stated that they recognised the need for a new market and abattoir, but felt that another site would be more readily acceptable to them. After a long debate, Councillor Wilson withdrew the motion, condemning the actions and motives of the butchers in endeavouring to frustrate the efforts of the council to provide a new market on Copley Hill. Finally, by a considerable majority, the council resolved that a draft reply prepared by the Town Clerk should be forwarded to the Local Government Board, along with the request from the Butchers' Association. A letter outlining the reasons for the site on Copley Hill and a request that the Board give their sanction to the proposals of the corporation should be sent. (*Leeds Mercury*)

APRIL 29TH

1877: An attempted burglary was reported in Headingley, where shots were fired at the police. At a late hour the previous night, a sergeant and a police constable were making sure that a property belonging to Mrs C. Kirk at Buckingham Villas on Headingley Lane was secure. The two policemen had been checking a gate from which a padlock had been broken, when rapid footsteps were heard and a pistol was fired at the constable. The sergeant chased the villain down Buckingham Road, and two more shots were heard. However, when the man reached the bottom of the road, the sergeant lost sight of the man in the dark of the night and returned back to the house, where he found the family awake and much alarmed at the gun shots. It was quickly established that the house had not been broken into, although there had been an attempt to force open a dining room window. Rather more than a year previously the adjoining house had been entered by burglars, and much property had been stolen. A watchman had been kept for these houses during the winter, but his services had been dispensed with a short time before. (*Leeds Express*)

APRIL 30TH

1849: Two suspicious characters were brought into court today, who gave their names as John Ackroyd and Henry Chickey. They had been found on the premises of farmer George Bride of Pontefract Lane, York Road. A little before 1 a.m., the family was disturbed by the barking of a dog and four of them, including Mr Bride, got up and hid in the yard. The two prisoners were caught and locked in a shed until the constable could be called. The two men, who are well known to the police, tried to make out they were walking on the track at the bottom of the garden, but Mr Bride pointed out that the yard was well away from the track. The magistrate, on hearing of their past history, sentenced them to prison for three months as rogues and vagabonds. (*Leeds Mercury*)

———◆———

1892: It was announced that the Mayoress of Leeds gave birth to a daughter yesterday. It was said that many years had elapsed since such an event occurred in connection with the municipality, and it was a time of great rejoicing. 'It is understood that the birth will be commemorated in the usual manner, which is by the presentation to the Mayor, Alderman Boothroyd, of a silver cradle'. (*Leeds Mercury*)

MAY 1ST

1833: On this day, a very handsome memorial, subscribed to by many hundreds of his fellow townsmen, was presented to a surgeon, Mr Flood of Leeds, at the Music Hall. The memorial had been presented to him for his services during the cholera epidemic of the previous year. Mr Flood had worked tirelessly on behalf of the sufferers of the epidemic, and had appointed nurses to offer help to those patients in their own homes where possible. In his role as the Medical Officer of Health for the town, he was also responsible for strategies of the prevention of spreading the epidemic further, for which his fellow townspeople were exceedingly grateful. The memorial bore the following inscription; 'As a testimony of esteem, this inscription, accompanied with a purse of gold, is presented by those who have abundant cause for deeply felt gratitude to Mr Flood, surgeon, for his great skill and valuable exertions, in arresting the progress of the dreadful epidemic disease called Cholera Morbus, by which the town and neighbourhood of Leeds were awfully visited, during the year 1832'. Mr Flood offered his thanks for the memorial and drunk the health of the Lord Mayor and the people of Leeds. (*Leeds Intelligencer*)

MAY 2ND

1866: The town of Leeds was visited today by some very curious visitors who were described by a local reporter. He stated 'the party consisted of the Chinese giant Chang, his wife and attendant. Mr Chang is 7 feet 9½ inches without his shoes, and it was generally agreed that he was an intelligent, handsome and agreeable young man and a most remarkable member of the human race. Apart from his gigantic stature, he was interesting as a specimen of the Chinese scholar and gentleman, for he is said to be a mandarin, who writes poetry, and is an incarnation of the mild Oriental type of wisdom. With him was his wife, a beauty of the Flowery Land, who in addition to the charms of face and manner of which she could boast, was distinguished by the possession of the smallest foot in the world – a wee distorted member scarcely four inches in length. Then there was a Tartar dwarf, called Chung Mow, smaller than Tom Thumb and a grotesque little "Celestial" who enlivened his distinguished comrades' entertainment by singing a comic song in "pigeon English"'. The article said that these were the chief members of the party, but they were also attended by three servants, who cooked for them. (*Leeds Mercury*)

MAY 3RD

1940: It was reported that the Leeds town council had threatened to prohibit Sir Oswald Mosley from holding meetings in corporation property, if he did not withdraw remarks he had made at a mass meeting held at Leeds Town Hall. At a meeting of the council, the leader of the Labour Party, Mr Joseph Armistead, complained that Sir Oswald had challenged the Leeds police about a charge, which was without real substance; he also said that if they refused to do a certain thing, it would prove that Leeds City Council was Jewish governed. Mr Armistead stated that until an apology was offered and the comment withdrawn, Sir Oswald would not be allowed to speak in rooms which were council property. The Liberal leader agreed, describing it as a gratuitous insult to the council, yet he warned that they must not be seen to deny 'free speech' for the citizens of Leeds. The quickest way to make the Fifth Column effective was to deny an expression of people's views. The Conservative leader stated that 'we are out to win the war. These doctrines are against unity in the country and are of assistance to our enemies'. The minutes were passed unanimously without any special resolution being proposed. (*The Observer*)

MAY 4TH

1865: On this day, a statue of the Prince Consort which had been sculpted by Mr Noble, arrived at the Leeds station and was transported to the Town Hall on a huge wagon. The town council had arranged for the statue to be erected on one side of the vestibule of the Town Hall, facing the statue of his wife, Queen Victoria, on the other side. Workmen had been employed for several days to erect scaffolding for the removal of the statue of Her Majesty from a pedestal in the centre of the vestibule, to the other side. It took several workmen many hours before the statue itself was successfully lowered and put into place. The *Leeds Mercury* reported that: 'Several weeks will elapse before the entire work is finally completed, and it is probable that the memorial of the Prince Consort will be inaugurated with a public ceremony. Early visitors to the Town Hall have already commented on how fitting the repositioning of the statues was, despite the fact that much scaffolding is still in place. It is to be hoped that the work will be completed some time next week'. (*Leeds Mercury*)

MAY 5TH

1923: It was announced today that the Queen, Princess Mary and Viscount Lascelles are amongst those paying tribute to the family of Mr Willie Hodgson, the ex-Lord Mayor of Leeds, who was killed in a motoring accident at Stanningley, between Leeds and Bradford, late on Friday morning. Mr Hodgson had been part of the welcoming committee who received the Queen and Princess Mary when they visited Harewood, following the announcement of the latter's engagement to Viscount Lascelles last year. The telegram, which was dated May 3rd, stated: 'The Queen is grieved to hear of the tragic death of your husband and desires me to express to you and your family their Majesty's deep sympathy in your great sorrow'. The telegram was signed by a private secretary. Viscount Lascelles also telegraphed the family. His telegram simply read: 'Princess Mary and I wish to express our deepest sympathy in your sad bereavement'. The funeral of Mr Hodgson took place at St John's Church, Roundhay, yesterday and a fitting gesture of the city's tribute to his memory was demonstrated by a crowd of over 20,000 people. The crowds lined the route for over a mile and there was a full attendance of members of the City Council. (*Guardian*)

MAY 6TH

1823: A case was reported today about the fate of one of Leeds climbing boys (chimney sweeps) 'whose abolition was required by the populous of Leeds and the country in general'. The *Leeds Mercury* gave details of his miserable life: 'The boy, Thomas Lee, was born an illegitimate son of an African woman, who had died from drowning the previous year. At the age of nine he was apprenticed to Joseph Haddock as a climbing boy, and the township of Leeds agreed to pay Haddock 2s a week. As was usual with this trade, the child developed sore knees and elbows which were exacerbated by being forced to sweep as many as seven chimneys in one day. He was not allowed respite, despite his wounds, and was often goaded up the chimneys with a fork. On several occasions when he said he could not work, he was taken to a nearby lane and beaten severely. On Wednesday last he ran away and was brought back to the workhouse where his sores were attended to.' Mr Haddock was reported as being 'a good master', but the newspaper asked, 'if such revolting scenes are what boys can expect under good masters, what must be the situation of those in the hands of bad ones?' (*Leeds Mercury*)

MAY 7TH

1857: Mr Swale, the Chief Inspector of Nuisances, appeared at the court house at the request of one of the magistrates, Mr Darnton Lupton Esq., and made a statement to the bench. He told them that on the previous day an Irishman called at the Board of Works and stated that there was a woman lying dead in a lodging house in Harrison's Court, York Street, in a very offensive state. Her friends were unable to bury her and the relieving officer for the workhouse refused to give them either a coffin or the burial dues. Mr Swale had gone to the house and found the body of a woman laid near the fire; a number of men, women and children in the same room. The body had been lying there since Tuesday and the smell was most offensive. He ordered the fire to be put out and the people to leave the room immediately, after which he saw the relieving officer. A coffin was sent and the body interred the same night. Another magistrate commented that, 'this was becoming a common practice and was an attempt of relatives and friends to relieve themselves of the cost of internment'. (*Leeds Mercury*)

MAY 8TH

1945: Today the city of Leeds celebrated VE-Day with open-air dancing, which took place in front of the lions at the Town Hall. It was reported that 'a total of 70 people lost their lives in nine air raids which took place in Leeds during the years of World War Two. The worst attack was suffered on March 14th and the early hours of the 15th in 1942, when the Town Hall, City Station, goods yards and the famous Quarry Hill Flats were all bombed. People who lived in the city counted themselves lucky not to have had more damage. Indeed, it was said that the black pall of smoke which lay over the city saved it from more bomb damage. In reality Leeds was saved because of its inland position and having no industrial targets of any significance'. In order for Leeds people to be able to celebrate VE-Day suitably, music was supplied and hundreds of couples, many of them women, danced in the front of the Town Hall, thankful that they had survived the five years of the war. (Feather, J.W., *Leeds: The Heart of Yorkshire*, Leeds, Basil Jackson Publications, 1967)

MAY 9TH

1930: A controversy broke in Leeds over the absence of Miss Kathleen Merry, aged fifteen, from school; her absence was discussed at the Leeds Town Council on this day. Miss Merry, the daughter of a local golf professional, defiantly stayed away from school to take part in a women's golf tournament after being refused leave of absence by the headmistress of the West Leeds High School. When she returned to school, she was sent back home on suspension. Alderman Alfred Massey said that, 'I do take exception to the idea that is prevalent today in this city and in the educational world that a headmistress has right over a child and the parents have none. If this is what we have to tolerate from the education authorities, the sooner we transfer the custody and upbringing of our children to the State and the education authorities the better'. Mr Fred Barraclough, an ex-president of the National Union of Teachers, maintained that the headmistress was perfectly justified in taking the action that she did. Alderman Simpson, chairman of the Education Committee, expressed the hope that the heads of school would use 'tact, discretion and discrimination in such circumstances and they will find that they would be firmly supported by the authorities'. (*Leeds Mercury*)

MAY 10TH

1846: An unusual scene took place in the Borough Court this morning. A poor woman, named Elizabeth Stainsby, told the magistrate that she lived in Pottery Field and was in receipt of parish relief of 6s a week. On the last pay day she spoke to relieving officer Mr Wrigglesworth, who told her that her relief money had already been paid out to someone else in her name. It seems that the relieving officer was at fault, as he had paid out the money without a ticket from the party applying for it. The magistrate told him that he would have to pay the cost out of his own pocket 'even if he lives on bread and water for a week'. Wrigglesworth refused to pay it and walked out of the court, amid a storm of hisses and boos, but before he got very far, he was once again recalled back into court. The judge told him, 'I consider you totally unfit for the situation you hold, and I will do anything in my power to get you turned out of it'. Wrigglesworth, without any reply, turned and left the court once more. (*Leeds Mercury*)

MAY 11TH

1874: It was reported today the Miss Sarah Robinson was visiting Leeds and other towns in the north of England. Her aim was to improve the lives of soldiers, particularly when they were off duty. She states that in Portsmouth most of the soldiers are quartered when they have served abroad for twelve or eighteen months, before moving onto other stations. She told a large crowd at the Assembly Rooms that 'there is nowhere to pass their time, except those that offer vicious temptations and spending money on drink'. The *Mercury* records that: 'More than 1,000 public houses and beer shops throw open their doors to our soldiers in the town, many of them presenting as companions the most dissolute and abandoned of the population; but the house "without the drink" is still wanting. Mrs Robinson's intention is to open such a house in Portsmouth and is collecting subscriptions from some of the best and most distinguished officers. No help was expected from Government quarters but private benevolence has already provided more than half of the £6,000 needed. The Soldiers Institute is expected to open by the end of June and we trust that Leeds will do its share and contribute towards that end'. (*Leeds Mercury*)

MAY 12TH

1870: Today's newspaper recorded an attempted suicide in Leeds, when a man named John Wood was brought into the dock. He was charged with trying to take his own life on Sunday May 8th. PC Mylands stated that about 1 p.m. on Sunday he went into the Horse and Jockey Yard, Holbeck, and found the prisoner lying on his back with a dreadful gash across his throat. The wound had been inflicted in a privy with a razor. The prisoner was taken to his brother's house, and there his throat was dressed by Dr Scott and Dr Pearson. At the time he said that he wished he had completed the job and asked Dr Scott to 'chop his head off'. The prisoner was moved to the Holbeck workhouse, where he remained until Tuesday night, when he was discharged. He was then taken into custody by Mylands, to whom he said as they were on the way to the police station, that 'at the time he made the attempt on his life, he was both drunk and mad'. He had been recognised by a neighbour who raised the alarm, and his brother took the razor away from him. The prisoner was remanded for a week. (*Leeds Express*)

MAY 13TH

1876: A meeting was held in the library of the Friends Meeting House in Woodhouse Lane, Leeds, to hear about the Christian mission work undertaken in Belleville – the Communist district of Paris. Miss De Broen told the assembly that her work had begun soon after the termination of the siege of Paris. The work had started amongst the women who formed their own sewing classes, which were attended weekly by 300 people. Each worker received five pence for a day's sewing, and whilst at work the Gospel was read and hymns taught to the class. Other agencies had since been established in that same district including; Bible classes, Sunday schools, night schools, children's meetings, visitation of the sick and poor, and a dispensary and medical mission. An iron church had been erected in order to comply with certain Government regulations, and subscriptions were asked to support the church and the people of the mission. The chairman stated that, 'having witnessed for himself the success of the mission in Paris, he knew of no better contribution of funds than to the establishment of a new church'. Miss De Broen was thanked for her talk and the proceedings were then concluded. (*Leeds Mercury*)

MAY 14TH

1856: It was reported today that the architect's plans for the new tower for the Leeds Town Hall had been exhibited in the shop window of Messrs Hardwick & Sons, woollen drapers of Briggate. The architect, Mr Broderick, stated that the new tower would be an important addition to the building; not only would it be pleasing to the eye, but it would also be in keeping with the architecture of the noble edifice. The whole of the tower was to be surmounted by a dome. It was reported that 'the tower gives a splendid finish to the hall; whilst removing the objection raised by some against it being of a too spiral appearance of the former design. The height will be 220 feet and will have a superior adaptation for public clocks. The design was exhibited to the members of the Town Council at the quarterly meeting and, although no decision was come to on the subject, the general feeling of members of the council seems to be in favour of the new design. The decision rests with the Town Hall Committee, a meeting of which is convened for tomorrow afternoon'. (*Leeds Times*)

MAY 15TH

1866: The flax spinning mills at Saynor Lane, Hunslet, belonging to Messrs Parker Brothers, were destroyed by fire this morning. Work commenced as usual at six o'clock, and shortly before eight, smoke and flames were observed issuing from a large wooden shed about six or seven yards away from the mills. The shed was filled with tow, and the inflammable nature of this substance caused the fire to spread with great rapidity. A second wooden erection, also containing tow, was in flames within a few minutes, and as the wind fanned the fire in the direction of the main building, the situation became very alarming. Fire brigades attached to the various insurance offices and several engines were dispatched to the scene of the conflagration. Before the exertions of the firemen could be of any avail, the mills had caught fire; flames bursting from every window. The roof fell in shortly afterwards, and the attention of the fire brigades were principally devoted to confining the fire to the mills, and to saving the adjoining houses in which the workmen lived. The efforts of the firemen in this respect were fortunately successful, but the mills were completely gutted. No cause could be assigned for the fire. (*The Guardian*)

MAY 16TH

1856: It was reported in the *Leeds Mercury* that 'the Crimean photographs now on view at the Music Hall in Leeds, conveyed a more vivid idea of the incidents of camp life and the scenery around Sebastopol than endless pages of descriptions in newspaper'. The photographs not only showed distinguished generals and officers, but also the scenes and events of the struggles on the shore of the Black Sea. Other photographs showed councils of war, which were held by Lord Raglan and his officers. Similarly, the likeness of Marshall Pelissier and Omar Pacha were depicted, along with landscapes and portraits in what amounted to be a collection of about 320 photographs. The reporter stated that: 'The magical skill of the photographer has preserved not only for the amusement of an idle hour, but has furnished thoughts at once sad and ennobling. These pictures have an intrinsic value as a work of art, yet also convey the conditions in which our valiant soldiers fight for the Empire'. The exhibition would continue to be on show for another fortnight before being transferred to Wakefield. (*Leeds Mercury*)

MAY 17TH

1847: On the morning of this day an explosion of fire-damp occurred at Beeston Main colliery, near Leeds, resulting in the loss of nine lives. The colliery of Messrs Harding and Co. was visited later today by the General Manager and some of the colliery owners. It was thought that the explosion had been caused by the sudden intrusion of foul air from some old workings into the section where the deceased miners were at work. The list of those unfortunate men and boys who were killed were:

Aaron Bell, of New Hall, Beeston, aged 22
George Bell, of the same place, aged 15
Charles Duxberry, Beeston, aged 14
William Westerman, Lee Fair Road, aged 12
John Orrell, of Churwell, aged 28
Joseph Longstaff of Beeston, aged 56
John Hall, of Beeston, aged 10
John Jessop of Beeston, aged 32

It was also reported that William Richardson, of Churwell, aged 40, was taken out alive, but died in the course of the day. Mr James Harding told the reporter 'that an investigation into the explosion will be held without delay'. A subscription was expected to be started for the wives and families of those miners who died. (*Leeds Mercury*)

MAY 18TH

1887: It was reported that there had been a case brought to the attention of the magistrates at the Town Hall, of an assault on two bailiffs in the course of their duty. Joshua Fox (aged 45) of Ebony Street, Pottery Field, Hunslet, was charged with assaulting Matthew Normington and Arthur Stanbridge. The two men had gone to his house to serve a warrant on Fox for 12s 9d, which was owing to Dr Smith. They alleged that Fox refused to pay the money, or to go with them, but instead took up a shovel and attempted to hit them. After a short struggle, they endeavoured to take the shovel out of his hands and place him in handcuffs, but during the course of the struggle received several blows from him. In defence, Fox said that he offered to pay the money later that week when he had received his wages. When they would not agree to that, he further suggested to them that they could take him to his brother, who would pay the amount. He maintained that there had been no struggle and he offered to go quietly without handcuffs on. Despite this the magistrate, Mr Bruce, sentenced him to one month's imprisonment. (*Leeds Daily News*)

MAY 19TH

1848: The *Leeds Mercury* offered some advice about the prevention of accidents for passengers travelling on trains. The article stated: 'We have this week received several communications from respectable correspondents, developing plans for the prevention of accidents on railways. In some of them there is great similarity of principle. One of the writers thus speaks of the advantages of his plan: "When a danger has been identified a secret signal can be given to the guard from three different compartments of a carriage, and from the guard to the engine driver, with instantaneous effect, without causing the slightest excitement to any other passenger in the train. Thus the alarm which would attend any signal by sound would be avoided in cases of no immediate danger". It has been noted that there has been some concern over the last year or so regarding accidents to passengers of railways, who had been attacked whilst travelling in carriages. It is felt that if some system of notification to the engine driver can be adopted it will be of great value and may even save lives'. The letters were directed to the directors of the Midland Railway for their attention. (*Leeds Mercury*)

MAY 20TH

1873: In pulling down some buildings today for the improvement of New Market Street, a portion of an ancient building known as the Old Red Lion, which was occupied by Mr Alfred Taylor, came down with a crash between 1 p.m. and 2 p.m. The collapse gave but a brief warning, and fourteen or fifteen men who were in the tap room of the Red Lion, barely had time to obey the landlord's summons to 'come out' before the lower part of the old-fashioned hostelry was a complete wreck. Just before the crash came, however, Pearson, the brewer and a waiter, made a dash back into the tap room to rescue his two favourite cocks and he became buried in the ruins. He was rescued immediately, but he received such injuries that rendered his removal to the Infirmary necessary. His birds were unhurt, but a dog was injured by falling rubbish. It was found on investigation that the outer wall on the side of the excavation had given way, which demolished the floors and chimney pieces of the tap room. The landlord told a reporter that 'he had lost almost two thousand gallons of ale which had been stored in the cellar below and was now undrinkable'. (*Leeds Mercury*)

MAY 21ST

1838: A pickpocket was brought into the Leeds Town Hall court and the corresponding report in the *Leeds Independent* related that: 'A well known little strumpet named Harriet Marshall was brought before the magistrates charged with having picked the pocket of a man, named Samuel Robinson, in the central market, on the evening before. Robinson stated that he was passing the prisoner, when she took hold of him and stopped him. She then put her hand into his pocket, and eased him of the burden of nine shillings. Seizing the opportunity, she then ran from him, but Robinson stopped her before she had gone three yards from him. Still holding onto the girl, a watchman was called, who took the prisoner into custody. He told the magistrates that he knew that she had thrown some silver, or something like it, into the street, because he heard the jingle of it as it hit the cobbles. On searching, however, he could not find any money at all. Marshall was committed for trial at Wakefield'. When she appeared at the assizes on July 18th Marshall was sentenced to a month at the Wakefield House of Correction. (*Leeds Independent*)

MAY 22ND

1858: A letter to the editor of the *Leeds Mercury* brought a dangerous practice to the attention of other readers today. The reporter stated that: 'A correspondent complains that the practice prevails in Leeds, and no doubt in other places, of men and boys amusing themselves by shooting at marks, and sometimes at small birds, in fields adjoining public roads. These fields are in many cases frequently at a very short distance from the paths where passengers and horses are continually travelling, and it is inevitable that accidents will happen'. The reporter commented that 'our correspondent mentions some accidents from this inconsiderate and wanton conduct that have nearly proved fatal, within the last few weeks in Leeds. We strongly urge the police to address the necessity of bringing these delinquents without delay before the magistrates. We also beg that this notice quickly brings an end to the unpardonable conduct complained of'. The reporter concludes that: 'It is hoped that the local police force and the magistrates will deal harshly with perpetrators of such serious offences and efforts will be made to wipe out such behaviour'. (*Leeds Mercury*)

MAY 23RD

1807: The election riots of the previous Tuesday and Wednesday nights were reported in today's *Leeds Mercury*, in particular that 'on Wednesday night the Militia mounted their horses without orders from their own officers or from any civil authority, and proceeded galloping down the footpaths of most of the public streets with their swords drawn. They were riding in the most furious and menacing manner thereby stirring great terror to the peaceable inhabitants of the town'. The magistrates ordered that the soldiers concerned were to be placed under confinement for acting in such a dangerous and uncivil manner and particularly without orders from their superiors. The *Mercury* tried to excuse such behaviour, stating that 'perhaps they are certainly entitled to some indulgence, as it is universally admitted that there was perhaps more occasion for military interference on the Wednesday night as on Tuesday. For a considerable time after the soldiers had scoured the street, some mischievous men and boys assembled about the Mayor's house which is situated about half a mile from the town and broke quite a few of his windows'. (*Leeds Mercury*)

MAY 24TH

1839: A fire in a wagon was reported as it made its way from Leeds to Ripon. The newspaper recorded that: 'As the wagon belonging to Mr John Richmond of Ripon was travelling from Leeds to that place, two females who were travelling in the wagon told the Wagoner that there was a smell of burning. While removing some of the packages in order to ascertain where the smell was coming from, flames burst forth. The wind being high at the time, fanned the flames with great violence. Before any of the goods could be entirely removed several valuable packages were destroyed and greatly damaged. It fortunately happened that the occurrence was discovered so near to a dwelling that assistance was almost immediately procured, or the consequences would have been serious. Various are the estimates of the amounts of damage, and the origins of the fire, but the most authentic seems to be that the fire started due to friction between two large French millstones which are iron hooped and were at the bottom of the wagon. It is thought that the damage will estimate to be around £100 which will fall on the proprietor'. (*Leeds Mercury*)

MAY 25TH

1874: Today's newspaper reported a theft from the Leeds post office of a letter. The article stated: 'At Leeds Borough Court on Saturday, Thomas Fisher, 22, a sorter in the Leeds Post Office, was charged by Detective Officer Reeves with the theft of a postal letter'. It appears that for some time letters had been going missing from Leeds, and in order to trap the thief, Detective Officer Reeves inserted into an envelope a marked half sovereign and four dozen postage stamps. Resealing the envelope he posted it in Skipton to an address at Halifax. The post office authorities ensure that the Halifax letters are re-sorted at Leeds, and it was found that the bag in which they were placed had been searched, but the letter posted by the detective was missing. Fisher, who had been the worker responsible for sorting the letters, was accused of having taken it. This he denied, but on being searched, the marked half sovereign and the stamps were found in his possession. He was remanded for a week until further investigation could be made into his character. The following week he was found guilty and sentenced to three months in the House of Correction. (*Leeds Express*)

MAY 26TH

1857: During a sitting of the magistrates at Leeds Court House today, a woman named Elizabeth Thompson was brought in by Inspector Lister on a charge of imposture. The woman, who was dressed respectably, was addressed by Councillor Joseph Wright. He claimed that she had called on him earlier that morning stating that her husband, who was a cloth dresser, had recently died, leaving her with four very young children, now dependent on her. She showed him a petition on which was several names, the last one being that of the Mayor, Mr Fairburn, who, it was alleged, had given the woman 10s. Councillor Wright, who was aware that the Mayor was in London, questioned her closely. At first she stated that Mr Fairburn had given her the money, then changed her mind and said it was the butler who had given it to her. Keeping her confined at his house, Mr Wright sent a note to the Fairburn house and when he was told that no such person had been to the house that morning, he gave her into custody. The signatures on the petition were forgeries and the bench thanked Mr Wright for bringing the case to their attention. The woman, who was single, was found to belong to a gang of travelling thieves, and was sent to the Wakefield House of Correction for three months. (*Leeds Mercury*)

MAY 27TH

1863: A letter was received in Leeds from the President of the United States of America, in response to a resolution which had been passed at a meeting at the Music Hall on February 3rd, regarding the abolition of slavery. The letter, which was addressed to Mr Baines, the Leeds Member of Parliament, was sent from the Legation of the United States, London and was dated May 20th 1863. The letter stated: 'Sir, I am directed by the President of the United States to acknowledge on his behalf the reception of the proceedings of the citizens of the Borough of Leeds, which were duly transmitted to him through the medium of this Legation. It gives him great pleasure to observe that these proceedings are distinguished by an earnest desire that peace may and for ever be, preserved between the United States and Great Britain, and that the union of this country, which is the bulwark of its safety, may be maintained, and especially that it may not be overthrown so as to give room to a new nation to be founded on the cornerstone of human slavery'. The letter goes on to say that the same response had been made to delegations from Manchester and Bradford. (*Leeds Mercury*)

MAY 28TH

1874: 'Today a dinner was given to 50 people who were assembled to eat a meal of Australian Meat, which, it is hoped, would be a step towards introducing the idea to working class people. The invited people who principally represented trade societies, met at the Black Lion Inn, Mill Hill, Leeds, and the meal was under the personal attention of Mr D. Tallerman, the promoter of the Australian Meat Agency of London. After the different meats, which consisted of boiled beef, Scotch collops, ox cheeks etc., had been served with hot vegetables, several of the invited guests made speeches, in which they highly praised the quality of the meat. Mr Tallerman stated that he looked upon this movement as a most important one, and as it spread it would be certain to have the effect of lowering the price of fresh butchers meat. "I have tried Australian meat in my own family with the best results and had known scores of working men who had adopted it with advantages to themselves and their families. Of course they cannot be compared to roast beef and mutton, but they might be used as supplementary and as a change to their own meals".' (*Leeds Mercury*)

MAY 29TH

1743: On this day, the great Methodist John Wesley came to Leeds. He recorded in his diary that not a year before, he had visited Leeds, 'and found that no man cared for the things of God, but a spark has now fallen in this place also, which will kindle a great flame. I met the infant society; about 50 in number, most of them justified, and exhorted them to walk circumspectly. At seven o'clock I stood before the door of Mr Shent's and cried to thousands, "Ho! Every one that thirsteth, come ye to the waters!" The word took place. They gave diligent heed to it, and they seemed to be a mass of people prepared for the Lord. I went to the great church [parish church] and was shewed to the minister's pew. Five clergymen were there, who a little confounded me by making me take the place of my elders and betters. They obliged me to help in administering the sacraments. I assisted with eight more ministers, for whom my soul was much drawn out in prayer. But I dreaded their favour more than the stones of Sheffield'. (Feather, J.W., *Leeds: The Heart of Yorkshire*, Leeds, Basil Jackson Publications, 1967)

MAY 30TH

1865: Mr Emsley, the borough coroner, held an inquest on the body of Alfred Henry Fielding, a gentleman who had died suddenly whilst staying at the West Riding Hotel on Sunday. The deceased was aged about forty years of age, and was employed as a commercial traveller by Messrs Pearce and Co., surgical instrument manufacturers of London and Bristol. He had been staying at the hotel for about a week and on Friday he complained of a pain in the region of his heart. On Saturday night he went to bed partially intoxicated and about 2 a.m. on Sunday afternoon, he was discovered in a dying condition, though he had been seen previously by a maid and had appeared to be fast asleep. The surgeon, Mr H. Price, was called in immediately, but he was too late to be of any service. The coroner requested that Mr Price undertake a post-mortem on the body and he gave evidence at the inquest to state that he could not find any disease of his heart and offered his opinion that he had an attack of apoplexy accelerated by intemperate habits. (*Leeds Mercury*)

MAY 31ST

1918: 'Today the King and Queen's tour of the West Riding came to an end, as the royal couple returned back to London. During the first two days of the visit they visited manufacturers of clothing for "our own and Allied armies". The King visited the Army Clothing Depot in Leeds, and the Phoenix Dynamo Manufacturing Company's works at Thornbury, where the production is largely associated with munitions of war. Hundreds of men and girls wearing silver badges boisterously cheered the King and Queen. One of the men in the excitement of the moment shouted "Good old George" and the King just laughed at the unconventional greeting. The King's attention was brought to Mr James Young, a Crimean veteran, eighty-three years of age, who had brought his grey-haired wife to see their Majesties. The old soldier was asked many questions, and both the King and the Queen heartily shook his hand. This afternoon, three VC's were presented; Sergeant Whitfield proudly received his decoration personally, whilst sadly the other two were handed to the widows of Acting Lt Col. William Herbert Anderson and Private Walter Mills. The royal couple left Leeds to many loud cheers.' (*The Times*)

JUNE 1ST

1886: Today's newspapers recorded the disappearance of a woman and two children from Farsley. The *Leeds Mercury* recorded: 'A little excitement has been created by the sudden disappearance of a married woman named Prince, and her two children. Mrs Prince, who has resided with her husband at Farsley for about two years, is a woman under middle age, and up to now, has been looked upon as an estimable and respectable woman by those who came in contact with her. However, circumstances transpired just this last week which led to enquiries being made, and a meeting was held between numbers of people from whom Mrs Prince had obtained goods on credit. It seems that she had told certain shopkeepers that she was expecting quite a large legacy, and obtained goods on the understanding that they would be paid for as soon as her legacy had been obtained. It is understood that the matter has now been placed in the hands of the police, who are making an investigation into the matter. Any information about the woman's whereabouts should be given at the Town Hall or to her distraught husband.' *(Leeds Mercury)*

JUNE 2ND

1859: A meeting of the Ragged School Association met in a house adjoining Spitalfield's school. The annual report was read by Mr William Glover Joy, who stated that the Ragged School and Shoe Black Brigade had been set up the year before. It had been reported to him that Leeds did not contain enough homeless young people to qualify for help, but Mr Ambler, a town missionary, had disputed that notion. Mr Glover Joy stated that Mr Ambler had told him of the 320 homeless children of the town that he had spoken to, most of them lived by stealing; they had no shelter and simply crept into any hole or corner they could find. Some were taught by their parents to steal and told not to come home without any booty. Others lived with their mothers in houses of ill fame and frequently resorted to public houses, gin palaces and casinos. By Mr Amblers reckoning there were about 600 of these 'street Arabs' in Leeds alone. Mr Glover Joy thought that a 'Ragged School' and 'Night Refuge for the Homeless' would meet the needs of these street children. It was resolved to begin with a Ragged School and Night Shelter for the most destitute and Mr Ambler to be engaged as master. (*Leeds Mercury*)

JUNE 3RD

1858: A severe and protracted thunderstorm passed over Leeds and the neighbourhood, which the people of the town claimed to be the worst for many years. It was reported that 'during the torrential downpour, one of the pinnacles of St John's Church tower was struck by lightning, as was a house at Burley, but fortunately in neither case was the damage extensive. The rain caused the Bramhope tunnel on the North Eastern line to give way at the Leeds end, and the water rushed through in a perfect torrent with tremendous noise. A train which was proceeding through the tunnel about six o'clock, was met by the current and forced to stop. Rescue of the train and its passengers was affected very slowly, the train being in the tunnel more than an hour before it could be brought out. The passengers for Leeds were forced to leave the carriages and walk through the accumulation of rubbish which had collected in the tunnel. Thankfully they arrived safely at Arthington and from there they were sent by another train via York. All the rescued passengers finally reached Leeds about midnight and preparations had been made to get them safely home'. (*Leeds Mercury*)

JUNE 4TH

1872: There was an account of an affray between a group of men who were disturbing the Sabbath by gambling. The report stated that: 'Four young men were yesterday brought up at the Leeds Town Hall charged with playing at pitch and toss on a footpath leading from the suspension bridge to Knostrop the previous Sunday afternoon. Following several complaints, police constables were sent to the area dressed in plain clothes, where they watched the operation for a while before descending on a crowd of over a hundred youths. Bricks, stones and other missiles were thrown, and some of them even pulled knives out, but ultimately – with the assistance of some civilians nearby – the four men were safely housed in the lock-up, with no further injury to their captors; Police Constable Pybus, the officer who had taken the lead in the charge, had his watch broken. Two of the men were sentenced to a month each in prison. One of the other men, who had been previously convicted (and threatened one of the policemen with what he would do when he came out), was sentenced to three months, and the fourth man, thought to be the ringleader, got six months in prison for assaulting the police.' (*Leeds Express*)

JUNE 5TH

1840: At Rothwell Debtors Gaol a meeting was held, including all of the inmates, for the purpose of amending the internal regulations of the establishment. The chair was taken by Mr John Stephenson, who in a very able speech, stated that 'the object of the assembly was to rid ourselves of the mismanagement that had taken place by our predecessors'. Many alterations were proposed, discussed and carried unanimously. Two gentlemen, Mr John Roberts and Mr John Wisdom, were appointed to wait upon Mr Jewison, the Governor, to point out 'the misery and inconvenience all had to endure whilst in the prison'. Mr Jewison admitted the complaints were justified. In the most handsome and humane manner he sanctioned the whole of the proceedings. Since then 'he has promptly provided new beds and linen, and has engaged a person for the purpose of washing and keeping the same in repair'. The deputation having signified Mr Jewison's assent, gave a vote of thanks to him. The debtors 'recommend to the flint-hearted Whig Marshall, the chairman of the Honour Court of Pontefract, the propriety of attending to the noble and humane example of Mr Jewison'. (*Northern Star*)

JUNE 6TH

1861: Today the magistrate courts were surprised to deal with a woman who had been married the previous week, and who arrived at the court in her full wedding regalia. The woman, Ann Lyons, *née* Carrol, of Allison's Buildings, was a rag sorter and worked for Mr George Smith of Swinegate. She had been in his employ for many years and as such held a position of trust. She was therefore allowed to weigh the goods and to give money to the persons bringing in the rags. Two months ago she told Mr Smith that a man named Patrick Malloy, who lived in Bells Yard, York Street, wanted to dispose of some woollen cloth rags on April 19th. Mr Smith's attention was brought to the bag of rags on the scales and he agreed a price of £1 15s 11d, which Malloy had told her to collect for him, and the money was handed over. Other similar transactions occurred in the name of Malloy and on one occasion when she appeared to be anxious to obtain the money on behalf of Malloy, Mr Smith became suspicious. No such man could be found and Mrs Lyons confessed that she had been taking old stock and re-selling it to her employer. Not having sufficient evidence, the case was dismissed. (*Leeds Mercury*)

JUNE 7TH

1934: Plans for extending the Leeds and Bradford municipal aerodrome at Yeadon, which is placed midway between the two cities, were disclosed at a meeting at the Leeds City Council today. Alderman F.H. O'Donnell, a member of the joint committee of the two corporations, outlined a £6,000 scheme to make the aerodrome, which was described as 'a very important terminal of trade routes'. Alderman O'Donnell told reporters: 'The West Riding does a large trade with Holland and therefore both Corporations hoped to see Yeadon linked with the newly opened Hull-Amsterdam service. At the moment there is about 62 acres in use for landing purposes, and in addition to this we are hoping to take another 35 acres. This would give the aerodrome a runway of over a thousand yards. It had been intended that the extension work would be completed in the next two or three years, but the two corporations of Leeds and Bradford had come to the conclusion that the extension work ought to be done immediately. The cost of the work will be shared between the Leeds and Bradford Corporations'. (*The Times*)

JUNE 8TH

1843: The newspapers recorded a correspondence from a member of the public asking for 'a call for public improvements' to the town of Leeds. Addressing his letter to the Editor of the *Leeds Mercury*, the writer noted that 'several streets at the north part of the town, namely Skinner Street, Mercy Street, Forest Street and Primitive Street, result in some areas which are entirely without sewers and paving stones. Others streets are imperfectly drained having merely open gutters, where filth of all descriptions is indiscriminately deposited and where the water in some places forms pools of several yards in extent, which quickly becomes stagnant, filling the atmosphere with impurities'. The correspondent suggests that as a result 'in this district there is a great amount of sickness, especially amongst children, which has proved alarmingly fatal. Steps should be taken immediately to remedy this state of things, as should the weather become warmer, which might daily be expected, the district will be in a shocking state'. The reporter urged that the town council take note to have this nuisance urgently dealt with as a matter of public health. (*Leeds Mercury*)

JUNE 9TH

1777: It was on this day that the Leeds Assembly Rooms were opened to the public. Now, it was announced, 'the people of Leeds have rooms large enough to hold balls and card parties for the Leeds nobility and the local gentry'. The ground floor formed the northern range of the third White Cloth Hall. The rooms were opened by Sir George Savile and Lady Effingham and admission fee was half a guinea for one gentleman accompanied by two ladies. The admission fee provided access to dancing and card games and musical concerts were provided. (*Leeds Intelligencer*)

1880: A case was heard before the coroner, on the death of a railway porter employed at the Great Northern railway station at Leeds. The porter, Mr Walter Jackson, was shunting some carriages and took off the brake without waiting for the signal; as a result the train collided with a stationary engine. The man was thrown violently to the floor, but he managed to continue with his duties although he complained of a pain in his side and he died a few days later of fever. After hearing all the evidence the jury retired and brought in a verdict of 'accidental death, there being no one to blame but the deceased himself'. (*Leeds Mercury*)

JUNE 10TH

1844: Tonight there was a clash between soldiers and the police in Leeds. About forty or fifty soldiers exited in small batches from the military barracks and, by pre-arrangement, assembled at the Green Parrot, Harper Street. About seven o'clock they left the public house in a body, armed with sticks and bludgeons, and went on a crusade against the police. They proceeded up Kirkgate, into Briggate, where they were met by a crowd of police and the battle started. The gang was so intent on inflicting some damage that the police, in almost every instance, suffered defeat and disaster. Constable Wildblood narrowly escaped with his life; Constable Robertson was also hurt and bruised badly, especially on the head and arms, and Constable Smith was nearly killed. During the affray the streets and windows in Briggate, Kirkgate, and Commercial Street were crowded with people who did not come to the help of the police. Indeed, the populace generally seemed to sympathize with the military. At length, reinforcements from the police arrived to finally quell the disturbance. Some of the soldiers took flight at their approach, and some were marched back to the barracks in Woodhouse Lane, where they were dealt with severely by the military authorities. Others were dealt with by local magistrates. (*Leeds Mercury*).

JUNE 11TH

1827: This evening a distressing accident happened to Mr Richard Mann, son of William Mann of Seacroft, near Leeds. The newspaper reported that 'the gentleman was intending to build himself a house at Thorner and along with several workmen was in the process of pulling down an old building for that purpose. The men had been trying unsuccessfully to pull down a wall using ropes, when Mr Mann, notwithstanding that he had been warned of the imprudence of such a step, went to the base of the wall to try to find out what was holding the wall erect, when it fell down with such a crash, and buried him in the ruins. Every means possible were used to remove the rubbish as speedily as possible, but he was found quite lifeless. Such was the violence of the crash that his body was nearly cut in two, and part of his skull was found in his hat. Mr Mann was about 27 years of age and was a gentleman of accomplished manner. He leaves a young widow to whom he was married about 12 months ago, to mourn his untimely fate'. (*Leeds Intelligencer*)

JUNE 12TH

1867: Today's newspapers carried the story of a dishonest lodger in Leeds. At the Town Hall yesterday, before Mr H. Oxley Esq. and Mr J. Bateson Esq., a woman named Sarah Crofton was brought before the magistrates. She had been charged with stealing a quantity of bed linen from the lodging house where she had been staying. The landlord, Mr W.A. Cooper of Nile Street, told the court that the prisoner had occupied a furnished room at his house for the past three months. During that time she had taken the opportunity to steal the property in question, and pledge it with various pawnbrokers. The prisoner was further charged by Mrs June Howgate with having illegally pledged 11½ yards of stuff and a quantity of calico, which she had given her to make up into a dress. The prisoner acknowledged her guilt in both cases, and from what she said in extenuation, it appears that she had been brought up respectably, but had been deserted by her husband, a printer, who had left her destitute. It was said that she 'was a woman of intemperate habits' and she was sentenced to two months imprisonment. (*Leeds Mercury*)

JUNE 13TH

1848: As a result of many complaints of furious driving from the coaches and omnibuses of the Leeds turnpike roads, proceedings were taken to put a stop to the cause of these complaints. Joseph Randall, the driver of a coach which ran between Leeds and Wakefield, appeared before the Justices to answer a complaint made against him by the police. Two witnesses named Thomas Fisher and James Vollans, who were in Hunslet Lane on Saturday, spoke to Randall about galloping towards Leeds at the rate of ten or twelve miles an hour, thereby endangering the safety of the passengers and other road users. In his defence, two of his passengers told the court that they had enjoyed the ride vastly and had not felt that slightest apprehension at the speed of the coach. In answer to questions from the magistrate, it appears that Randall had his horses ride at full gallop throughout the journey and flogged the horses to urge them on. In the end the magistrate thought the charge was fully sustained and therefore fined Randall 40s and costs. (*Leeds Mercury*)

JUNE 14TH

1844: Today saw the culmination of the military riots which had taken place in Leeds (*see* June 10th). A number of prisoners that had been implicated in these riots were brought before the magistrates. Some of the prisoners were identified by various witnesses and charged with having taken an active part, fighting with the soldiers in their attacks upon the police. The magistrates were resolved upon inflicting the heaviest punishments allowed by law. Ten soldiers and nine civilians were bound over to appear at the Borough Sessions. Others who could not obtain bail were committed to the Wakefield House of Correction for periods of between eleven days to one year. A great number were set at liberty, there being no sufficient proof to commit them. It was thought that the riot had started not so much by an attack on the police – which resulted from the riot – but when the soldiers attacked Leeds citizens in the town centre because they were incensed at notices which had appeared in the public houses. The notices stated 'No Irishmen or soldiers wanted here'. (Feather, J.W., *Leeds: The Heart of Yorkshire*, Leeds, Basil Jackson Publications, 1967)

JUNE 15TH

1964: It was announced today that a new bus scheme, the first of its kind, was to have its trial run in Leeds. If successful, it will probably be developed in all major towns and cities in Great Britain. The report states: 'The role of public transport in future traffic plans may be decided in Leeds after experiments over the next two years. A Park and Ride scheme and a system of express buses into the town centre will be developed within the city. The Park and Ride scheme is aimed at commuters from outside the city. They will be charged an inclusive fee for parking outside the congested areas and travelling in by bus. The express buses will bring those living within the city boundaries directly into the city centre'. Mr D.A. Quarmby of Leeds University, said that 'fifteen thousand cars come into the city each day at peak periods. We will study how motorists react to our experiment in order to remedy this problem. It is to be hoped that the new scheme will cut down on the congestion which has been experienced in Leeds for the last few years'. (*The Times*)

JUNE 16TH

1896: A case of cruelty to children was heard in the Town Hall before Mr Atkinson, the stipendiary magistrate. Michael Cairns and his wife Mary were charged at the instance of Inspector Backhouse of the NSPCC, with having neglected their children in a manner likely to injure their health. Last evening, a constable found a boy aged ten and a girl aged eight standing in the doorway of a public house, trying to sell matches. The girl was crying bitterly and when asked why, she said that her feet were sore. She was unable to walk and the police constable carried her to the police station. Whilst there she told the constable that they had been out all day, and had had nothing to eat since morning. Dr Tordoff examined the children and he found that the girl was shockingly dirty and had no underclothes on under a thin little dress. He weighed her and found that she weighed 7¾lbs less than she should have done. The boy was also 11lbs underweight and in the same filthy condition. It seems that the father was an industrious man, but his wife was addicted to drink. The case was adjourned for Inspector Backhouse to make a further report on the family and the charge against the man withdrawn. (*Leeds Mercury*)

JUNE 17TH

1853: It was reported that many dog owners in Leeds were destroying their pets rather than pay for a license. The *Leeds Mercury* noted that 'the Chancellor of the Exchequer had proposed an additional tax on dogs and that every person who keeps a dog will be compelled to pay a tax of 12s a year'. The newspaper noted that: 'To such an extent has this practice of destroying pets prevailed, that the surface of several ponds has been nearly covered with the carcasses of dead dogs and the stench proceeding from them is most foul. Last Thursday the subject was brought to the notice of the Scavenging and Nuisance Committee and as such nuisances were deemed to be injurious to public health, orders were immediately given to remove the carcasses and bury them in quicklime. The matter was completed in four days, when we were told that the numbers of carcasses of dead dogs buried were 483. If the additional dog tax is instrumental in preventing our labouring population from keeping dogs, it will have the effect of a great social evil'. (*Leeds Mercury*)

JUNE 18TH

1847: On this day it was reported that the town was in the grip of an epidemic of typhoid fever, which was no doubt exacerbated by poor conditions. The local newspaper recorded that: 'In the Rose and Crown Yard on Union Street, twenty-eight persons had the fever in seven houses, three of which were without beds. In Wellington Yard, ten people in seven houses, and in Goulden's Buildings four people in three houses were attacked. In another house in Brighton Court, in which there was not a single bed, twelve had the fever, and in a house in Brook Street six were attacked under similar distressing circumstances. As a result of the epidemic, the House of Recovery and the fever hospital were completely full. A temporary wooden shed for a hospital was erected in Accommodation Road and on Richmond Hill. At Cleveland Street, a mill was likewise temporarily occupied for the same purpose'. It was reported that two of the town's surgeons had also caught the disease. It was estimated that 'in the whole township, there were at least 400 persons suffering from the disease. Several individuals caught the contagion whilst ministering to the necessities of the distressed Irish. Between the 27th of May and the 30th of June four Catholic priests died whilst ministering to their parishioners'. (*Leeds Times*)

JUNE 19TH

1727: A ceremony took place in Leeds to proclaim the accession to the throne of King George II. This ancient ceremony, which would proclaim the accession at the Market Cross and at Kirkgate, was described as follows: 'Ordered that the Aldermen and Assistants of this Burrough, do waite upon Mr Mayor tomorrow, at twelve of the clock, at his own house, in their Gownes and on horseback, to go from thence in procession up the Back of the Shambles to the Markett Cross and there proclaim the Mighty Prince, George Prince of Wales, to be lawfull and Rightful King of Great Brittaine. From thence to go down the Shambles, and to make the like Proclomation at Kirkgate end, at the Vicaridge, at the north end of the Bridge, and at Boar Lane end, and from Boar Lane to adjourn to the house of Mr James Wainman's to Solemnize the day, where an entertainment is to be prepared at the Corporations charge, but the same is not to exceed the sume of fifteen pounds'. (Robinson, P., *Leeds Old and New*, Leeds, S.R. Publishers Ltd, 1972)

June 20th

1681: A meeting was held in Leeds regarding the news which had come to the town of the son of Alderman Foxcroft, who had been captured and taken prisoner by some Turks. It seems that the boy had been apprenticed to Captain Robert Newport, who was the owner of the ship *Adriatique*, as a burser. A report in the town council minutes record that: 'His master having lost his life with the vessel, the young man was taken captive and carried as prisoner to Algiers and there sold for seven hundred dollars. The sum required for his redemption will amount to £350 sterling at the least, and his father not being in a condition to raise the same, have craved the advice and assistance of the court; thereupon it is ordered, that a general collection be made from house to house in all constabularies and places in the said Borough. And that all persons, both householders and others, will be pleased to give their charitable contributions to so pious a work, for the Redemption of a Christian soul out of the hands of those barbarous infidels'. A letter was also sent to other towns in the West Riding to ask for their contributions to this 'pious cause'. (Mitchell, W.R., *A History of Leeds,* Chichester, Phillimore, 2000)

JUNE 21ST

1846: Today's newspaper contained the following account of the electric telegraph, which was now available on completion of the train line from Rugby to Leeds. The work, which had been finished the previous Wednesday, was described as 'that splendid masterpiece of scientific mechanism which may not inappropriately be called the railroad of the mind. From Leeds to Rugby, a distance of 122 miles, intelligence of any important event may be communicated through the instrumentality of the telegraph in such a short space of three minutes; and when the telegraph shall be constructed between Rugby and London, a further distance of 33 miles; it is probable that the inhabitants of Leeds may be put in possession of proceedings and decisions of national interest, almost as early as the immediate neighbours of Westminster Hall on the Surrey side of the Thames. The advantages of such a mode of communication, conveying intelligence with the rapidity of thought, are almost inconceivable whether considered in a national or social point of view. It is to be hoped that manufacturers and industrialist of Leeds will soon discover the importance of this new and innovative system'. (*Leeds Mercury*)

JUNE 22ND

1863: 'An invitation was given to the Prince and Princess of Wales to visit Leeds during their forthcoming visit to Halifax, where it was hoped that the Royal couple will take part in the ceremony of laying the first stone of the new Infirmary. A deputation from Leeds consisting of the Mayor, the former Mayor, and chair of the New Infirmary Committee – as well as accompanying local MPs, Mr Baines and Mr Beecroft – visited Marlborough House this morning and waited upon Lieutenant General Knollys, Comptroller of the Household to His Royal Highness the Prince of Wales'. It was reported that the deputation was courteously received, a free conversation ensued, and a memorial conveying the invitation was left with Lt General Knollys to be conveyed to the Prince and Princess. The *Mercury* stated that: 'It is impossible for us yet to offer an opinion as to the probability of their Royal Highnesses being able to accept the invitation, but it is expected that an answer will be received in the course of today'. Unfortunately, Lt General Knollys wrote the next day to Mr Baines to inform him that the visit would not go ahead due to the 'fatigue which the Princess of Wales has lately incurred'. (*Leeds Mercury*)

JUNE 23RD

1824: The Leeds (or Haigh Park) Races were to be held for the first time. The races had been roundly condemned by some who said that they will be 'an unfortunate event for the town, due to the fact that they will no doubt encourage a spirit of gambling, exercising an injurious influence upon public morals and interrupting the enjoyment and consequently diminishing the comfort of many who derive their daily bread from the produce of their hands'. However, others disagreed and praised the establishment of the races, stating that 'the course, which is admirably adapted for the purpose, is situated about three miles south of Leeds, on the new road to Pontefract. For the comfort of race-goers the grounds are provided with a grandstand and the usual appendages of such a place, with accommodation for horses and their riders'. Generally though, the populace of Leeds were in favour of the races and there was little doubt that the racecourse would become very fashionable with the people of the town and would bring in much-wanted revenue for public rates. (*Leeds Intelligencer*)

JUNE 24TH

1828: An announcement was made in the local newspaper of a couple of body snatchers at work in Leeds. Two men, by the name of James McDonald and John Curtis, were examined before the magistrates on a charge of disinterring a dead body, which was taken in a hand barrow, in an uncovered state, down Kirkgate the previous night at midnight. The report stated that: 'Some papers were found on the person of McDonald, with a list of medical gentlemen in this town, among others Dr Hunter, who was called into the court to give evidence. Showing great reluctance to give his evidence, Dr Hunter stated that McDonald had called on him on Sunday at his surgery and asked him if he wanted a skeleton. He replied that he did not. McDonald then asked him if he wanted a subject for dissection, to which he again replied in the negative, giving his reason that he was not at the time undertaking a dissection with his students'. After some not very material evidence, the parties were committed once again for re-examination. The report continues that 'at this time we understand the body does not appear to have been claimed or identified'. (*Leeds Intelligencer*)

JUNE 25TH

1848: Today it was announced that a cure of hydropathy had been tried on a horse and proved to be very beneficial to the animal, which had previously seemed to be dying. The *Leeds Mercury* announced that: 'The cold water remedy had been administered to the brute creation as well as to man. Several instances have been reported to us in confirmation of this statement. The most recent case is that of one of two horses who were accustomed to run a stagecoach between Leeds and Ilkley, and which yesterday week was obliged to be pulled up on the road, when it was dragging a heavy load of passengers. The horse appeared so strained and disordered as to require that it was taken out of harness, and its place supplied by another. Being near its journey's end, it was with great difficulty that the horse was got to the stables, where it was expected to die during the night. Whilst at the stables, the horse was tightly packed with a sheet saturated with cold water, and then surrounded by straw and other things to prevent evaporation, and to the amazement of the stablemen, it began to recover. By giving the horse another four or five similar applications in succession, it has been restored to a healthy condition, and is now able to undertake its work'. (*Leeds Mercury*)

JUNE 26TH

1847: News came to the town of Leeds about a robbery which had been committed on the person of John Kitchen, a quack doctor who claimed to be able to cure the deaf and dumb. Kitchen, described as an '82 year old corpulent man attired in ragged clothing and bandages instead of stockings', had been brought before the magistrates at Leeds Town Hall charged with drunkenness the previous Monday. He was so drunk that the police were forced to lock him up in the cells. Whilst they searched his cart, which carried all his possessions, they found a silver plate, eight watches, articles of gold and a bag holding 280 sovereigns. He said that most of the possessions had been his for over thirty years and had travelled around the country with him for forty to fifty years – his cart being his only home. The magistrates fined him 5s and costs for being drunk and advised him to put his belongings in the bank. As a consequence, as he left the town, he was robbed. There is little doubt that the perpetrators were probably in the Town Hall and heard of his hoard and decided to steal it. (*Leeds Mercury*)

JUNE 27TH

1812: An account was published of the first journey of a locomotive in Leeds, which had been made by Messrs Fenton, Murray and Wood, for the purpose of substituting steam for horses. 'The machine had a steam engine of four horsepower with the agency of cranks turning a cog wheel, and iron cogs which were then placed at one side of the railway, allows the locomotive to be capable of moving at ten miles per hour'. The article stated that: 'At four o'clock in the afternoon of June 24th, a machine ran from the coal staithes to the top of Hunslet Moor, where six and afterwards eight wagons of coal, each weighing 3¼ tons, were hooked to the back part. With this immense weight, to which, as it approached the town, was added to the weight of about fifty of the spectators who had climbed upon the wagons. The locomotive set off on its return back to the coal staith, and performed the journey, a distance of about a mile and a half, principally on a dead level in twenty-three minutes without the slightest accident'. (Feather, J.W., *Leeds: The Heart of Yorkshire*, Leeds, Basil Jackson Publications, 1967)

JUNE 28TH

1852: At the Leeds courthouse today there appeared before the magistrates a man named Luke Booth, who was charged with using abusive language and demonstrating disorderly conduct in a railway carriage the previous Saturday. The men who brought the complaints were Mr John Kay and Mr Joseph Forrest, both of Leeds. It seems that the two men were on the Manchester to Leeds train and, arriving at Huddersfield, they were joined by the prisoner, who, in a state of intoxication rudely entered the carriage, taking a seat between Mr Kay and a lady. A short time after leaving Huddersfield he fell asleep, making use of Mr Kay's shoulder as a pillow. When the latter pushed him away and remonstrated with him, the prisoner began to use the most abusive language towards Mr Kay and Mr Forrest, which he continued through the whole of the journey. On arriving at Leeds station, the two men made a complaint and the prisoner was given into custody and locked up. The magistrates fined him 20s and costs, which he immediately paid before leaving the court. (*Leeds Mercury*)

JUNE 29TH

1890: The escape of a prisoner from Wakefield Gaol was reported in the local newspaper. It seems that Leeds man Robert Hipps was found to be missing from his cell at Wakefield by the warders. Prior to his imprisonment for theft he had lived at 22 Farrar Street, Leeds. During his confinement it was said that 'Hipps had been more than once in trouble with the police who regarded him as "a determined character"'. Local police reported that he had served several prison sentences in the past for charges ranging from burglary to arson. The newspaper reported that 'up to last evening the missing criminal had not been captured'. Hipps was a shoemaker and supposedly he picked the lock of his cell with an awl. It is then supposed that he made his way out of the prison and then, incredibly, leapt over the high wall which surrounded the prison. The Leeds police were informed and were on the lookout for this notorious character. The paper requested that: 'Anyone who has any information on his whereabouts is asked to contact the Chief Constable at the Town Hall as soon as possible'. (*Leeds Mercury*)

JUNE 30TH

1869: Today the town of Leeds saw the last of what had become a local landmark. The *Leeds Mercury* reported that the old Briggate clock, which had served the public of Leeds for more than a century, was taken down and sold in the Crypt, being offered to the highest bidder. Mr H.B. Legg had offered to give it an appropriate refuge in his new building at the corner of Briggate and Upperhead Row, but this was turned down and the clock was put up for auction later in the day. There was a good attendance at the sale and the auctioneer, Mr Weatherly, read out the inscription on the dial: 'The clock had been erected by George Goodall of Aberford in 1787 and it had been repaired by William Bowling in August 1795'. The auctioneer invited offers for the clock and its machinery, which included three clock bells made by Mears of London in 1787 – the largest bell weighing upwards of 5cwt. Mr Turton of Marsh Lane finally bought the clock for £50. For a further 30s he also acquired the iron vane and copper fleece which surmounted the clock, five cast-iron pillars (which supported the cupola and the timber), tye bolts and nuts connected with the machinery. (*Leeds Mercury*)

JULY 1ST

1718: The first edition of the *Leeds Mercury* was printed by John Hirst from his office 'over against Kirkgate end'. The original newspaper consisted of twelve small quarto pages and carried a huge woodcut representing the Golden Fleece. There was also a depiction of a fat old postman wearing a wig and a low crowned, broad brimmed hat. The woodcut showed him blowing a straight horn and galloping on a heavy horse, with a banner proclaiming 'THE LEEDS MERCURY'. The paper cost 3*d* and it contained nothing but brief extracts from the London and other paper's foreign and domestic news, together with an account of local trade and markets. It also had columns which gave news from abroad, which had been received in letters from places as far away in the Empire as India and New York. During times of epidemics the paper would print weekly metropolitan lists of mortality and casualties. But the editor, Hirst, refused to print news about Leeds as he thought that news of the local affairs of Leeds were too well known to people of the town to require printing. Despite this, the newspaper became very popular and sold in its hundreds. (Read, D., *Press and People 1790–1850 Opinion in Three English Cities*, London, Edward Arnold, 1961)

JULY 2ND

1861: Today it was reported that Lt-Col Woodford had inspected the Leeds police force in the Coloured Cloth Hall yard. The Mayor was present, as well as some members of the Watch Committee. The force, at this time, consisted of one Chief Constable, six Inspectors, twenty-six sub-inspectors and sergeants, four detective officers and 168 constables. The Chief Constable informed Lt-Col Woodford that four sub-inspectors and sergeants, and nine constables were not in attendance because of being on duty. (*Leeds Mercury*)

***

1930. It was announced that a memorial plaque to Louis Aime Augustin Le Prince, who was said to be 'the father of the film industry', was to be placed on the wall of his workshop at 160 Woodhouse Lane, Leeds, a studio which he occupied from 1887 to 1890. The tablet reads: 'Louis Aime Augustin Le Prince had a workshop on this site, where he made a one lens camera and with it photographed animated pictures. Some were taken at Leeds Bridge in 1888. Also he made a projecting machine and thus initiated the art of cinematography. He was assisted by his son and by Joseph Whitely, John William Longley and Frederick Mason of Leeds'. The Lord Mayor of Leeds consented to unveil the tablet and the French Ambassador was represented by Sir Charles Wilson. (*The Times*)

JULY 3RD

1871: Today it was noted that 'by the use of commendable energy, the authorities for the Census Office have now been completed and have issued a preliminary report upon the population of Leeds'. It was reported that 'the census had been carried out extremely well and there had been little problems, which could not be dealt with by the census enumerators. One of them spoke about a wealthy spinster of a very advanced age, who fastened up her doors and windows, and forbade access to the enumerator, saying that even a fine of £20 would not induce her to give him the required information. However in answer to a soothing letter, she sent her completed schedule to the central office and therefore had been included in the census. Another enumerator was insulted and assaulted by a man who also refused to allow him onto his property, but on the whole, the great task of 3rd April appears to have been accomplished in a very smooth and satisfactory manner. From the report it has been established that the population of Leeds in this year is 52,036 and generally speaking the increase is much greater than the ten years from 1851 – 1861'. (*Leeds Mercury*)

July 4th

1827: On this day the local newspaper reported that smoke which had been issuing from the surface of the ground in St Peter's Square had increased in such quantities, that it created much alarm in the neighbourhood. An excavation was made where a large body of fire was found, which, as soon as it reached the air, burst into flames. Fire engines were procured and a quantity of water was thrown into the hole, which appeared for a time to have extinguished the fire. However, over the next two days, the smoke was seen to issue from several other places and in such very considerable quantities, that once more there was cause for concern that the area might become engulfed in flames. A number of excavators were employed in digging more holes to remove the earth and to ascertain the cause of the fire. It seems that they discovered a bed of coal, about 2 feet in thickness and only 5 feet beneath the surface of the ground, was on fire and was the cause of the smoke. It was found that the ignition had been created by the furnace of a pipe maker, which had been erected over the coal bed, causing it to ignite. The furnace was removed and the hole was filled up with gravel, which was well saturated with water. (*Leeds Mercury*)

JULY 5TH

1891: A show which was visiting Leeds, run by Colonel Cody and 'his interesting troupe', had its final performance in Cardigan Fields. The entertainment, which had been in Leeds for a fortnight already, was said to be a tremendous success and thousands attended as they preformed two shows a day. The troupe 'which gained so much favour each day, was so entertaining that last Saturday saw "the largest house they have had since they left Brussels two months previously".' Colonel Cody told a reporter that 'in a financial sense, the visit to Leeds has been highly satisfactory'. His kindness also extended to entertaining forty-one children of Holbeck workhouse and forty-five of its elderly residents at his show, which was judged to be a great success. The inclusion of his trained horses and cowboys held the rapt attention of the children; as did the Indian encampment scene. The finale – the attack of the wagon train – was realistically performed and carried out. (*Leeds Mercury*)

JULY 6TH

1864: 'The first Commission of Assize for the West Riding of Yorkshire was opened in Leeds this day, amidst the enthusiasm of all classes of the inhabitants. Thousands of sightseers gathered, the morning trains conveying thousands of people from all surrounding districts, in time for the hour arranged for the judges to arrive in the borough. The time at which their Lordships were expected to arrive from York was 4.45 p.m., and a strong barricade was erected between the station platform and the central entrance. A clear passage was left for the judges between the station and the Queen Hotel, where the procession was to commence. At the west entrance to the hotel a number of gentlemen had taken up their position, and respectfully saluted the judges as they passed within to change into their robes. A few minutes later their Lordships appeared dressed in their judicial wigs and red gowns. A body of mounted police then entered the square, followed by two carriages, one containing the Under-Sheriff (Mr W. Gray), and the other the judges' marshals. Having drawn up in front of the Hall the Mayor and other dignitaries received their Lordships, who, on alighting, were repeatedly cheered. The learned Judges, preceded by the Mayor, passed up the steps and into the Town Hall where refreshments were to be served.' (*Leeds Mercury*)

JULY 7TH

1908: Today the King and Queen, accompanied by Princess Victoria, arrived in Leeds for the opening of the university extension. The local newspaper stated that: 'Decorations were being installed right up to midnight on the previous night, which had transformed the streets beyond recognition. Boar Lane, the most central thoroughfare, was a notable sight and was so bedecked and garlanded, so bristling with Venetian masts, festooned and be-flagged that the familiar frontages were lost to view'. Soon after 1 p.m. the Royal train drew up at the platform and the Princess and the Royal couple were transferred to the Town Hall, heralded by a flourish of trumpets. A guard of honour, made up of the men of the Leeds Rifles, was mounted in Victoria Square and nearly fifty Crimean Veterans were on parade. The King, the Queen and Princess Victoria were then conducted to the Victoria Hall, where, on a high dais, chairs of state had been set and, in a very unusual ceremony, the Lord Mayor of Leeds was knighted Sir Wilfred Hepton. After these proceedings their majesties were escorted by the Leeds Squadron of Alexandra, Princess of Wales's Own Hussars, on the next part of their visit. (*The Times*)

JULY 8TH

1853: The *Leeds Mercury* reported that a case of a boy named Isaac Jennings, aged thirteen years (who had been in custody four or five times before) was placed before the Justices on Monday; he had been charged with pocket-picking. About 10 p.m. the previous Saturday, a girl named Priscilla Smith, living in Brewery Street, Hunslet, was in Kirkgate market. Feeling somebody at her pocket she turned round sharply and found the prisoner's hand in it. The lad bolted and she shouted out 'stop thief' and he was caught by another female. When Smith grabbed hold of him and told him she was sending for the police, he got her hand in his mouth and bit it, in an attempt to make her let go of him. When he realised he had failed, he became penitent and offered her the money he had stolen (10*s* 9*d*) saying, 'I beg your pardon' and 'let me go'. Policeman Sharp was called and the boy was arrested and taken to the police station. The bench, on hearing the case, felt that a mere prison sentence would not deter the boy from stealing in the future and sentenced him to be taken before the assizes for trial. At the next assizes, the judge found him guilty and he was sentenced to six months with hard labour at the Wakefield House of Correction. (*Leeds Mercury*)

July 9th

1870: It was reported that an alarming omnibus accident happened on the Roundhay Road at 10 a.m. this morning. The bus, which had travelled from Boston to Leeds, was just opposite the Leeds Barracks, when it overturned without warning. The bus was licensed to carry twenty-six passengers – twelve inside and sixteen on the roof – and it was reported that several of the outside passengers had been injured after being thrown to the ground. The inside passengers, which consisted principally of women, suffered slightly better. There had been a good deal of luggage on the vehicle, which was consequently scattered all over the road. The inside passengers were extricated with some difficulty as the bus had been thrown onto one side and the passengers were all in a heap. Assistance was quickly given by people living near to where the vehicle had overturned, and three surgeons were soon on the scene. Several policemen and Inspector Ball from the Sheepscar station attended, who rendered some timely aid and, under their care, three of the injured passengers were taken to the Infirmary. It seems that the accident was caused by one of the large wheels giving way, the spoke of which had been broken off from the centre. (*Leeds Mercury*)

JULY 10TH

1894: Today, readers of the *Leeds Mercury* were informed about a day's holiday which had been given for some of the poorest children of the town. Subscriptions had been collected over the last few weeks and over £150 had been spent on events throughout the day, resulting in over 200 children being selected and entertained at Roundhay Park. Through the kindness of Mr Winslow, the manager of the Roundhay Electric Tramway, the children were given a ride both ways, free of cost. They started the proceedings at 12.30 p.m., when they were given tea and spiced buns. Kindly neighbours had helped to make the little ones presentable by the loan of hats, cloaks, boots etc. and the children seemed to have enjoyed themselves thoroughly. Races were run and games of tug-of-war were organised, in which the children competed amongst themselves, and prizes were awarded for the winners. The children had plenty to eat; supplemented by a halfpenny-worth of sweets each and chocolate and nuts. The *Mercury* said: 'It is to be hoped that this will become an annual event in order to provide these most vulnerable young children with at least one good day out, away from the cares of their parents'. (*Leeds Mercury*)

July 11th

1871: A report about an inquest into the death of a man named John Stewart, who died in a colliery accident at Killingbeck Colliery, appeared in today's newspaper. It seems that Stewart, who was aged twenty-four years, was employed by the trustees of Messrs Garside in a sinking pit in the colliery. On the morning of Tuesday last, whilst the deceased was at the bottom of a shaft, three or four yards of heavy chain broke off and fell upon him. He was standing in a stooped position and because of this, his back was greatly injured. He was extricated from the shaft and taken to the hospital, where it was reported that he died on Thursday. Representatives from Messrs Garside attended the inquest and reported on the safety rules and regulations which were in place for workers in the colliery. Witnesses stated that they had seen the accident, but that it happened so quickly that they were unable to prevent it. The coroner, in summing up for the jury, stated that the accident could not have been prevented and that no one was to blame for his death. The jury returned a verdict affirming that to be the case. (*Leeds Express*)

JULY 12TH

1882: There was a report on an adjourned case of night poaching at Adel cum Eccup, on land belonging to Mr Francis Darwin JP. Thomas Teale, William Morris and Stephen Hird had been brought into the West Riding Court the week before, charged with the offence. The gamekeeper, James Child, said that he was watching the woods about 1 a.m. in the morning with two assistant gamekeepers and two police constables. They saw five poachers who, when they saw the gamekeepers and the police constables, attempted to run off. Two of them escaped but Teale, Morris and Hird were caught and taken into custody. In their possession was found twenty-two rabbits, a number of nets, pegs and other appliances for poaching. It was noted in the newspaper that 'they did not carry guns or have dogs or ferrets in their possession'. It seems that their peculiar manner of poaching was to spread a large net and to frighten the rabbits into it by dragging a piece of cord over the ground, forcing the rabbits to run into the nets. The case was adjourned for a week to look into the men's antecedents, where it was found that none of them had been charged with poaching previously. All three were given six-month prison sentences with hard labour. (*Leeds Mercury*)

July 13th

1626: On this day, King Charles I gave the First Charter of Incorporation constituting the town and parish of Leeds to be a Municipal Borough. The charter stated that: 'Whereas our town of Leeds in our county of York, is an ancient and populous town and the inhabitants for many years past, have had and skillfully exercised, the art or mystery of making and working, woollen cloths commonly called in England "northern dozens" to their perpetual praise, and great increase of the revenue of the crown of England for the custom of the same cloths. And whereas divers clothiers of the same town had begun to make deceptive cloths to the damage and prejudice of us, subversion to the clothiers of the town and the discredit of the inhabitants there'. The Charter then went on to outline that 'from henceforth the town was to be governed by an Alderman, nine principal Burgesses and twenty assistants with the power to act for life and to fill up vacancies as they arose'. (Robinson, P., *Leeds Old and New*, Leeds, S.R. Publishers Ltd, 1972)

JULY 14TH

1873: An action was heard at the assize court against the Leeds Corporation, for injuries to a horse that had been brought by a soda water manufacturer named Barnet and Co. It was claimed that on April 1st, a horse and van belonging to the plaintiff was passing along Meadow Road, under the charge of a man named Thackster. The Corporation steamroller was there and the plaintiff's van passed it, between two carts. The driver of the steamroller had stopped the engine whilst the two carts had passed, but it was alleged that it was started as the van was alongside it. The noise startled the horse, which took fright, reared up on his hind legs and then fell, cutting the animal quite severely. The harness was damaged and the van shaft was broken; the horse had to be put down. The defence claimed that the van did not pass the steamroller on the same side as the carts, and that the engine was not started again until the van was thirty yards in front. After several witnesses had been examined, the learned judge said he did not believe the incredible story of the witnesses for the defence, and he gave a verdict to the plaintiff against the Corporation and awarded him damages and costs. (*Leeds Mercury*)

JULY 15TH

1847: Today the local newspaper announced that the Leeds Borough Gaol was now completed at a cost of £43,000. The report states that the building 'is pleasantly situated near Armley, on the south side of the picturesque valley of the Aire, about a mile and a half west of the town. It is a noble castellated stone structure, presenting a massive pile of masonry, and is visible from many distant points. Messrs Perkin and Backhouse, of Leeds, were the architects. Previous to its erection, the prisoners convicted at the Borough Courts were sent to the Wakefield House of Correction. The discipline of this gaol was that of the "Silent System", and the employment of the prisoners is reproductive labour. Each inmate has a separate cell (of which there are about 334), where he follows the occupation to which he may have been accustomed. Those who have no defined calling are employed in picking oakum or making matting, the proceeds of which are applied in aid of the establishment. In addition to the persons committed from the sessions, convicts are also confined here, at the cost of the government, preparatory to their departure for their penal settlements. The arrangements are on the most improved system of prison discipline'. (Mitchell, W.R., *A History of Leeds*, Chichester, Phillimore, 2000)

JULY 16TH

1839: On this day, two women described as being 'of the gypsy tribe' were brought before the magistrates at the courthouse charged with having obtained from two women the sum of 3*s*, under the pretence of telling their fortunes. The two foolish young women duped in this way were both servants to Mr D. Whiteley of the Horse and Trumpet Inn in Briggate. The prisoners were sisters and they gave their names as Mary Cunningham and Sarah Boswell, the former being the elder of the two and married. It appears from the statement of the girls that on Monday afternoon, the two women were in the Horse and Trumpet, and after drinking a glass of ale proceeded to the kitchen where, finding the girls alone, they at once proposed to tell them their fortune. Fortunately, Mr Whiteley was within hearing, and could also see all that transpired; he therefore stepped out and called in Policeman Spiers, who was on duty in the neighbourhood, and into whose custody 'the unravellers of future events' were transferred. As there was no proof that the younger girl had received any of the money, she was discharged, but Cunningham was sent for a month to the Wakefield House of Correction. (*Northern Star*)

JULY 17TH

1926: 'Today ends the ten days' long festivities of the Tercentenary programme to celebrate the 300 years of the First Charter of Incorporation as a municipal borough from Charles I. The intention was to not only make merry, but to also advertise the city in the eyes of the world. The celebrations started on Thursday 8th July, and during that time the city was decorated to such a degree that has not been seen, apart from Royal visits. Traders and businesses on every street raised as much as £500 towards the decorations and made themselves responsible for their own street. A replica of the Old Moot Hall, which stood on Briggate, has been erected in wood and plaster by the London, Midland and Scottish Railway outside the station. Indeed, so lifelike is the building, that even a statue of Queen Anne, which stood in a niche in the building, has been replicated. To open the festivities a military tattoo was held at Roundhay Park, as well as a pageant in the park showing the history of Leeds. The weather has been remarkably warm and dry which added to the success of the programme, which was attended by thousands throughout the celebrations.' *(The Observer)*

JULY 18TH

1891: The editor of the *Leeds Mercury* received the following letter regarding bathing costumes at the East Coast watering places. The correspondent wrote: 'A short time ago the swimming clubs throughout the country took a vote on the question of male swimming costume, and most emphatically condemned the drawers hitherto used by male swimmers as indecent and unfit to be used in public. At regattas and swimming galas regulation costumes are insisted upon. These costumes extend from the shoulder to nearly the knee and are supplied to members of clubs at 1s 6d each. I suggest in the interests of public decency, that all bathing machine proprietors should be compelled under a penalty to supply their customers the regulation or similar garments especially at bathing places within say, a fixed distance of 200 yards of machines used by ladies. I further suggest that an Inspector be appointed to see that this rule is carried out in all our watering places alike. In fact let it be regarded as an act of public indecency, which it is, to violate this general rule'. The letter was signed 'Lover of Decency'. *(Leeds Mercury)*

July 19th

1876: An open-air meeting was held this afternoon in front of Leeds Town Hall to protest against the Contagious Disease (Women's) Acts of 1866 and 1869. This Act gave policemen the power to arrest prostitutes and bring them into police stations to have compulsory checks again venereal disease, undertaken by police surgeons. As a result of this, many working class and respectable women had been forced to submit to these humiliating processes. At the meeting, the Revd George Hines requested that the following resolution be passed: 'We the inhabitants of Leeds consider the Acts unconstitutional, unjust and immoral in principle and degrading to the nobler features of manhood and an insult to women. We therefore pledge ourselves to use all possible means to erase such Acts from the Statute Books of the Realm'. The Leeds Working Men's National League also sent a petition to Parliament to immediately repeal these Acts and to ask 'that your honourable House will not again attempt to legislate for the protection of immoral men, who suffer solely from their own misconduct and will not seek to deal with prostitution except by laws dealing justly and equally with both men and women alike'. (*Leeds Express*)

JULY 20TH

1847: A young man called Robert Coates was brought before the magistrates at the courthouse, for sending threatening letters to the Duke of Wellington. When the prisoner was brought into court, the Chief Constable told the magistrates that some days ago the man had been arrested for sending a letter to the Queen, asking her to put him on the pension lists. As the contents were of a harmless nature, he had been dismissed with a reprimand. A letter was forwarded from the Metropolitan Police Commissioners in London, to the police office in this town. The letter to the Duke of Wellington had been signed 'Mr A. Hilson', but comparison with the letter written to the Queen proved to be identical to Coates' writing, and once again he was taken into custody. The letter, which called the Duke 'a pest' and 'a down right villain', stated that if the letter writer was near to him he would 'daub you all over with pitch and tar and set fire to you'. It was agreed by the magistrates and the jury that the letter was that of a madman and Coates was sent to the lunatic asylum at Wakefield; to be held there at Her Majesty's pleasure. (*Leeds Mercury*)

July 21st

1810: Today's newspaper held a report of a man named Keighley, who had been brought before the magistrates at the Town Hall charged with ill-treating his wife. The reporter stated that: 'It appeared from her evidence which was confirmed, indeed by the marks of violence upon her person, that he had repeatedly treated her with the most outrageous cruelty'. She told the court that he had recently attempted to stab her and she had only got away from him by the interference of neighbours. It seems that she appeared before the court with the intention of proffering Articles of the Peace against him; but on hearing that the result of this would be to confine him to prison for life, she relented and consented to forgive him on his promise of better behaviour; which he readily made. The reporter concluded that, 'during his recent confinement, this poor woman and her two children, had to subsist or rather languish, on two shillings a week, allowed her by the overseers of the township of Mirfield. Her evident distress excited much commiseration in the court room, and as a consequence some silver was collected at the table and given to her'. (*Leeds Intelligencer*)

JULY 22ND

1898: It was announced that the Yorkshire Show, which was being held at Leeds in Roundhay Park, was a great success. *The Observer* newspaper explained that 'the park is situated on the prettiest side of Leeds and within easy distance of the city. The Yorkshire Agricultural Society agrees that, with its sandy soil and gentle slopes, it is an ideal site for a big country show. Leeds is not an agricultural centre, but the Society knows that an occasional visit to a manufacturing district pays them well. The Leeds show promises to be a record one. Yesterday by five o'clock, it was estimated that 8,554 visitors had passed through the turnstiles, compared with 6,838 at Harrogate on its opening day and 5,801 at York. The entry of stock, even though there are no pigs (and Leeds is a pig breeding centre), have only twice been exceeded in numbers, in 1832 and 1890. The display of sheep is a record one and the cattle and horses are just about as numerous as they were at Harrogate, twelve months ago. At a meeting of the council, presided over by Mr E.W. Beckett MP, it was decided to hold next year's show at Hull'. (*The Observer*)

JULY 23RD

1853: A very sad affair occurred on the premises of Mr Henry Barker, a plumber of Kirkgate, Leeds, today. It seems that a quarrel had taken place between an apprentice named Peter Dawson, and a journeyman named Wallace Waddington, over some tools which had been lost. Waddington accused Dawson of stealing them and the two came to blows. In temper, Dawson grabbed a heavy long brush and dealt Waddington a violent blow over the head. Seeing that the man was badly injured, some of the other workmen, who had heard sounds of a quarrel, endeavoured to pull Dawson away from the body of Waddington, which by now was on the floor of the workshop. Waddington was seen by a surgeon, Mr Watson, who immediately sent him straight into the hospital. Unfortunately a few hours later, and without regaining consciousness, he died. At Dawson's trial the surgeon, Mr Bond, told the court that he had undertaken the post-mortem and found that the heavy blow had caused a fracture of the skull. There was also evidence of effusions of blood on the brain. The jury found Dawson guilty of wilful murder and he was committed to the assizes on a charge of manslaughter. At the assizes in September 1853, Dawson was sentenced to three months imprisonment. (*Leeds Mercury*)

JULY 24TH

1867: At the Astor House in New York, 200 members of the Ingraham family met together to assert their right to the possession of the piece of land – covering eighteen square miles of land – on which the City of Leeds is built. Two hundred years ago, the owner of all the land was a man called Joseph Wilson, and when he died he bequeathed it to his granddaughter, Sarah Cowell. In 1680 she married Timothy Ingraham, and the will, which had not been seen for four generations, was thought to be lost; until the city was built. In 1802, Solomon Ingraham, of New York, attempted to make a claim on the estate, but he died shortly afterwards. In 1825, advertisements were seen in the *Times* asking for heirs of the estate, and an attorney was sent to England to search for papers. None were found and there the matter rested, until the will was found in the hands of someone who asked $10,000 for it, as well as one tenth of the estate. In order to raise the money, each Ingraham was asked to forward $5 towards expenses, and in the case of those who could not offer the money they would lose their part of the estate. (*The Times*)

July 25th

1827: At noon today, there was a report of a man who had been attacked by a lion. The *Leeds Intelligencer* reported that a man named Jonathon Wilson was looking at the lion, who was called Wallace, in the Wombwell menagerie, 'which is now exhibiting in this town', when he incautiously placed his hand in an aperture at the bottom of the bars. 'The ferocious animal made a spring at him and, with his claws, succeeded in drawing the unfortunate man's hand towards the grating, into which he thrust his open jaws. At this critical and dangerous moment, the keeper happened to approach, and by his prompt, spirited and sufficient exertions, pulled him away from the bars. Some of Mr Wombwell's servants assisted in removing Mr Wilson to the Infirmary, where he now lies, and hopes are entertained that amputation will not be necessary.' The reporter warned that 'people cannot be too cautious how they approach the den of such animals; curiosity might be gratified without incurring the like danger as has befallen this unfortunate man, who appears to be upwards of fifty years of age'. It was later reported that Mr Wilson died on Friday August 4th, after his arm had became infected and inflamed. He died at his own home after requesting, the day before, to be removed from the Infirmary. (*Leeds Intelligencer*)

JULY 26TH

1834: In a field adjoining the Leeds barracks, a disgraceful fight took place between two men; one of whom was a soldier. It was reported that 'a large crowd of people had assembled to witness the fight and a great deal of excitement prevailed. After the fight was over, which took just over an hour, some of the soldiers drew their swords and chased several people, who had been shouting abuse, out of the field. One of the soldiers, named Joseph Clibbron, struck with his sword several times a person named John Beckett, a cloth-dresser at Gott's factory, who resided at Westminster Place, New Road End, as he was getting over the wall, and inflicted such wounds as to cause his death on the following day. Clibbron was committed to York on a charge of wilful murder. At the spring assize in the following year, the indictment for wilful murder was ignored by the Grand Jury, and the prisoner was then advised to plead guilty to a charge of manslaughter. He was sentenced to be imprisoned and kept to hard labour in the House of Correction, at Wakefield, for the space of two years'. (*Leeds Mercury*)

July 27th

1785: At the General Quarter Sessions of a local borough today, it was reported that 'James Coupland, one of the bailiffs of the Adwalton Court, was ordered to be confined in the House of Correction at Wakefield and kept to hard labour there for six months'. His crime was described that he had 'for a violent and cruel trespass, committed in this town, distrained and taken away goods to the value of upwards of £5 for a pretended rent of only five shillings. As a result of this the poor owners were thereof deprived of all their furniture, and left without a bed to lie on, or a blanket to cover them. William Chappell and Samuel Cook, two brother bailiffs, were indicted along with him for being assistants in the above matter and, both being found guilty, were committed to the same House of Correction until they could produce proper security to try and traverse their indictment. On Friday, they were conveyed under a strong guard to Wakefield and further surrounded as their departure from prison here was watched by some thousands of spectators, who testified their approbation of the sentences by repeatedly shouting "huzzas".' (*The Times*)

JULY 28TH

1863: Today the new Corn Exchange was unofficially opened in Call Lane for the transaction of business. Although the building was still incomplete, it was opened in its present state for the convenience of the people using the Exchange. It seems that there had been some unpleasantness which had existed between the tradespeople and the council, arising out of the proposed charge for admission to the building. The *Leeds Mercury* stated that 'this issue has now been amicably settled'. Two years prior, the plans of the architect, Mr C. Broderick, had been accepted, and under his supervision the work was undertaken by contractors. The site in Call Lane was purchased by the Corporation and the work began on May 7th 1861. Mr Alderman Gill, the chairman of the committee, accompanied by several members of the Council, entered one of the galleries of the Exchange and announced that the building was open. He added that, as the erection would not be completed until September, any official ceremonial would be deferred until that time. The building was then inspected by a large number of gentlemen who spoke in the highest terms of the beautiful manner in which the place was lighted. (*Leeds Mercury*)

JULY 29TH

1826: The *Lancaster Gazette* printed an account of Leeds described by a foreigner who had recently visited the town. He stated: 'Leeds is described as one of the most interesting towns in England, by the great appearance of industry, which it displays. It has assumed for armorial bearings two of Minerva's birds, because this goddess presided over the weaving of silk and wool, as well as over other useful arts. Leeds is the centre of orders for, and the principal market of, woollen cloth manufactured in the West Riding, of which it is the commercial metropolis. The cloth market is a building which is 380 feet long by 180 feet wide. It has six double rows of stalls and is the Palais Royal for mercers, and this building is celebrated for the perfect manner in which it is lighted. The internal police and regulations, by which sales are carried on in this beautiful establishment, are of less remarkable than its architecture. The city has a public school, with 100 presentations; a school on the Lancastrian plan. For 1,000 children, schools of industry and Sunday schools, two commercial and political newspapers. Such are the intellectual resources of a population which in 1811 was reckoned at 62,534 inhabitants, but which now amounts to 83,796'. (*Lancaster Gazette*)

July 30th

1872: A most unusual atmospheric phenomenon was witnessed between 1 p.m. and 2 p.m. today. The *Leeds Times* reported that, 'the sky, which had been quite clear throughout the morning, by mid-day sounds of thunder could be heard in the distance. In the central part of the town, little or no rain fell in Boar Lane, Briggate, and the immediate neighbourhood remained perfectly dry. But in North Street, Camp Road, Meanwood Road and the neighbourhood of Sheepscar, a perfect hurricane of wind commenced, accompanied by a tremendous shower of rain, hail and ice. Large pieces of ice, as much as an inch and a half in circumference, were picked up during the storm. Whilst Boar Lane and Briggate presented every appearance of a long and continued drought, in some parts of North Street, the occupants of cellars could be seen emptying their dwellings of the overflow of surface water. Loud claps of thunder were heard in the afternoon and in the evening more heavy showers fell. Meteorologists stated that they had never known such a phenomena taking place in the town within living memory'. (*Leeds Times*)

July 31st

1873: Today there was a report of a stabbing case, which had taken place in Leeds on Monday night. A collier named William O'Brian, aged nineteen, was committed by magistrate Mr Bruce on a charge of cutting and wounding. The man had been in the company of a woman named Jane Clark, who resided with her mother, Ellen Clark, in Randall's Court. O'Brian, claiming to be a relative from Scotland, had supper with the mother before going out with Miss Clark, returning at some time between 11 p.m. and midnight. Mrs Clark refused to admit them, but was at length persuaded to open the door. The prisoner immediately set upon her, knocked her down and kicked her and, as she alleged, stabbed her twice in both arms. The daughter, whose conduct was anything but filial, was put into the witness box, but gave her evidence very reluctantly. She contradicted her mother's statement, and added that four gallons of beer were drunk by the trio that night, and that her mother had more than a fair share of it. It was proved that the woman had been cut on both arms. Mr Bruce, after listening to the case with obvious disgust, dismissed the case. (*Leeds Mercury*)

AUGUST 1ST

1846: Five cases under the Factory Act were heard before the Leeds magistrates, which had been brought before them by the Factory Inspector, Mr Baker. He told the court that he had been given information that under the direction of Mr Jackson, the manager of Messrs Hargreaves & Sons of the Union Street woollen mill, some boys had worked excessive hours under the Ten Hour Bill Act. He told the court that the boys, who were all under eighteen years of age, had worked for two days from six in the morning to eleven at night. Mr Jackson appeared before the magistrates and told them that he was ignorant of the fact they were under the age of eighteen, as they had made false statements regarding their age. He told them that in mitigation, one of the boys was only a day short of the age of eighteen. Due to this fact, and that it was the first case brought before them from Messrs Hargreaves & Sons, the magistrates fined Messrs Hargreaves & Sons the lowest penalty of the law, namely 40s in each of the five cases. (*Leeds Mercury*)

AUGUST 2ND

1870: Today the *Leeds Mercury* gave a report on the condition of the water supply to the town. It stated that: 'Our attention has been called by a correspondent to the state of the water which is being supplied to Leeds at this present time. Our informant suggests that this may have something to do with the excessive mortality that we are at present experiencing in the borough. We have at our office a sample of water from the north district of the town and it appears more like clarified sewage than filtered water, and as far as we can judge, without a chemical analysis, it consists very largely of earthy and peaty matter. We have also received a piece of white linen (through which the water has been allowed to run for six hours), which as a consequence is stained the colour of coffee.' It was requested that the Inspector of Nuisances' attention be brought to the state of the water, and the Medical Officer of Health to complete a report on it for the Board of Guardians. (*Leeds Mercury*)

AUGUST 3RD

1841: It was reported that a sad and terrible death, caused from destitution, had occurred in Leeds. An inquest was held before the coroner Mr E.C. Hopps at the house of Mr Thomas, the Royal Oak Inn, Kirkgate, on the body of an aged man whose name was unknown. The man had been found dead at the lodging house of Mr Glover at Wellington Yard, Kirkgate, that same morning. From the evidence, it appeared that the deceased had only taken lodgings at the house the night before and soon after he arrived he went to bed, having had nothing to eat or drink. There were six other beds in the room in which he slept and the room was little more than four yards square. Several people, of both sexes, occupied the other beds. In the morning, the poor man was found dead. The surgeon, Mr Teale, was called and he examined the body. He told the coroner and jury that he had not found any poisonous substances in the body, but there was an absence of any food in the body, which appeared to be very malnourished. He gave his opinion that death had ensued from natural causes, hastened by the want of the necessities of life. The jury returned the verdict accordingly. (*Leeds Mercury*)

AUGUST 4TH

1801: It was reported in the *Leeds Mercury*, on this date, that: 'The practice of holding political meetings at midnight has now become very frequent in the town and county. We are authorized to state, that one of these meetings was held on Saturday night last, at Hartshead Moor, near Clifton in this neighbourhood. There are strong reasons to suspect that the persons who compose these assemblies are influenced by bad designs; it is indeed thought that a secret correspondence exists betwixt them and the Government of France, and that they are countenanced and supported by men of consequence in this country'. A reply was inserted the following Friday, also dated August 4th, stating that: 'Having seen in your paper of today a paragraph stating that being perfectly acquainted with Leeds, I am convinced that the idea of any number or indeed any person in the West Riding carrying on a correspondence with France is to the injury of this Kingdom'; it was signed from a West Riding magistrate. An annotation was added that 'we know this comes from a respectable Magistrate'. (Read, D., *Press and People 1790–1850 Opinion in Three English Cities*, London, Edward Arnold, 1961)

AUGUST 5TH

1867: Today the Leeds Band of Hope held their annual concert and demonstration within the beautiful grounds of Kirkstall Abbey. It was reported that the weather was particularly good and contributed to the success of the day, bringing two or three times the crowd that would normally have attended. The gates were thrown open to the public at noon and by dusk it was estimated that between 10,000 and 12,000 visitors had paid their admission fee. Councillor Kershaw opened the concert and talked about 'the physical, social and moral evils brought about by intemperance and the desirability of organising more Band of Hope concerts in connection with the Sunday school, and the varied advantages of abstinence was urged upon those present with much energy on the part of the speakers'. There then followed a concert from 'youthful abstainers' who sung a variety of temperance melodies under the conductorship of Mr F. Wilkinson. More lectures were given on the debilitating habits to which people who were addicted to alcohol suffered. The concert closed with a prayer and the crowd was then free to walk in the grounds of the Abbey. Other attractions, to which they enthusiastically joined in, were boating on the river, football, and dancing competitions, as well as many little stalls with 'delights of all kinds'. (*Leeds Mercury*)

AUGUST 6TH

1853: It was reported that three strangers to the town had been caught the previous week calling upon the benevolence of people, asking for subscription for the relief of miner's families following a colliery accident. Two of the men had been captured and one of them, Thomas Jackson, was brought into court this morning. There had been no accident and, according to the books carried on one of the men, they had been most successful in Leeds and Wakefield and other places. Due to the vigilance of Demaine of the Leeds detective force, one of the trio had been brought into court last Monday and was already in the Borough Gaol serving his sentence. During his trial, Demaine told the court that he had seen the prisoner, John Holt of Barnsley, with two other men, all neatly dressed, calling on houses in Park Lane. When he realised they were begging he brought them into custody, but one of them escaped. The book made a long statement to the effect that John Holt and Thomas Jackson were miners at Springfield Colliery, near Barnsley, where there had been an explosion in which nine men and three boys had been killed, and asking for donations. The book listed names, although some were thought to be fictional, other listed donations of between £10 to a few shillings. The magistrates sent Jackson to prison for three months as a vagrant. (*Leeds Mercury*)

August 7th

1825: Today a Leeds dog called Billy was set to kill 100 rats in twelve minutes for a purse of 100 sovereigns. The place was an unoccupied house adjoining the South Market, where about 150 people had gathered, paying an admission of 2s each. The rats were turned into a square pit, although a circular one would have been of greater advantage to the dog and would not have allowed the rats to accumulate. The dog, which was of a bull and terrier breed, was then introduced to its task, but it was soon discovered that he was unlikely to perform that which had been allotted to him. He managed to kill about one third of the rats in seven minutes, when he sat down, panting from his exertions, and immediately retired. Three other dogs were brought forward, who proved to be worth nothing and, even with assistance, all the rats were not destroyed within the given time. A fifth dog was handed in, which demolished the remainder immediately. The *Leeds Intelligencer* reported: 'It is our belief that if this dog had been chosen first, he would have completed the performance within the set time'. The whole performance only lasted eighteen minutes. (*Leeds Intelligencer*)

AUGUST 8TH

1871: It was announced in the local paper that a 'British Workmen' public house had been opened at Stanningley the previous Saturday. This was a public house which did not sell alcohol. The proceedings were started by the Friends to the British Workmen, accompanied by the Stanningley Brass Band. They assembled at the station to meet about 500 members of the Friends from Leeds. From the station the visitors and Friends walked in procession to the new British Workmen public house. The house was declared open by Mr Benjamin White from Farsley. The house had an inscription which read: 'A public house without a drink, where men can sit, talk, read and think, then safely home return'. The premises were described as being well adapted for the purpose. The *Leeds Mercury* reported that: 'There are two large rooms and three smaller ones, which will be used as reading rooms and classrooms. The walls are decorated with pictures and instructive mottoes, and the tables are well filled with daily and weekly newspapers, magazines etc. The house is central to Stanningley and in every way convenient for the purposes of a British Workman'. (*Leeds Mercury*)

AUGUST 9TH

1895: An experiment had been carried out in Leeds, in order to cure alcoholics with Dr Tyson's Drink Cure, and the results were published today. Dr Tyson's 'cure' had been tested in America for some time and other successful tests had been carried out in the towns of Birmingham and Belfast. A provincial representative of Dr Tyson addressed the Leeds Working Mans Temperance League at their hall on New York Street. He told them that 'eleven most extreme cases of alcoholics had been chosen from the population of Leeds that belonged to the labouring classes, two of them being female.' The selected persons attended the hall and gave an account of the treatment they had undergone for twenty-one days commencing on 20th July. Three out of the eleven had failed to observe the conditions laid down by Dr Tyson; the result was that only eight cases had drunk the fluid provided for them, which had been invented by Dr Tyson. Following the cure, these eight cases said that they had been restored in body and mind, ate heartily and slept soundly. In answer to several questions, the representative told them that it was not necessary to continue the treatment indefinitely, as Dr Tyson's fluid was an antidote for the disease. (*Leeds Mercury*)

AUGUST 10TH

1897: It was announced today that three of the Leeds Volunteer Battalions; the Rifles, the Engineers and the Artillery, had returned back to the city after a week's encampment on the coast. The Rifles had been based at Redcar, the Engineers at Seaton Carew, and the Artillery had been camped near Morecambe. Although it was raining quite hard, the streets around the station were crowded to watch the battalions march to their headquarters. The first to arrive were the Engineers from Seaton Carew, who arrived back at 11.45 a.m. and they marched to their headquarters via Briggate, where they were addressed at the drill hall in Claypit Lane by Colonel Dawson. The second to arrive was the Rifles from Redcar, who got back to Leeds shortly before 2 p.m., and they marched through the streets headed by the band. When they drew up at the barrack yard at Carlton Hill, they were addressed by Colonel Wilson. The last to arrive was the Artillery, who had been camped near Morecambe, at 7 p.m. and they proceeded to their headquarters in Fenton Street, and were addressed by Colonel Cogalan. A local reporter was told by Colonel Dawson that these kinds of exercises were crucial to develop the team spirit needed by volunteer battalions, who had all worked very hard during the last week. He stated that these annual events were important for the morale of the soldiers. (*Leeds Express*)

AUGUST 11TH

1859: A young man called Thomas Franks was brought before the magistrates, on a charge of illegally pawning a musical box. The box had belonged to a Mrs Penny, who he had travelled with for some time as a 'sweetener' or decoy to induce people to speculate on the Wheel of Fortune. Franks had tired of the life and in order to return to Malton, where his parents lived, he had stolen the musical box. The magistrates disapproved of the way he had earned a living and, in order to become a witness against Mrs Martha Penny for defrauding the public, he was discharged. He told the court that he had travelled with her from town to town, charging people *6d* to try their luck. There were prizes of small value along with others of greater value; such as the musical box. Mrs Penny had taken a shop in Kirkgate, and the Wheel of Fortune lottery was opened every day for a week. He told the court that the tickets he had taken from customers were dropped on the floor, whilst he took tickets from another box. By pretending to be a customer and encouraging others, he would 'win' bigger prizes such as the musical box, which he would later return. Mrs Penny was sent to gaol for six months for deception. (*Leeds Mercury*)

AUGUST 12TH

1874: Today a handsome illuminated clock, which was erected in Briggate, Leeds, was unveiled and large crowds turned out to see it. The Mayor and members of the council were in attendance, along with the donor of the clock, Mr R. Scott. The Mayor told the assembled crowd that the Town Council had accepted a proposal from Mr R. Scott, a watchmaker and silversmith of the town, to supply a three dial clock at his own expense, on the condition that the gas to illuminate the clock was provided free of charge by the Gas Company. The Mayor stated that 'the clock cannot fail to be of great convenience to the people of the town'. The three dials were described as being 'four feet in diameter and placed in such a position on Briggate that it can be seen equally well on Vicar Lane, on the east, and Guildford Street, on the west, and from the bend on Briggate, from the north'. It was said that the clock, including incidental expense, the strengthening of the house which supports it etc. has cost Mr Scott above £200. The Mayor took the opportunity to thank Mr Scott for his kind donation, 'which will serve the people of the town well for many years to come'. (*Leeds Express*)

AUGUST 13TH

1841: Two young boys, named James Little and James Riley, were brought before the magistrates this morning on a charge of picking pockets the day before in the Free Market. The two boys, who were aged about fifteen, looked dirty and dishevelled as they were placed in the dock. Inspector Childs attended the court and stated that every Sunday 'that place was made a scene where Socialists, Jumpers, Ranters and other political and theological quacks, deal forth their nostrums to crowds of gaping greenhorns'. Thieves, such as these two boys 'find this an excellent field for the exercise of their vocation and consequently lose no opportunity of reaping a harvest of stolen goods'. One of the magistrates stated that there had been numerous complaints of the people assembling for these occasions, and 'such disgraceful proceedings were going on as he never saw in all his life'. Inspector Childs said that at times there were half a dozen sects holding forth at the same time, and the noise was incredible. After some discussion on the bench, the two boys, who had no previous record of offences, were dismissed with a suitable reprimand. (*Leeds Mercury*)

AUGUST 14TH

1857: A case was brought into court today which was hoped to serve as an example to beggars. A girl aged fifteen, named Margaret Williamson – described as one 'whose appearance betokened health and good living' – had been found begging and recounting a tale of the most pitiful kind on the streets of Leeds. She told a passing stranger that her father was ill in bed, and had been so for several months, and that there were four children at home in a starving condition and they only received 4s a week from the workhouse for their support. Unknown to the girl, the passing stranger was a magistrate, Mr Darnton Lupton Esq., and he offered to go to the house to see what he could do. When he offered to help, the girl tried to run off but was caught by a constable and taken into custody. Mr Lupton, accompanied by the police officer, went to the address and found the father of the girl hard at work cleaning and repairing hats. He told the court that in fact the whole of her story was an utter fabrication. The bench agreed and the girl, who wept bitterly during the hearing of the case, was sent to the Wakefield House of Correction for two months. (*Leeds Mercury*)

AUGUST 15TH

1876: A report was published on the laying of the foundation stone for a Ragged School near Jack Lane, Hunslet, which was laid by Miss Croft – daughter to the Mayor of Leeds. The site of the new building was described as being 'close to the room in which the school has been carried on for a number of years. The present building only accommodates 100 children, whilst the new building, which is about to be erected, will provide for 300 children. The design is of a Gothic style and will be eighteen yards long and eleven yards wide. The total cost including the land is about £1,000 and there is still around £800 to be raised'. As part of the ceremony the secretary read a report, which stated that the school commenced in 1857, with the object of gathering in children who attended neither a place of worship nor a Sunday School. Alderman Buckton, after depositing a bottle beneath the foundation stone, gave a brief address. He said that he believed the time would soon come when there would not be a necessity for such a school; universal education would make such a change in the rising generation as some of them would be delighted to see. (*Leeds Express*)

AUGUST 16TH

1843: In today's newspaper, there was an account of a Gala at the Public Gardens on the previous Wednesday evening. The Gala, which was held to raise funds for the Infirmary, comprised of a series of splendid fireworks and 'Signor Rossini's wonderful and hazardous ascent on a rope. The rope on which he walked across was elevated at a surprising height above one of the lakes, with which the grounds are beautified'. This feat was described as 'certainly an imposing one, but the grandeur of its effects was undoubtedly attributable to the blaze of beautifully diversified fireworks, by which the scene was most brilliantly illuminated during its performance. The rockets displayed a very peculiar effect, the night being misty, and immediately on the ascent of each, it soared out of sight in the heavens, and was lost to the observer until the instant of its explosion, when it produced a peculiar effect exactly resembling a bright flash of sheet lightening'. The evening was counted to be an enormous success and the number of people who visited the gardens estimated to be from 5,000 to 6,000, and the money taken for admission amounted to £50. (*Leeds Mercury*)

AUGUST 17TH

1853: The first stone of the Leeds Town Hall was laid today by the Mayor, John Hope Shaw Esq., in the presence of a vast concourse of spectators. The whole of the council, joined by members of several groups, formed a procession of enormous length which was enlivened with banners and the music of military and other bands. Mr Alderman Hepper, the chairman of the Town Hall Committee, commenced the proceedings by asking the Mayor to lay the foundation stone, and presented to him a richly embossed silver trowel with an ivory handle, and a mallet of polished oak. The Mayor then proceeded to lay the stone at the south-west corner of the new building. At the conclusion of the ceremony the vast audience signified their approbation by a loud unanimous burst of applause, which was caught up by the mass of people, and the cheers were re-echoed through the surrounding streets and by the crowds estimated to be more than 60,000, some of whom had collected on the tops of the surrounding buildings. The Mayor said that 'there had long been a need in Leeds for such a magnificent building and at last that need had been achieved'. (*Leeds Times*)

AUGUST 18TH

1819: Today's *Leeds Independent* gives details of an uprising of a group of Chartists in the town of Leeds. Similar groups were demanding reform and were operating in large cities all over Britain; the Government was determined to quell such rebellions. The local newspaper reported that: 'On the proceeding afternoon in consequence of an express message, a troop of the 4th Dragoons set off for Manchester; and at seven o'clock, four troops of the same regiment had just arrived, and expected orders to proceed for the same place. It is understood that a very numerous meeting was held last night on Hunslet Moor, near this town. They have been assembled in so private a manner that we did not hear of the circumstances until after the meeting was over. It had been resolved to hold another meeting, on the same place, this day. Today remains perfectly tranquil, up to the hour of this paper going to press (after midnight). However numerous bodies of men (at times to the amount of a thousand) have been loitering in Briggate during the whole day and even after dark. Fresh meetings have been announced, one at Bolton, on Saturday next, and another at Preston on Monday. They are both called by the reformers themselves after their requisitions to the local magistrates for the said purpose had been very properly dismissed with a negative'. (*Leeds Independent*)

AUGUST 19TH

1875: The annual treat for the inmates of the Leeds workhouse and the children of the Industrial School was held at Roundhay Park today. About 540 people were present when they arrived at 11 a.m., accompanied by the master and matron of the workhouse, Mr and Mrs Grosvenor, and the master and matron of the Industrial School, Mr and Mrs Driver. Over 300 of the paupers started the excursion with a steamboat trip out on the lake, whilst others paid a visit to the entomological museum and the 'camera obscura' exhibition; all of which were gratuitous for the day. A meat tea was provided in Mrs Brayshaw's large refreshment room, which the inmates ate heartily. After tea the Chair of Guardians, Mr Wray, addressed the assembled crowd and said that 'he did not think that in any union in England there was a better Board of Guardians, who did all that they could for the poor old men and women of Leeds. Great care was taken to meet their wants and he hoped that the ratepayers of Leeds would not grumble at what they had to pay for their support'. Thanks were also given to the Chair and Mrs Wray for their exertions in promoting the happiness of the people gathered there today. (*Leeds Mercury*)

AUGUST 20TH

1852: The statue of Sir Robert Peel was inaugurated at Leeds at noon this day, in the presence of an immense assemblage of people, said to be between 30,000 and 40,000 people. It was reported that 'the statue was placed exactly opposite the newly erected and handsome Unitarian Chapel, which fronts onto Park Row. The procession of the town council headed by the Mayor wearing his chains of office, the magistrates, etc., left the court house and took up their places within a railed area adjoining the statue. A raised platform was prepared for the speakers and invited guests, and on their appearance, headed by William Beckett Esq., they were loudly cheered by the assemblage. A signal flag was fixed at the top of the court house, and at the sound of a trumpet, it was unfurled and the statue was uncovered. Amidst the acclamations of the thousands of spectators, William Beckett Esq. then delivered an address and presented the statue to the Mayor, the aldermen, and burgesses of the borough of Leeds, in the name of the subscribers. The cost of the statue and pedestal was said to be 1,500 guineas, which was raised by subscription amongst 8,000 subscribers, who varied in donations from £100 to £1.' (*Leeds Times*)

AUGUST 21ST

1873: Complaints heard from a man signing himself as 'Traveller' were printed in the *Leeds Mercury* today. He was concerned about a group of card sharps that he had witnessed travelling on the Leeds to Stalybridge train. He stated that: 'He had not long been sitting in the compartment of the train, when a "gentleman" came to the carriage and asked if he objected to smoking, to which he replied that he didn't. The man took his place in the carriage along with four others and immediately, as the train pulled out of the station, the cards were produced. One of the men appeared to be winning and retired when he had won £2, after which our correspondent was induced to try his luck. Fortunately for him he declined. He pointed out that between Leeds and Stalybridge, there are many dark tunnels which are a danger to travellers, in particular when they are accompanied by other men, men who had confessed to him that they "lived" off the public. Our correspondent admitted that his blood ran cold throughout the journey and that he did not breathe freely until he stepped off the train at his destination'. (*Leeds Mercury*)

AUGUST 22ND

1881: It was announced today that Leeds was entertaining a group of 'American Midgets' on a tour of the provinces, who could be seen at the Assembly Rooms on Briggate, Leeds. The local newspaper covered the show and described it in great detail. The newspaper states that: 'Mr Frank Uffer, who exhibits the Midgets, contrasts the troop by placing alongside the little people, Miss Jenny Quigley, aged 26, born in Glasgow, and Commodore Foot aged 32, who is of German extraction and both who are about of the same stature as General and Mrs Tom Thumb. General Mite who was born in the state of New York weighs only 9lbs and who is fittingly termed the Prince of Lilliput, is 16 years of age, whilst his tiny companion, who is Mexican, is two years his senior. The General is fair to look upon and altogether pleasing. He wears evening dress, and whilst at times he skips about like the merriest of children, at others he is gentlemanly and dignified. The company has not the slightest restraint and has afforded immense satisfaction to all who have seen them including Her Majesty the Queen and several Royal personages. Both afternoon and evening receptions are daily held at the Assembly Rooms and we are told that they have been very well attended'. (*Leeds Mercury*).

AUGUST 23RD

1933: The King and Queen had an enthusiastic welcome today when they came to Leeds to formally open the handsome new Civic Hall. The royal couple, who had been staying with the Princess Royal and the Earl of Harewood, travelled in motor cars by the Harrogate Road into Leeds, where a mass of spectators along the route waved in greeting. As the cars drove slowly along Briggate, Boar Lane, Park Row and Victoria Square, the King and Queen waved to the crowd and they received a hearty welcome in return. A royal salute of twenty-one guns signalled the arrival given by the 69th (West Riding) Field Brigade of the Royal Artillery. After a short ceremony at the Victoria Hall, where the Mayor of Leeds welcomed their Majesties to Leeds, the King and Queen drove the short distance to the Civic Hall, where the Royal Standard had been raised. A gold key was presented to His Majesty and as he unlocked the blue and gold covered grille, a fanfare of trumpets announced to the gathered crowds that the ceremony was complete. Their Majesties made a tour of the building and their appearance at one of the windows was the signal for yet another loud cheer. Luncheon was served and the royal party left just after 3 p.m. to return to Harewood House. (*The Times*)

August 24th

1884: Today's newspapers carried a report about the visit of the Bishop of Ripon to Bramley, on Thursday, in order to consecrate a piece of ground recently added to the existing churchyard there. Two years previously it had been decided that no more burials could be held there, as the ground was overcrowded. Following an order from the Burials Department of the Home Office, the town council had been looking for a nearby piece of land to become available and was fortunate to secure the additional ground, which was about an acre in extent. The Bishop of Ripon was received with due ceremony by the Revd S.W. Cope MA, vicar of Bramley. Many of the parishioners of Bramley had turned out to watch the ceremony, which was solemnized with due reverence. The petition of consecration was read by the Revd Cope and the deed was signed by His Lordship and witnessed by Revd E.C. Lister MA, rector of Stanningly and the Revd H.J. Wilkinson, vicar of Kirkstall. The *Leeds Mercury* said, 'It is to be hoped that the new burial ground will be sufficient to receive the dead of Bramley for many years to come'. (*Leeds Mercury*)

AUGUST 25TH

1876: News was heard about a fire at the Leeds Foundry, which almost destroyed the building. The foundry, in Hunslet Road, was owned by Messrs Holroyd and Co., millwrights and engineers. The alarm had been given at Hunslet police station, which was close at hand, and the reel cart was retrieved and a jet was up and running within a few minutes. Information was sent to the Town Hall, and Superintendent Baker and the Corporation fire brigade turned out with the steam fire engine. The Insurance Company's fire engine turned out shortly afterwards. The building was about fifty yards long and twelve yards wide and consisted of two storeys. The fire appeared to have broken out on the second floor and flames could be seen coming out of the roof in the centre of the building. In less than ten minutes, the entire roof was ablaze and fell in. With the aid of water from a reservoir in St Helen's Street, the fire was subdued in just over an hour. The upper storey and its contents were entirely destroyed. The ground floor was occupied by machinery and no damage had been sustained, apart from those caused by the deluge of water. (*Leeds Mercury*)

AUGUST 26TH

1858: On this day, there were reports about an unwarranted attempt to hoax a Leeds tradesman. It was reported that: 'Some persons, more ingenious than honest, yesterday attempted to perpetrate a "lark" of the most ridiculous kind upon Messrs Smithson Brothers, tea merchants of Boar Lane'. A letter dated August 25th, addressed from Woodsley House, and beginning 'Mr Smithson, Sir', was received at the shop. It requested for them to send up to Mr Fairburn of Woodlsey House, the Mayor of Leeds, a list of almost eighty articles of the very best quality, followed with the request to let them be at Woodsley House by 10 a.m. on Saturday precisely. The document was signed Mrs Fairburn and the articles included large quantities of almost the whole of the produce sold by the firm. Suspicion was aroused by the ignorance of the communication and the police were notified. When they made enquiries, no one was surprised to find that no such note had been sent from Woodsley House. Several police constables secreted themselves around Woodsley House on the Saturday morning at 10 a.m., but the dishonest thieves were not found. The reported added that: 'We mention the circumstances to induce other tradesmen to be on their guard, and not run the risk of being duped by these thieves'. (*Leeds Express*)

AUGUST 27TH

1861: A case of an attempted murder of a young woman was reported in the *Leeds Mercury*. 'It seems that for a time a young, unnamed lady, who is a resident of Leeds, has been subjected to a series of annoyances, in consequence of her refusal to encourage the attentions of an unnamed artist. Whilst she was standing near the door of the vestry of Brunswick Chapel, a pistol was discharged at her: the contents passing close to her face, though fortunately not inflicting any injury. The police were informed and it seems that, as well as the pistol attack, numerous anonymous and threatening letters have been sent to her and also to her close relatives. It is, however, thought that the artist, who is at present in Rome, has a local companion who forwards the letters onto her. It is thought by the police that it was the same companion who fired the pistol and committed the outrage last night. The young lady was reported to be greatly alarmed at the incident and was staying at the home of relatives for the time being. Meanwhile, the matter is now being investigated by the Leeds police.' (*Leeds Mercury*)

AUGUST 28TH

1877: It was announced in the local newspaper today that there was to be a class for the training of teachers in Cookery and Domestic Economy at the Leeds School of Cookery. 'The central committee of the Yorkshire Training School of Cookery, has offered free scholarships to two of the candidates who, after a month's trial, prove themselves to be the most able to become teachers of Domestic Economy. One further scholarship is to be offered by the Leeds Ladies Educational Association; preference will be given to a governess who is already on the register of the Association. As well as the academic and scientific nature of learning about food and nutrition, a course of lectures will be delivered by Mr London on such topics as "The Nature and Properties of Food" and, "Domestic Economy, the Home and its Arrangements". Last night the school was open to a number of young women who attended in the hope of becoming teachers of Cookery. The teacher training shows the housewives and mothers of the future, how to make cheap and nutritious food for their families by using the freshest ingredients at the lowest prices. It is hoped that soon these teachers will teach the subject throughout all the schools in the borough'. (*Leeds Mercury*)

AUGUST 29TH

1861: Today, St Peter's, the parish church, was re-opened for public worship, after being closed for several months. The wear and tear of more than twenty years, with constant daily services, had rendered cleaning, repairing and a certain amount of redecoration absolutely necessary. In the beginning of the present year, a subscription had been started among the leading parishioners and a committee formed to carry out the work. 'Since 8th April last, the church has been given over to the architect and artisans for a complete overhaul, and the whole of the church has been cleaned and renovated. All the stalls, pews and seats have been repainted and varnished and the stonework carefully cleaned and restored. The ceiling has been entirely re-painted, grained and ornamented in a light oak pattern and the bosses gilded. The picture of "Christ's Agony in the Garden of Gethsemane" painted by Correggio, which has been placed above the altar, had been so indistinct for so long it was almost impossible to tell what the subject was, has now been cleaned and greatly improved'. It was reported that the parishioners were extremely pleased with the way in which the renovations have been carried out. (*Leeds Express*)

AUGUST 30TH

1874: The entertainment of Mr Heller's was moved from the Leeds Mechanics Institute to the Music Hall in Albion Street, which afforded an opportunity for the *Leeds Mercury* to call attention to the remarkable character of his entertainment. The reporter stated that: 'Mr Heller had been described as no ordinary conjurer, but his feats of necromancy are performed with an ease and adroitness which baffle the keenest observer. Although Mr Heller is an accomplished musician and a clever humorist – the jokes with which his entertainment is spiced are witty enough to keep the audience in high spirits – this pales in significance when compared with his daughter. Miss Heller sits at a table blindfolded, yet she can describe articles which are touched or exhibited in the hall; she can tell the time of watches and read sentences written moments before by members of the audience, which have been enclosed in sealed envelopes. How is it done? Those anxious to attempt a solution of the puzzle should pay Mr and Miss Heller a visit'. It was reported that the show would appear at the Music Hall for a further two weeks. (*Leeds Mercury*)

AUGUST 31ST

1914: Today by mid-morning, the recruiting office at Hanover Square was inundated by as many as 300 men wanting to enlist, and it was quickly realised that the office was too small. Because of the massive crowds collecting in front of the office, many applicants were told to use the rear entrance which was in the basement, passing through some unoccupied, dungeon-like cellaring, thick with filth. Undeterred, the men waited patiently but when they were told by the recruiting officer at 12.30 p.m. that no more men would be admitted until 2.30 p.m. there was an angry outburst. One man claimed, 'I have been waiting since 9 a.m. this morning and have not been able to get a turn yet'. He and several others got up and left. Captain Kelly assured a representative of the *Yorkshire Evening Post* that they were doing all they could to process the applications. Over 100 men had been seen that morning and the rest of the queuing men would be dealt with by nightfall. Many young men from the Jewish community in Leeds had turned up to join the army, but after waiting for hours at the recruiting office, many had given up. The newspaper stated that 'It is hoped that by tomorrow better arrangements will have been made'. (*Yorkshire Evening Post*)

SEPTEMBER 1ST

1844: It was reported that a young man named Richard Clarke was travelling in a train in a state of intoxication, thereby breaking one of the by-laws of the North Midland Railway Company. The Superintendent of Leeds station, Mr Thackeray, appeared before the magistrates on Monday to state that, to the great alarm of other passengers, Clarke had tried to throw himself out of the carriage several times whilst the train was travelling at full speed. It was with the greatest difficulty that he was restrained and prevented from carrying out his mad design. The prisoner was perfectly sober when he appeared before the magistrates and seemed quite at a loss to account for his insane conduct. The bench dealt leniently with him, only imposing upon him a fine of 5*s* and costs, but intimated their determination, should a similar case come before them, to inflict the full penalty of 40*s*. (*Leeds Mercury*)

September 2nd

1924: Local opposition to the project of a rodeo with headquarters at Leeds was already finding expression in the city. At a meeting today held at the Town Hall, which was addressed by Miss E. Ward, a letter was read from the vicar of Leeds, the Revd B.O.F. Heywood, announcing that he was entirely against the rodeo in Leeds, or anywhere else. Dr Hawkyard, a prominent Liberal member of the city council, also spoke against the rodeo, saying that it 'was calculated to gratify the primitive instinct of men' and therefore should be banned. But the largest opponent to the show was Miss Ward, who spoke very passionately on the subject. She told the meeting that 'as a Yorkshire woman who resented cruelty to animals in any form, I am totally against the cruel treatment of horses that throughout these disgusting exhibitions were often thrown to the ground. We do not wish to be killjoys, but there was such a strong feeling in the country, against the practice of making horses buck by artificial means that I feel it my duty to object to it'. It was agreed that a vote would be taken among those present; it was unanimously against the rodeo headquarters being based in the city. (*Leeds Mercury*)

SEPTEMBER 3RD

1895: Today's newspapers carried a report of the suicide of a young woman from Leeds, who drowned herself in the River Aire on Sunday night. A witness, Mr Joe Lockwood, saw the woman jump off the Crown Point Bridge and he heard her shout 'goodbye' followed by a response from a man who called out to her 'don't go Nelly'. Then he heard a splash of someone falling into the water. On running to the spot, Lockwood saw the man in the act of climbing over the parapet of the bridge, who sent him to fetch the constable before he jumped into the water. Police Sergeant Spink was called to the river and found a shawl floating in the water. He left to fetch grappling hooks, but meanwhile the body of a dead woman was pulled from the water by a boatman, further down the river. At the inquest held at the Town Hall yesterday, the deceased was identified as Ellen Wilson, the daughter of Ann Wilson. The other witness was a man called Sutcliffe Lincoln, to whom the deceased woman had been engaged. He told the court that they had quarrelled, which he believed was the reason why she had put an end to herself. The verdict was suicide whilst in a state of temporary insanity. (*Leeds Mercury*)

SEPTEMBER 4TH

1872: A young man aged twelve years was brought into the West Riding Court at Leeds, charged with stealing ginger beer from the premises of Mr James Hutchinson at the Old Hall Inn, Horsforth. The boy, who was named Samuel Swales, was the son of a labourer. Mr Hutchinson appeared at the court and told the jury that for some time he had missed several dozen bottles of ginger beer. On Thursday last, Swales was caught in the act of taking one from the yard at the back of the inn; a constable was called and the boy was taken into custody, Superintendent Pollard, in answer to an enquiry from the magistrates, stated that the boy had been up before the bench on a charge of damaging grass. He stated that Swales was well known to the police and he had given a great deal of trouble to his parents. He had run away for a week on one occasion and slept out anywhere; his father and mother having no control over him. Superintendent Pollard added that he had made enquiries and it seemed that the young culprit had never been to school in his life. The magistrate directed him to be sent to prison for a month, and then to be detained in a reformatory for five years. (*Leeds Express*)

September 5th

1823: On this day, Mr Green ascended from the area of the White Cloth Hall in his large and splendid balloon, which was estimated to be 107 feet in circumference, composed of 700 yards of silk, and capable of containing 136,210 gallons of gas. The ascent started at 10 a.m. after the gas had been taken on board. With Mr Green in the car were two Leeds businessmen, Mr James Holtby and Mr William Forsyth. After a fine and lofty voyage, which was enjoyed by all the passengers, Mr Green and his party descended at Haxey, nine miles north of Gainsborough, where they found the lower currents of air were blowing a hurricane. As a result, the moment his grappling iron caught firm hold of a tree, the cable broke, and he and his companions were thrown out of the car. Thankfully none of them sustained any serious injury; the balloon, lightened by its burden, re-ascended to a vast altitude and speedily disappeared. The balloon was later reported to be somewhere near the coast of Holland, where it was found by a Dutchman, who required no less a sum that £18 for its restoration. The balloon was later returned to Mr Green, although it was much torn and the barometer had been lost. (*Leeds Mercury*)

SEPTEMBER 6TH

1853: Mrs Harriet Beecher Stowe visited Leeds, where she had been invited in order to receive a testimonial from the readers of Leeds in honour of her book *Uncle Toms Cabin*. The book, which had been published the year before, depicts everyday life for slaves in America. Accompanied by her brother, the Revd Charles Beecher, her sister-in-law, Mrs George Beecher, and her son, she arrived from York, and immediately proceeded to the house of Mr George Baines, the Leeds MP at Headingley. Unfortunately, due to a sudden illness, the large meeting arranged to be held the next day had to be cancelled, and a smaller private meeting took place at the house of Mr Baines at 1 p.m. today. Most of the company, which included the Mayor, were members of the Leeds Anti-Slavery Association, and during the ceremony a highly ornamental silver basket containing one hundred sovereigns was presented to Mrs Beecher Stowe. The illustrated testimonial was also presented to her by the Mayor, where she was represented as being 'The Friend of the Slave'. Mrs Beecher Stowe, described as an abolitionist and author, captured the hearts of both America and Great Britain and added to the call for the end of slavery. Mrs Beecher Stowe then recalled some of her experiences whilst writing the book, which reduced many of the audience to tears. (*Leeds Mercury*)

SEPTEMBER 7TH

1858: Today Queen Victoria opened the new Town Hall at Leeds, where her reception was said to be an absolute triumph. *The Times* stated that: 'It would indeed be difficult to imagine a knightly prince of the Middle Ages, or a Highland chieftain of the last century received with louder enthusiasm or more fervently expressed fondness, than that which was given to our dear Queen on her arrival at Leeds. It was estimated that not far from a quarter of a million people, from all parts of the neighbouring country, are said to have come together for the purpose of gazing upon and welcoming the Sovereign. The people of Leeds had been cleaning and decorating the town for weeks before, in expectation of the important day. Every street was crammed with shouting sightseers; every housetop had its knot of loyalists eager to look on Her Majesty and give deafening proof that they enjoyed the sight. It is indeed wonderful to find such freshness of heart and feeling in this island of ours'. It was also reported that tens of thousands of people had been congregating in the streets yesterday in order to secure a suitable site to see the Queen, 'who is associated with national greatness and happiness'. (*The Times*)

SEPTEMBER 8TH

1831: A celebration was held in Leeds on the occasion of the coronation of King William IV and Queen Adelaide. The early morning was ushered in by the ringing of church bells and other demonstrations of a public holiday at 6 a.m. About 500 Sunday school teachers partook in a public breakfast in the Music Hall. About 10 a.m. a procession consisting of the Mayor, Aldermen, assistants, clergy, staff of the 1st West Yorkshire Militia, several orders of Oddfellows and others, formed at the courthouse. They proceeded to the parish church, where a service of thanksgiving was heard. After the service, the same procession proceeded back to the courthouse, where an elegant light repast had been prepared. It was estimated that as many as 12,000 Sunday school children later assembled on Woodhouse Moor. There they sang hymns appointed for the occasion before returning back to their respective places of worship to take tea. At 4 p.m. Mr W. Russum ascended in his magnificent balloon from the White Cloth Hall, to which the public were admitted free. The rejoicings were much marred by very unfavourable weather; 'at times the rain fell in torrents'. The festivities were concluded by a splendid ball in the evening in the Assembly Rooms. (*Leeds Mercury*)

SEPTEMBER 9TH

1811: Today an account of an electric storm was reported in the *Leeds Intelligencer*, when the workshops of Messrs Butterworth, Livesey and Butterworth, engravers of Leeds, were struck by lightening. It noted that: 'Witnesses stated that the electric matter was discharged down a bell wire, near a cupboard containing glass, china, silver teaspoons, and a Britannia metal tea pot. The spoons, being laid across each other, were partially fused at the point of contact and adhered firmly together. A circular hole was melted in the side of the teapot, and the cupboard was wrenched from the wall and fell to the floor. A number of flower pots containing shrubs etc., were driven from their places on the window seat with great violence and dashed against the wainscoting on the opposite side of the sitting room. Thankfully, despite all the damage, little injury was sustained. John Atkinson, an apprentice, was struck by the lightening, which succeeded in forcing him from his seat on which he was working. As a result of this he was temporarily deprived of the use of both legs; he was later restored in little more than a week. Relatives of the manufacturer, Mrs Dinah and Mrs Ann Butterworth, were seated near to the cupboard but providently sustained no injury'. (*Leeds Intelligencer*)

SEPTEMBER 10TH

1855: On this day the announcement of the fall of Sebastopol produced the liveliest sensations in all parts of the kingdom. 'In Leeds the bells of the parish church rang a merry peal nearly all night. For several days the joy of the inhabitants was unbounded. Bands of music paraded the streets and crowds of people waved and cheered. In the evenings especially, the excitement was very great, and an immense quantity of fireworks and coloured fires were let off in Briggate, and other streets. There was scarcely a warehouse, shop, or private house, without a banner or flag hung out, many of them really handsome, and bearing appropriate devices and inscriptions. Two or three immense banners were hung across Briggate; a monster tri-coloured one was thrown across the north end of Leeds Bridge, bearing the words "Honour to the Allies". Mr Appleby exhibited in front of his shop in Briggate the head of a bear, stuffed and muzzled, with a flag suspended above it, inscribed "The Russian Bear muzzled at last". The Mayor and town council recommended to the inhabitants that they illuminate their houses on the 17th, in honour of the event, which was responded to with great alacrity'. (*The Telegraph*)

SEPTEMBER 11TH

1881: Leeds was preparing itself today for the visit of the Prime Minister, Mr Gladstone, on Friday and Saturday next. *The Observer* noted that 'there are plans which have been made by the Leeds Liberal Association for the Cloth Hall to be covered over and suitable platforms, galleries etc. will be erected there for the reception of the premier. It had been announced by the Liberal Association that next Friday there will be a banquet in the Cloth Hall, to which the price of admission will be one, two, three and five guineas respectively according to situations. At the banquet the speaker's platform will be reserved purely for the accommodation of the ladies. Priority will be given to subscribers to the Leeds Liberal Association for two tickets each. For the remainder of the gallery, admission is priced at one shilling per ticket, which are at this present time on sale at the post office. We understand that invitations have been sent to several members of the Cabinet and other prominent Liberals to be present at the banquet. The Association has also made arrangements for the Hall to be lit by electric light'. (*The Observer*)

SEPTEMBER 12TH

1838: A young man had been enjoying a glass of ale at the Gas Makers Arms, the house of a Mr Joseph Holmes, on Meadow Lane, Leeds. A quarrel arose in 'which he became implicated' and his wife flew to his defence. In less than a second she had the landlady's cap torn into shreds and a brave soldier, fully equipped in his regimentals, sprawling out on his back. The newspaper report continues: 'She then used her best endeavours to gather her beloved out of the crowd, but before she was aware, some powerful though unseen hand, pitched her right out of the house and into the street. The doors were immediately fastened against her. Notwithstanding this she repeatedly tried, though ineffectually, to regain admission; and in order to induce the parties inside to open the doors, she set to work to break the windows, and in two or three seconds smashed not fewer that half a dozen. The scheme succeeded and the door was speedily opened and all the parties turned into the street'. During the affray the husband was attacked and almost strangled by the landlady, due to his wife's interference. The case was brought to court on the part of the landlord, Mr Joseph Holmes, in an attempt to claim damages from the woman and her husband. However, the magistrates decided that the evidence was exceedingly contradictory and they dismissed the case. (*Northern Star*)

SEPTEMBER 13TH

1852: This evening a most successful matrimonial hoax was played out at the Bull and Mouth Hotel, Leeds, upon a Mr Winter, who had advertised for a wife in the London papers. The *Leeds Times* reported that 'one or two wags thinking to share a joke at his expense, forwarded to his published address, a delicate and perfumed *billet deux* purporting to have been written by a Miss Bailey, and thus a correspondence satisfactory to both parties resulted, which eventually led to a meeting at the above hotel. Miss Bailey agreed to introduce Mr Winter to her relatives. A young gentleman, whose face was not encumbered with facial hair, was encouraged to act the part of Miss Bailey. Mr Winter arrived and was ushered into the room to meet Miss Bailey. After a while, Miss Bailey introduced firstly her affectionate brother; then followed in rapid succession with her uncles and cousins. With the first half dozen, the lover shook hands with vigorous cordiality, but when they poured upon him in one unbroken tide, he found that he had been hoaxed in a most gratuitous fashion. His only means of escape from Miss Bailey's many relatives was to treat them to wine and drink, after which he managed to escape, albeit with great difficulty.' (*Leeds Times*)

September 14th

1835: At ten o'clock this morning, the Royal party consisting of the Princess Victoria and her mother the Duchess of Kent, left Harewood House and passed through Leeds, on their way to Wentworth House – the seat of Earl Fitzwilliam. News of the journey had been given and as a result the thoroughfares were so busy that it was estimated that more than 80,000 people lined the streets to wave at the Royal personages. It was reported that: 'Indeed the streets were so crowded that the royal carriage could only proceed at a very slow pace, and at some points of the route the vehicle was so completely hemmed in by the crowd, as to render it impossible for the postilions to proceed. The carriage being closed, the Royal occupants were in a great measure secured from the public gaze, and the result was, that numbers of persons attempted to get upon the wheels for the purpose of having what they called "a right good look". In an act of loyalty, an attempt was made to take the horses from the carriage, and draw the carriage through the town by several men. However, it was thought that such proceedings would have given great offence to the Duchess and, in the mind of her illustrious daughter, to have excited no small alarm'. The cavalcade, however, passed through the town amidst every manifestation of loyalty from the people of the town. (*Leeds Mercury*)

September 15th

1839: Today's newspapers carried a report about four boys who had been caught stealing turnips from a field on Roundhay Road. The boys were observed by the owner of the field, Mr John Baker, who saw them escaping through a gap in the hedge, each with turnips in their possession. He gave chase and succeeded in capturing them; he then summoned a police constable and the two men escorted the boys to the police station. On passing Marsh Lane, a number of people were assembled, made up principally of men who abused him for taking the four young boys into custody and attempted a rescue, which was prevented by the constable. Mr Baker told the police officer that the thefts from his fields had been so bad that for several Sundays he had been forced to employ men to guard the fields. As a consequence of this he had missed church for the last four weeks. He admitted that on occasions he had taken the law into his hands, flogging boys rather than take them before the magistrates. The boys' parents were called and they consented to their sons being flogged, rather than be sent to the Wakefield House of Correction. The urchins were accordingly taken down into the cells to undergo the ordered punishment. (*Leeds Mercury*)

SEPTEMBER 16TH

1914: Colonel Stead announced to the press that the Leeds Pals Regiment, which had recently been formed, were to start their training at Colsterdale on the Yorkshire Dales. The training camp, which is situated about five miles from Masham and set in beautiful countryside, is ideal for training men to fight. Some of the men would be housed in the navvies' huts, which had now been vacated, but the rest of the men would be accommodated in tents until additional tents could be provided. A hundred tents had been donated by the War Office and subscriptions would be required to provide another fifteen. Colonel Stead told reporters from local newspapers that 'a recent appeal had resulted in half the 2,000 blankets needed, and sixteen rifles and 50,000 rounds of ammunition have been given to the battalion. A Leeds manufacturer had also donated a knife, fork, and spoon for each man, and a further appeal asking for fieldglasses had been made. The men who had been given the cutlery and the fieldglasses were told to scratch their name on the items which would be returned after the war'. (Milner, L., *Leeds Pals,* Leeds, Pen and Sword Books Ltd, 1998)

September 17th

1859: The new vicar for Leeds, Revd James Atlay BD, was formerly inducted into the possession of the vicarage of Leeds. Reverend Atlay arrived at St Peter's about 3.30 p.m. and was met in the schoolroom by several of the Trustees and Revd E. Cookson, who held the Bishops Warrant. Immediately after he was welcomed, the introductions and refreshments were served. Afterwards, Revd Cookson and Revd Atlay walked round the church, preceded by Mr Moore the parish clerk, who carried the keys. On arriving at the vestry entrance at the east end, the Revd Cookson took the hand of the vicar and handed him the keys of the church, stating to him, 'I induct you into the real and actual possession of the vicarage of Leeds, with all its profits and appurtenances'. The door was then opened and the vicar entered alone, after which it was again closed until he had tolled the bell to summon the parishioners and the public to the church; they were then admitted. Reverend Atlay remained for the afternoon prayers, but took no part in conducting the service. At the next Sunday service he would read himself in and preach two sermons. (*Leeds Mercury*)

SEPTEMBER 18TH

1888: An attempted robbery from Woodhouse cemetery was reported today in the *Leeds Mercury*. The newspaper reported that: 'Yesterday at Leeds Borough Police court a man named James Keathing, described as a traveller, was charged with frequenting the cemetery with intent to commit a felony or felonies. He had previously been seen attempting to pick pockets of bereaved families in the cemetery by an off duty police detective, and arrested. Since then he has been identified as a well-known pick-pocket known to Scotland Yard detectives as James Golding, also known as John McGee and James Cox. He has been sentenced to terms of imprisonment many times during his criminal careeer, dating from April 1859, when he received his first prison sentence. The man is known to be active in both the cities of London and Manchester. When sentencing him the magistrate reproved him, saying: "The public should know you are living entirely by crime, so that they may be warned against you. It is desirable that you should be known out of gaol as well as in gaol. It is a shocking thing for poor people who attend funerals to have their minds disturbed by such a ghoul as you are". He was then sentenced to be imprisoned for three months'. (*Leeds Mercury*)

September 19th

1920: Today the people of Leeds heard of the generosity of Sir Edward Wood MP, who handed over to the city of Leeds his historic seat of Temple Newsam – to be in the city's possession forever. The house is a fine example of a Tudor-Jacobean mansion, along with its woodlands and farmlands, designed by Capability Brown. The house and grounds are expected to be a permanent source of pleasure to the people of Leeds, as they enjoy the house and grounds of, what has been described as, the Hampton Court of the North. The house and the estate, consisting of 960 acres, were handed to the Leeds council for a nominal sum of £35,000. In return, Sir Edward was given a honorary law degree and the Freedom of the City of Leeds. The house was incorporated into a much older house of the Tudor period, which was the birthplace of Lord Darnley, born in 1545, who became the ill-fated husband of Mary Queen of Scots. It is also associated with the Darcy family, some of whom were executed in the early sixteenth century for their part in the Pilgrimage of Grace. The house and grounds are still open to the public today. (*The Times*)

SEPTEMBER 20TH

1890: 'Sir James Kitson Bart., leaves Leeds this morning for Liverpool and from there he will sail by the RMS *Servia* for New York, on a business trip. The ship was built in 1881 in Glasgow for the Cunard Shipping Group, and was the first ship which was authorized to carry the Royal Mail. Sir James is travelling to America as the President of the Iron and Steel Institute, to represent Leeds. He has also been invited to take the chair at the meetings to be held over the next few months in New York, and also at the International Congress of Mining Engineers, to be held at Pittsburg in November. Sir James will be accompanied on his travels by the Misses Kitson, and also by Sir Lothian Bell, and other leading members of the Leeds Iron trade. Mr Butler of Kirkstall Forge has also been invited as another member of the Iron and Steel Institute. Coincidently it has been reported that Sir George Morrison (the Town Clerk) will also be a passenger on the RMS *Servia,* as he is going to America for a short holiday with his relations. It is expected that the town clerk will begin the return journey on or about October 11th.' (*Leeds Mercury*)

SEPTEMBER 21ST

1865: Today it was announced that the Home Secretary, Sir George Grey, had written to the Lord Lieutenant of West Riding of Yorkshire, Earl Fitzwilliam, directing him to communicate with the magistrates of the West Riding, to ascertain their feelings as to the desirability of having a separate assize for the West Riding. 'The number of cases being tried at the assizes at York has been steadily increasing, and it is thought it would be beneficial to have a separate one in the West Riding for the cases from the West Riding itself. The place of the assizes has been suggested to be on sites somewhere between Leeds and Wakefield. The Lord Lieutenant, in compliance with the request, instructed the Clerk of the Peace to communicate with the West Riding magistracy. Therefore, copies of the letter have been sent to each magistrate requesting an answer to be transmitted to Earl Fitzwilliam, in order for his reply to the Home Secretary to be dealt with as a matter of urgency. We understand that a similar communication has been sent to the Lord Lieutenant of the North and East Ridings for them to give their opinion on the matter'. (*See* July 6th 1864) (*Leeds Mercury*)

September 22nd

1830: Today, an anti-slavery meeting was held in the Coloured Cloth Hall Yard at Leeds. The meeting was to discuss whether an 'Address' should be sent to the 'Throne', and petitions to both Houses of Parliament, praying for the total abolition of slavery in the British Colonies. The Mayor took his place at 12.15 p.m. and there were several addresses condemning the trade to the large numbers who had gathered there. It was finally agreed that the resolution, which was addressed to 'The Kings Most excellent Majesty', read as follows: 'We exult in the institutions of civil liberty, and the frankness and generosity of your Majesty's character, by which we are permitted and emboldened to declare our decided and uncompromising conviction, that the unhappy and injured beings, who toil in our colonies, are just as much entitled to liberty as either the peasants or princes of England: and that we have no more right to hold them in a state of slavery than they have to reduce us to the same condition, and that every principal of justice and of religion, as well as the spirit of free constitution, and the dictates of a sound and enlightened policy, demand that they should be totally and for ever emancipated'. A similar resolution was sent to the Houses of Parliament. (*Leeds Independent*)

September 23rd

1834: Today's newspaper held an account of the opening of the Leeds and Selby Railway, which took place yesterday at the early hour of 6 a.m. in order to reach Selby before the Hull and Selby packets left at 8 a.m. Only one engine was launched, which was described as 'a handsome piece of mechanism, made by Messrs Fenton, Murray and Jackson of Leeds. It is estimated to be eighteen-horse power and is called *Nelson*, to which there were attached three first-class carriages and six carriages for second-class passengers. The former will carry eighteen passengers each and the latter twenty-four'. It was reported that overnight rain had made the rails so slippery that the engine only achieved two miles in forty minutes and it was agreed that one of the second-class carriages would have to be left behind. The account went on: 'Several bystanders hooted with laughter as the train continued on its slow way and calls were made to police officers to put their shoulders to the engine to help her on the way. Finally the train arrived at Selby just in time to catch the packet to Hull. The route all the way into Selby was crowded with spectators at this novel and interesting sight'. (*Morning Post*)

September 24th

1846: It was reported today that the 2nd West Yorkshire Yeomanry Cavalry made a stop at Leeds on the way to their camp at Harrogate. The news of the battalion's stop at Leeds had been broadcast in the local papers. As a result, many people came out to watch as all the Squadrons arrived in the town *en route* from Halifax, Bradford and Huddersfield. The battalions were headed by an excellent regimental band and arrived in Leeds at half past ten in the morning. The men were disbanded in Briggate for a short interval, which gave them time to take refreshments and to walk around the town. The men were re-assembled again at half past twelve, when they proceeded once more on their way to Harrogate. Thousands of spectators had assembled in Briggate to witness their departure and they crowded along the route, waving and cheering. Under the command of Col. Pollard, the Mayor congratulated the men, stating that: 'We have never observed a yeomanry corps equally well mounted, in better order, or in higher spirits. They are evidently in a state of admirable discipline, and present a very soldier-like appearance'. The soldiers marched off and the crowds did not disperse until the spectacle was lost to sight. (*Leeds Times*)

September 25th

1934: Today the eight-year-old Princess Royal came to Leeds to carry out one of her first official duties. It had been requested that she pay a visit to Leeds in order to unveil a bust of the King in the Civic Hall. The bust had been presented to the city by Alderman R.H. Blackburn, who had been Lord Mayor when the King opened the Civic Hall the previous year. The bust, which had been carved of white marble and was the work of Mr W. Reid Dick, had been on show at the Town Hall for over a month. Many people had visited and admired the bust. Alderman Blackburn told the Royal visitor that 'not only was the unveiling of the bust of the King a commemoration of the royal visit but also an expression for all times of the city's loyalty to the throne'. The Princess Royal then unveiled the bust to great applause. Lord Harewood, speaking on behalf of the Princess, stated that she had asked him to express her gratitude for the reception the people of Leeds had given her, and to say what a great pleasure it had been to come to Leeds to carry out such a pleasant task. He congratulated the City of Leeds, and was happy to commemorate the visit for future generations with so noble a work of art as they had seen unveiled that day. (*The Times*)

SEPTEMBER 26TH

1823: On this day, whilst working on the new road from Hunslet to Belle Isle, near Leeds, a group of workmen uncovered a stone coffin. The coffin contained some remains of bones which were identified as being part of a thigh, leg and arm bones, and a skull. The remains were found under a thin covering of plaster. When the plaster was removed, the workmen found a human body, which still had the impression of the linen it had been enveloped in. The face, which was partially decomposed, appeared to have been somewhat covered with a semi-circular piece of glass. The skull had virtually perished, but the teeth remained in an excellent state of preservation. A considerable number of glass beads of various colours and sizes were found scattered around in the coffin. There was also the remainder of a sword, although there were no markings visible on it. Though the coffin and its contents were carefully washed, no coin or inscription was found to fix the date of the interment or to give any clue as to the occupant's name. Mr Blenkinsop, the secretary to the Leeds Philosophical and Literary Society, took charge of the coffin, which appeared to be made out of Bramley Fall stone and was covered with a lid five feet thick. The *Leeds Intelligencer* reported that 'the coffin is hoped to be on show to the people of the town as soon as possible'. (*Leeds Intelligencer*)

SEPTEMBER 27TH

1894: Today's newspapers reported on Mr Chamberlain's visit to Leeds, and the breakfast which had been given in his honour at the Town Hall. Mr Chamberlain was received by loud cheering as his train pulled into the station. A band from the 10th Hussars greeted him as he stepped out. When he met the Mayor at the Town Hall he told him, 'I feel it to be a great honour, as well as a great pleasure to have received the hospitality of the Leeds and County Unionist Club; and I take this opportunity of expressing on behalf of both Mrs Chamberlain and myself our deep sense of the kindness with which we have been received in the City of Leeds. We have had a Yorkshire welcome and we shall always look back on it with gratification'. Loud cheers were given to Mr Chamberlain and his wife at this point. He went on to talk about the distress of the working classes at that time in Leeds, and spoke about policies being put in place by the government to 'steer that class away from anarchy and revolution'. Mr Chamberlain later visited the Leeds and County Unionist Club, before leaving at 1.30 p.m. for Birmingham. In the Midland Railway Station a considerable crowd had gathered, whose cheering the Right Honorable gentleman acknowledged courteously without attempting to make a further speech. (*The Times*)

September 28th

1876: The Midland Railway Company decided to permanently adopt a new style of carriage for their line. They proposed that 'a first-class carriage will be almost similar to the Pullman drawing room cars at present in use upon this railway, to ride in will be no extra charge above the ordinary first-class fares. Furnished with mahogany tables, each carriage will have its own landscape painting as well as mirrors for the benefit of the ladies who are travelling in them. The carriage will be open throughout, but for persons of a retiring disposition, a space will be provided at the end of each carriage, so that all the semi-privacy attached to a present first-class compartment may continue to be enjoyed. The third-class carriage will be laid out upon the same plan, but they will, of course, not be so elaborately fitted up. The fittings will be made of pine, but will lose nothing in the comfort of the first-class passengers. The wheels of the new carriages will be on the "bogie" principle and the carriages will, in weight, be equal to three of the present carriages. It is hoped by the Midland Railway Company that the new carriages will add to the comfort of the railway passengers'. (*Leeds Mercury*)

SEPTEMBER 29TH

1837: 'It was announced today that on Monday last, Whitworth Russell Esq., the Inspector of Prisons, and Captain Jebb of the Royal Engineers, have been asked to render advice and assistance to the town council of Leeds, to examine the various sites which have been offered for the erection of a Borough Gaol. The committee met at the house of the mayor and we understand that three sites have been proposed for the erection of the new Gaol'. (*Leeds Mercury*)

———— • ◆ • ————

1959. In today's *Times* it was announced that Leeds police would be upgrading their police cars. It reports: 'Four £1,000 sports cars, coloured moonstone and black and clearly marked "Police" have been added to the motor patrol section of Leeds City Police, in an attempt to regain the pre-war title of "courtesy cops". Mr A.J. Paterson, the Chief Constable, said yesterday that the new cars are the first of their type to be used by any police force in Britain. The drivers will be selected, not only for their ability, but also for their courteous approach to the public. A motorist exceeding the speed limit would probably be politely cautioned, except in cases where the speed was obviously dangerous to the public; in such cases proceedings would definitely be taken'. (*The Times*)

SEPTEMBER 30TH

1894: Mr John Ryan, a Corporation employee, received a letter from his wife, who had recently been cured of rheumatism at St Winifred's Well at Holywell, North Wales. Sent as a pilgrim by subscription from the local Catholic church, along with four others, the party had left Leeds at the beginning of August. In the letter to her husband, who was employed as a night watchman, she states that she has been cured of an affliction which she has had for ten years, and which left her unable to get around without the help of crutches. She delightedly told her husband that she had only been dipped in the miraculous well on two occasions and was now able to walk about quite easily with just the aid of a stick. She was hoping to go into the well for a third time before she was due to arrive back in Leeds. Mr Ryan told the *Mercury's* reporter that he couldn't quite believe this miracle and needed to see it with his own eyes before he accepted it as true. His wife was believed to be due home within the next two weeks. (*Leeds Mercury*)

OCTOBER 1ST

1879: Today the Mayor announced to the members of the Corporation that several gifts had been promised to the Leeds Recreation Ground, from donors who had been impressed by the recent gift of 600 trees planted on Woodhouse Moor, by Councillor J. Hardwick. The Mayor, Alderman Addyman, announced that one of Leeds' businessmen, Mr North, had promised a new fountain – 'the best that could be had' – to be placed on the recreation ground. Alderman Gaunt said they 'only wanted a clock now' and Councillor A. Brown agreed to fund a new clock; Mr Geenty suggested that the gas committee should illuminate the clock for free, and the Mayor said 'there was no doubt they would do so'. Mr Emsley offered to 'give as good a fountain for Hunslet Moor as Mr North had promised'. To more cheers and shouts of 'Hurrah' Councillor Brown promised to supply some trees for the recreation ground. Mr Scupham suggested that something similar should be done for 'Paddy's Park' on Pontefract Lane, and offered to plant some trees there. The Mayor pointed out that the land of Paddy's Park did not actually belong to the Corporation, that it was only rented, and Mr Scupholme agreed to supply the trees all the same. (*Leeds Mercury*)

OCTOBER 2ND

1897: Today the members of the 21ˢᵗ Hussars, who were stationed at Leeds, held their annual athletic sports on Cardigan Field, Kirkstall Road. In spite of dull, threatening weather, there was a large assembly of spectators, including several officers of the regiment and their friends. The sports kicked off with a half mile foot race which was followed by several contests in sword *vs* sword, sword *vs* lance, lance *vs* lance, and finally, a lance *vs* bayonet. The proceedings at this stage were varied with an encounter between a 'Zulu Chieftain' and a British Hussar. The costume of the Zulu was said to be 'admirable', and though he displayed considerable valour, he was no match for the mounted Hussar. Other competitions followed which included a tent pegging contest, lemon cutting, and tilting at the ring. Throughout the day there were trapeze, horizontal bar and other gymnastic exercises, and a tug-of-war brought the proceedings to a close. It had been announced that all the proceedings of the day's sports would be donated to charitable organisation. (*Leeds Mercury*)

OCTOBER 3RD

1865: The city saw the formal opening of the Leeds Medical School, erected in Park Street, by Sir James Paget FRS of St Bartholomew's Hospital, London. For the last thirty-five years, the school had operated from the small and most inconvenient premises in East Parade. The new building 'comprises of a lecture room, museums of human and comparative anatomy, pathology and laboratories for the use of students and lecturers. The theatre is placed in the centre of the building and below the platform is the anatomical department, which consists of three rooms, a receiving room, a lecturer's private dissecting room and the student's dissection room. The library floor of the building is attached to the resident curator's rooms. The library is 40 feet by 20 feet and is lighted by three double windows in front, and dormer windows at the back. The style of the building is Italian Gothic, and the cost of the building is about £5,000, which it is understood will be met by the proceeds of the sale of the premises in East Parade. The school is open to all medical gentlemen on payment of an annual subscription'. (*Leeds Express*)

OCTOBER 4TH

1844: Today's newspaper reports on the proliferation of 'monster trains'. The *Leeds Mercury* comments that: 'In this day of wonderful inventions and improvements, perhaps no object on which the eye can rest, affords a more striking example of the advance of science and the arts than is exhibited by a monster train. A fortnight ago we recorded the astonishing fact that no fewer than 6,600 persons were conveyed from Leeds to Hull at 6 a.m. and the last train arrived back in Leeds at 2 a.m. the following morning. The train consisted of four divisions and comprised of 240 carriages and nine engines. A pleasing feature of this unparallel performance was, not withstanding the great pressure consequent on such masses of people, all eager to be setting off on their trip, not one serious accident occurred. It was gratifying to see rational enjoyment so conducive to health, brought within the power of so many people who happily availed themselves of such an opportunity'. The editor concludes that he was 'pleased that the general prosperity of the next twelve months will see many such excursions leaving from Leeds'. (*Leeds Mercury*)

OCTOBER 5TH

1928: It was announced today that Messrs Lewis's Ltd, proprietors of retail stores in Liverpool, Manchester and Birmingham, have acquired a site of over 5,000 square yards in the centre of the city. 'It is to be on the new main street which the Leeds Corporation proposes to cut across Leeds. Messrs Lewis's will build a modern store on the site in accordance with the general design, prepared for the Leeds Corporation by Sir Reginald Blomfield. It is believed that the purchase price paid for the site is £150,000 and that the total cost will be £750,000. Mr F.J. Marquis, the director of Lewis's Ltd, admitted that "It was the attraction of the new road that Joseph Chamberlain aimed to construct that caused the founder of the firm, Mr David Lewis, to decide to open a business in that city. As a board we are enormously impressed by the enterprise of the Leeds Corporation in proposing to construct a new road right through the centre of the town". It is supposed that work will commence as soon as Lewis's can get vacant possession, but this is not anticipated to be in the next twelve months'. (*The Observer*)

OCTOBER 6TH

1894: Today's newspaper reported on the visit of the Duke and Duchess of York, who arrived in Leeds to tumultuous applause. Following a short delay, their Majesties finally entered the city in an open carriage. The pair were taken aback by one enthusiastic member of the crowd who, evading the police, ran to the Royal Carriage, jumped on the step and leant into the carriage. His Royal Highness extended his hand as if to shake hands with the man, but the escort of Lancers were quick to react. One rode straight at him, whilst a second struck at his hands with the flat of his sword. The man held on and by this time it was felt that an attempt on the Duke's life was being made, and another charge was made. During this attack the man was trampled underfoot and he was cut about the face, though not seriously hurt. The Duke watched as the man was rescued and taken to the Town Hall, where he was identified as Joseph Thackerah, known to the Leeds police as being 'of weak intellect'. On reaching the Town Hall themselves, the Royal couple were met by the Mayor and Mayoress, who presented an address from the Corporation. (*The Times*)

OCTOBER 7TH

1842: Mountjoy, the celebrated pedestrian, completed the very remarkable feat of walking from Leeds to Bradford and back again three times within fourteen hours, on six successive days; a distance of sixty-two miles each day. He was well known for his athletic feats in the local area. On the 17th of last month, at the Victoria Cricket Ground, Woodhouse Moor, Mountjoy ran a mile in which he walked forwards and another mile which he walked backwards, in the space of half an hour. He also trundled a hoop half a mile, and wheeled a barrow half a mile. He then hopped upon one leg for 200 yards, then ran backwards for 200 yards, picked up forty eggs with his mouth, placed each a yard apart (without his knees touching the ground or his hands touching the eggs) and then collected each egg in his mouth, and deposited it in a bucket of water without breaking any of them. After a rest of thirty minutes he then ran seven miles, leapt over sixty hurdles (at an elevation of nearly 4ft), the last twenty of which he did with an egg in his mouth. (*Leeds Mercury*)

OCTOBER 8TH

1830: Immense sensation was caused today by the news that John Stanley of Crimbles Lodge, Camp Road, a most respectable wool merchant and broker, had been apprehended on a charge of bigamy. It seems that on June 16th at Knaresbrough, Mr Stanley married Ann Daniel – a governess to Mr Gott's children, another manufacturer of Leeds. Last night a woman described as a 'good looking female attended by her son aged 22 years' arrived in Leeds from Cumberwell, near London. She brought a letter to a respectable resident, and immediately introduced herself as the wife of Mr Stanley, whom she had married in 1806. She stated that she had born him eleven children, six of whom were still living, and the eldest of whom had accompanied her to Leeds. In support of these and other allegations, she produced a regular marriage certificate. Mr Sowrey, the constable, was instructed to take charge of the prisoner at Crimbles Lodge, where Mr Gott and Mr Barr were present. By some means or another the prisoner escaped and was not heard of again. (*Leeds Mercury*)

OCTOBER 9TH

1822: On this day a swindle was uncovered, which had been perpetrated in the town. The *Leeds Intelligencer* wrote: 'A set of swindlers have for some time infested this town and neighbourhood, and practice a species of fraud, which requires exposure. They are a bill-drawing gang, purporting to reside at Halifax, from whence they date their spurious paper. The mode they adopt to raise the cash, is by one of the party going to a public house, pretending to be short of change, offering his bill for discount, with the allowance of the usual premium; if he succeeds, the person discounting the bill is plundered of the whole amount; if not, he seldom fails to borrow a few pounds, leaving the bill as security, for which of course, he never calls again. The following is a copy of the bill offered on Monday last, in Leeds:

Halifax, 9th September

Two months after date pay to Mr Isaac Wilman,
Sixteen pounds, Sixteen shillings.
JOHN ROBINSON
To Jones, Loyd and Co., Bankers, London

Wilman is well known amongst the butchers of this town and, it is said, has raised hundreds of pounds in this way'. (*Leeds Intelligencer*)

OCTOBER 10TH

1849: Today ended a plague of cholera. The first case in Leeds had occurred on June 12th, in the family of an Irishman named McCartney, in Wheeler Street, Bank. The next case was that of Jonas Brook, Market Street, who died on June 14th. The disease then spread rapidly until September, when it began to diminish. The disease was singularly fatal to a family of the name of Craven, in Cavalier Street, no less than eight deaths having occurred in that family alone. In the borough of Leeds, the total deaths considerably exceeded 2,000 in the four months that it raged. The *Leeds Murcury* then reported that 'it may be mentioned here that Captain Waterton's cholera powder proved very useful in the first stages of the disease, and the Captain's house was literally besieged by parties anxious to possess it'. The same paper also reported that during the cholera in Leeds, the following articles were destroyed by order of the town's surgeons; namely, 888 flock beds, 258 flock pillows, 12 pillowcases, 15 bed ticks, 373 coverlets, 540 blankets, and 282 cotton sheds. These were then replaced out of the poor rates. (*Leeds Mercury*)

OCTOBER 11TH

1865: 'The Queen of the Sandwich Islands [Hawaii] arrived in Leeds this afternoon, accompanied by the Bishop of Oxford. They reached the Town Hall at about half-past two, where a guard of honour of the Leeds Volunteer Rifles were on duty. The Mayor was wearing the Insignia of his office. The Vicar, Canon Atlay, and a large concourse of ladies and gentlemen, were present to give Her Majesty a cordial reception. The Mayor immediately conducted the Queen to his official suite of rooms, where a splendid collation was set out. At a quarter-past three, a meeting on behalf of the Hawaiian Church Missions was held in the Victoria Hall, at which the right royal lady attended and occupied a seat on the platform. The Vicar presented an address of welcome to Her Majesty from the clergy, and the Queen graciously replied. The Bishop of Oxford delivered an address in which he eloquently pleaded the cause of the mission, and a collection was made at the close. The Queen and the Bishop of Oxford, together with the Queen's suite, left soon after five o'clock for York, where they were to be the guests of the Dean.' (*The Times*)

OCTOBER 12TH

1663: On this day it was decided to abandon the Farnley Wood Plot. This had been an attempt by hundreds, if not thousands of men, to attempt to overthrow the Royalist stronghold of Leeds city centre. Plans were put in place 'to restore the rebel Parliament, to reinstate ejected pastors and to remit the taxes'. It had been anticipated that about 300 people were to have gathered at Farnley Wood, with the intention of seizing the city. But few people turned up for the revolt and it was lost. It was estimated that only thirty men had turned up and spent the night in the wood, before returning home in the morning of October 12th. The men hoped that no one would find out about the plot and it would not reach the ear of the authorities in Leeds. However, one of the ringleaders, a man named Joshua Greathead, turned police informer and alerted the authorities and twenty-six men were captured and sent to York to take their trial, being imprisoned in Clifford's Tower. All the men were found guilty and sixteen of them were hanged, drawn and quartered in one day. (Feather, J.W., *Leeds: The Heart of Yorkshire*, Leeds, Basil Jackson Publications, 1967)

OCTOBER 13TH

1919: The Executive Committee of the Leeds Free Church passed a resolution criticizing the treatment by the Leeds County Council, of Mr C.H. Broughton, the late head of the modelling department in the School of Art. The Council refused to re-instate him on the sole ground that he was 'a conscientious objector'. The reasons why he should be re-instated were listed:

- it is admitted that he is sincere and a man of irreproachable character
- he acted in harmony with the law
- he did work of national importance
- his past life in the School of Art is satisfactory, that he is the best man available for the post
- a large number of his former pupils (ex-soldiers) have appealed in writing for his re-appointment.

Whilst expressing no opinions of Mr Broughton's views, the Committee appealed to the City Council to re-appoint him to his former post. Copies of the resolution are to be forwarded to each member of the council who, at the last meeting, referred back to the Education Committee their recommendation that Mr Broughton should be re-instated. (*The Observer*)

October 14th

1805: On this day, a suspected murderer possibly suffering from remorse, killed himself. The *Leeds Intelligencer* announced: 'The recent murder of Mr William Stables, of Horsforth near Leeds, must still be fresh in the recollection of the public. This morning, the body of Mr John Stables, his brother, also of Horsforth, was found hanging from a beam in his own barn. At the time of the murder, strong suspicions were generally attached on this brother (who was the heir to the property) as well as being an accessory to the foul deed. Whether those suspicions were well grounded, we will not pretend to determine. However, what is known is that ever since his brother's death, Mr John Stables never seemed to enjoy one moment's peace of mind. His own house he dared not inhabit and such strong sensation of fear perpetually agitated him so that he would seldom be left alone. Judgement cannot be made by friends and relatives of the dead man, who will be judged by a higher authority from whom the truth can never be hidden'. (*Leeds Intelligencer*)

OCTOBER 15TH

1825: There appeared an appeal in the *Leeds Independent* for sympathy for the striking Saddler Journeymen at present in Leeds. The appeal reaches out: 'TO the PUBLIC and JOURNEYMEN SADDLERS in particular. In consequence of an advertisement in the *Leeds Independent* on Tuesday last, for Four Journeyman Saddlers, we wish to let the world know that there is a sufficient number of men already in the Town to fill these posts, provided their employers would agree to the very moderate request of allowing them half an hour for *Drinking Time* in the afternoon, which request will generally be thought reasonable, when the Public are informed, that in the winter season, they are accustomed to work from dinner time to eight o'clock at night without any intermission. This request they made to their masters in the most respectful way, but were refused. In consequence of which they have struck. The hardship of their case will appear the greater, when it is known that they have been refused a privilege which other mechanics enjoy who work two hours in the day less than the Saddlers'. (*Leeds Independent*)

OCTOBER 16TH

1848: The Leeds Moral and Industrial Training School was formally opened on this day. It was described as being 'pleasantly situated at Burmantofts, occupying an eligible and elevated site of six acres in extent, including the playground and garden. It is built of brick, with stone facings, at a cost of £14,000. The style of architecture is Elizabethan. The front presents a commanding appearance, with bay windows and three large oriel windows. The interior is arranged for the separation of the inmates, the northern side being appropriated to the girls, and the south to the boys. Between the rear and front buildings there are covered colonnades, to enable the children to take outdoor exercise in wet weather. Admission to the school is vested absolutely in the Board of Guardians, and the inmates generally consist of orphans or deserted children, but there are also a few who are children of deserving, resident poor. They are received at an early age, and are immediately placed under the superintendence of the schoolmaster or schoolmistress to be taught industrial work. The building has accommodation for about 400 children and youths, and has often from 230 to 300 inmates'. (*Leeds Mercury*)

OCTOBER 17TH

1907: Today it was announced that the Suffragettes were holding meetings on Hunslet Moor. The week before, on October 12th, the police estimated that over 100,000 people had turned out to welcome Mrs Pankhurst and Mrs Mary E. Gawthorpe to Leeds. It was reported that on the journey to the moor, women waved their handkerchiefs and called out to Mrs Pankhurst and her party 'success to you'. Mill girls and shop girls shouted out 'votes for women', and doors and windows were crowded with women waving encouragement. Street corner meetings were very popular with two of the suffragettes, Mrs Baines and Mrs Massey, who toured the streets of South Leeds in a small wagon. A little bell would be rung vigorously as a summons to housewives to come out of their houses for five or ten minutes. By this method they would be told about the large evening meeting, usually held at night, and of the procession which would precede it. On Wednesday there would be a dozen dinner-hour meetings throughout the city followed by special afternoon meetings. (*Leeds Mercury*)

OCTOBER 18TH

1824: On this night, about ten o'clock, the horse keeper in charge of the horses belonging to the Amity Coach, took them as was his custom, to water them at Waterloo Ford in this town. Owing to the late rains and high winds that the town of Leeds has been experiencing, the water had risen to an unusual height, and the stream had become very strong. Suddenly the man, who was riding one of the horses and leading the others, was so overwhelmed by the current of water, that he and two of his horses were dragged into the water. The current was very strong as it pulled the man and the horses along. He was able, with great difficulty, to arrest his journey by the aid of trees overhanging the water. He managed to scramble out of the river with the assistance of some men working at Messrs Banks and Goodman's dye house, about 100 yards below the ford. Unfortunately, the horses were carried down the river and were found drowned the next morning. One was found at Thorp Hall about four miles out of the town, and the other at Fleet Mills, which was about seven miles from the town. (*Leeds Intelligencer*)

OCTOBER 19TH

1854: Today's newspaper carried an account of a soldier of the 83rd Regiment who shot himself on Wednesday last. The soldier, Alexander Macintyre, was a private in the regiment which had taken up its station in Leeds, and he was aged about twenty years. He had been in a firing party of a funeral for a fellow officer and was found fault with, by the Sergeant Major, for being dirty. This caused him to exclaim that if he was humbugged in this way any more he would shoot himself. This being addressed to the Sergeant Major was considered insubordination, and he was therefore brought before his commanding officer and sentenced to four days' drill in the dry room. After being incarcerated in the dry room for more than two and a half hours, the report of a musket was heard and on entering the room Corporal Southall was found dead. On Thursday, an inquest was held at the Barrack chapel and a verdict of 'temporary derangement' was returned. (*Leeds Mercury*)

OCTOBER 20TH

1873: The business of the Leeds Borough Police Court was abruptly adjourned today, due to an odour which was said to be offensive to the most delicate of sensibilities. Even the most experienced and 'nostril hardened' officers of the court expressed a high sense of dissatisfaction with the atmosphere of the court. The court had scarcely got to business when there ascended from the iron grating by which the building is warmed, the most offensive and sickening stench. One by one even 'the dirty looking occupants of the gallery', who had come to see after the fate of those whose names appeared on the list for the day, stole out into the open air. Then the officials of the court, with surprising unanimity, 'seemed to find their immediate presence required in other parts of the building' and lastly Mr Bruce, the magistrate who, with courageous devotion to duty, had remained upon the bench until he was no longer able to stand it, openly declared it so, and hastily quitted the bench. Mr Swann, the keeper of the borough jail, sent to make enquiries, found that the unwashed clothes of a prisoner had been placed in an oven and had caught fire. (*Leeds Mercury*)

OCTOBER 21ST

1861: It was noted today that, in response to complaints made some time ago, a public clock – regulated by Greenwich Time – had been applied for by the local manager of the Electric Telegraph Company in Leeds. The clock was to be similar to those placed at Birmingham, Manchester and Liverpool railway stations. In compliance with the application, one of Sandy's best clocks had been sent to Leeds and was erected today in one of the windows of the company's offices in Park Row. The *Leeds Mercury* stated that: 'The clock will be regulated by Greenwich Time daily, every morning at ten o'clock, and it will be maintained every two or three months'. However, the reporter noted that 'the dial is too small for ready observation from the street and it is felt that if it could be enlarged the advantage to members of the public would be greatly enhanced'. (*Leeds Mercury*)

OCTOBER 22ND

1825: Today it was reported that for the very first time, the lights in the parish church were lit with gas. The *Leeds Intelligencer* reports: 'This evening our Parish Church was for the first time, lighted with gas. The old chandelier has been furnished with thirty new branches, of exactly the same shape as the former ones. They had been designed by Messrs Taylor and Co. of Leeds to replicate the old ones, apart from the fact that the new ones were hollow for the purpose of admitting the gas. They were affixed to the body of the chandelier, which is also hollow and forms a receiver for the gas, previous to its consumption. The gas is conducted into the chandelier by means of a pipe from a false roof, which has been erected in the church. The experiment has been deemed to be such a success that it is intended to fix another one in the west gallery, and a third in the choir. Other branches will be distributed throughout the church. Such was the spectacle when lit that the excessive crowds in the church gasped with amazement and no doubt many others will visit the church to see this new innovation'. (*Leeds Intelligencer*)

OCTOBER 23RD

1874: The annual meeting of the Leeds Early Closing Association was held at the Parker's Hotel, on Briggate, and it was said that the audience was not very large. The president, Mr A. Megson, stated that: 'The committee felt rather discouraged by the lack of interest manifested by the assistants and apprentices in Leeds to the early closing movement. They felt compelled to notify that unless a more united and determined effort were made for those by whom the movement was organised, little good could be done by the committee on their behalf'. The president thanked those employers who had agreed to close at 7 p.m., and a resolution was passed, pledging the meeting to endeavour to obtain a half-holiday once a week. It was suggested that the half-holiday be organised for a Thursday at 2 p.m.. After a vote of thanks was given to Mr Megson, the meeting separated. (*Leeds Mercury*)

OCTOBER 24TH

1860: This evening, Lord Palmerston arrived in Leeds at 5.50 p.m. and he received a very hearty welcome. Even though news of the exact time his train would arrive was delayed until late afternoon, a crowd of around a thousand people assembled to greet him. Mr Symons, the station superintendent, had agreed to allow some people access to the arrival platform, but the crush had been so great that the gates had to be closed. However, once his train arrived there was such a surge that the gates were broken open and the crowd climbed up onto the carriage. More cheers erupted and the Premier, accompanied by his wife, stepped onto the platform and entered an antechamber. Lord Palmerston then came to the door and doffed his hat in recognition of the cheering crowds. The 'Great Lord' asked the crowds politely to make a 'lane' for him and his wife, and the crowds parted, allowing him access to his carriage, in which he was taken to the residence of Mr Beckett at Kirkstall Grange. Lord Palmerston will visit Wakefield and Pontefract before staying with Earl Fitzwilliam at Wentworth. (*Leeds Mercury*)

OCTOBER 25TH

1817: The *Leeds Intelligencer* stated on this day that: 'An inhabitant of Leeds, a Mr Clay who recently obtained a patent for certain machinery calculated to improve the surface of the roads, is making his first experiment on the road from Leeds to Wakefield. It has been attended with such success which is truly astonishing. Mr Clay's invention involves operating with other machines, by a stupendous roller that can be loaded to almost any weight. By such means, the road exhibits solidity and smoothness. The effect becomes almost that of magic. The roads are at once rendered smooth, hard and even; and what is most important, by the regular application of the machine, they must always remain so. A narrow wheeled wagon makes no impression and passes over the impenetrable surface of the road as if upon marble. The system eminently conduces to safety, as well as beauty and durability, for it is impossible that any loose stones or other material can exist upon the surface. All is reduced to one immoveable mass by the ponderous roller, which forces the larger stones into their bed, or crushes them to powder'. (*Leeds Intelligencer*)

OCTOBER 26TH

1904: A meeting was held in the Town Hall tonight to consider the problems faced by the unemployed men of the town. It was decided that three resolutions were to be pushed forward. They were:

- That the Leeds Corporation complete all works for which provision has already been made, and for which borrowing powers have already been obtained.
- That employment should be limited to men who have lived in the city or the borough for at least six months.
- That the system of dismissing employees who work for the Corporation in all of its departments through slackness should be discontinued.

'As an incentive, Leeds council voted for £10,000 to be donated to the cost of work for the unemployed, to add to the £500 already donated by Leeds Industrial Co-operative Society for the poor. There are at present 3,960 people on the register of the Corporation Labour Bureau, and about 2,000 of these cases have been found to be genuinely needy. Employment has been provided for 700 and another 100 will start work on Monday'. (*Manchester Guardian*)

OCTOBER 27TH

1953: 'The Prime Minister, Sir Winston Churchill, will receive at 10 Downing Street this afternoon, a civic deputation which will confer upon him the Freedom of the City of Leeds. This will be in accordance with a resolution passed by the city council on April 7th 1948. Sir Winston has never found it possible to go to Leeds to collect this honour, and he has now arranged for it to be conferred upon him in London. A deputation from Leeds, to include the Lord Mayor, Alderman D.G. Cowling, the recorder, the leader of the Labour Party on the city council, and the leader of the Conservative Party, will be travelling to London. After the Lord Mayor has addressed the Prime Minister, a scroll setting out the council's resolution will be read by the town clerk. Sir Winston will respond and will sign the roll of Honorary Freemen of Leeds, which will also be signed by the Lord Mayor and the town clerk. A silver cigar box is also to be presented to the Prime Minister by the Lord Mayor'. (*The Times*)

OCTOBER 28TH

1792: John Smeaton, who was born on June 8th 1724, in Austhorpe, near Leeds, died on this day. An inscription on his monument at Whitkirk Church reads: 'Sacred to the memory of John Smeaton FRS, a man whom God had endowed with the most extraordinary abilities, which he indefatigably exerted for the benefit of mankind, in works of science and philosophical research; more especially as an engineer and a mechanic. His principle work, the Eddystone Lighthouse, erected on a rock in the open sea (where one had been washed away and another burnt down in 1754) secure in its own stability and the wise precaution for its safety, seems not unlikely to convey to distant ages, as it does to every nation of the globe, the name of its constructor'. Smeaton was afterwards employed in a great number of useful undertakings and, amongst other things, he made the River Calder navigable. (*Leeds Intelligencer*)

OCTOBER 29TH

1860: Madame Clara Novello made her farewell performance of the Messiah, at the Victoria Hall in Leeds, at the first of the subscription grand concerts. Madame Novello was reported to be in splendid voice and it was said that she achieved one of her finest triumphs as a vocalist. The band consisted of the Yorkshire Orchestral Union and the chorus comprised of 200 members of the Yorkshire Choral Union. The *Mercury* then reported: 'We are requested however to state that some apology is due to the subscribers for an intrusion into the reserved seats by a few ladies holding tickets for another part of the Hall. The explanation is, that as these persons had travelled from a great distance, and could not possibly be accommodated elsewhere, it was felt by the committee that they could not with any degree of consideration and fairness, exclude themselves from hearing the performance'. (*Leeds Mercury*)

OCTOBER 30TH

1928: Today the Leeds Chamber of Commerce sent a deputation to the Leeds Town Council, asking for steps to be taken in order to make Leeds a municipal airport. A letter from the Hull Chamber of Commerce dealt with the question of securing an air mail service with the continent and expressed a view to establish other Chambers on the subject. Mr E. Hudson, the director of the Blackburn Aeroplane Company, said that it was vitally important that Leeds should become an airport and thus maintain connection with the United States and Canada. He warned, 'if you lose this opportunity it will be a disaster for Leeds in twenty or thirty years hence'. On Monday October 29th, a letter was received by the town clerk from the Air Council to invite the attention of the Corporation regarding the importance of civil flying. The letter explained that British Civil Aviation may be divided into two parts; 'that is the regular air service undertaken by Imperial Airways and air flying clubs, air taxis and provision for pleasure flying companies. Provision devolves onto local authorities who can see the possibilities for pleasure and commerce'. (*Manchester Guardian*)

OCTOBER 31ST

1812: It was announced today that the Leeds mail had been robbed yesterday on its way to London, and the guard was being interrogated at the Mansion House this morning. It seems that the mail was proceeding at a sharp pace between Kettering and Higham Ferrers, when the coachman had occasion to speak to the guard. The guard stated that he could not hear and went forward to speak to him. Returning back to his seat he saw that the lock of the lid of the hind part of the coach, where the mail was kept, had been forced. He instantly ordered the coach to be stopped; the guard and the coachman found that sixteen bags of mail had been stolen. The coachman was also interrogated and his evidence corroborated with that of the guard. The Lord Mayor, on the suggestion of the solicitor for the Post Office, sent off marshals' men and police officers in all directions to appraise the Bankers in London and Westminster of the extensive robbery, and to stop such persons who would present bills and drafts for payment from the town, whose mail had not reached the post office. Printed circulars were then forwarded to every post office in the United Kingdom (*see* December 3rd). (*York Herald*)

NOVEMBER 1ST

1845: The *Leeds Mercury* announced today that the town's Water Supply had been tested and the result was very good. The reporter stated that: 'We have great pleasure in copying, by permission of a gentleman to whom it had been addressed, Dr Prout's results on the quality of a sample of water supplied to the inhabitants of this town, by the new Water Works'. The gentleman, who sent the sample to the doctor, was anxious to know its character. He had therefore ensured that the sample had been drawn from a tap in his house and the water was allowed to run a few minutes before the bottle was filled. Dr Prout, who was one of the most distinguished, scientific members of the medical profession, stated that he had carefully examined the sample and recorded that, 'I find it is good water; there are traces of lime and common salt in it; and more than the usual quantity of sulphuric acid. It is probable that it contains a little gypsum and I therefore regard it as fit for all common purposes'. (*Leeds Mercury*)

November 2nd

1822: In today's newspaper, there was a report of a wife being sold at Leeds. The *Leeds Mercury* reported that: 'On Saturday last, one of those disgraceful scenes which unfortunately are not of infrequent occurrence, took place at our market cross, with the exposure of a female with a halter around her neck, the wife of some wretch totally regardless of public decency. A mock sale took place and the purchaser is said to be a resident of Chapeltown. It may be proper to state for the information of those who are likely to be restrained by no higher consideration, that the exhibition of these kinds are punishable as misdemeanours, by both the seller and the purchaser'. (*Leeds Mercury*)

———— ◆ ————

1859. Today it was reported that Mr John May, a pointsman on the Midland Railway at Leeds, received a certificate from the Royal Humane Society 'for his humane exertions on 7th July when he jumped into the Leeds canal to save a female who was attempting suicide'. At the presentation it was announced that May, who was an excellent swimmer, had recently rescued three other persons from drowning when a boat they were in capsized on the canal. (*Leeds Express*)

NOVEMBER 3RD

1870: It was reported that since Sanger's Circus opened a few days ago in Cookridge Street, it has been very well attended. It was reported that: 'The building had been renovated and re-decorated, and much taste has been displayed in the arrangement of the interior. The performers are, for the most part, new to the Leeds public, but they have brought a good reputation with them, and their abilities are above, rather than below average. Two of the clowns are especially clever in the not unimportant parts they have to play. The horses are all well trained and are splendid animals, one of them being a Treachery Colt, a thoroughbred bought at £1,700 from the stud of the late Lord Derby. There is a large elephant, which under the guidance of its keeper seems even more at home in the ring than the horses. The band is a good one, and under the leadership of Mr J.A. Emidy performed extremely well. The ringmaster and showman, Signor Scott, displayed a talent for controlling the acts and the audience alike. We encourage those who have not visited the circus to waste no time in attending these marvellous acts'. (*Leeds Mercury*)

November 4th

1849: It was reported that there had been a breach of the bye-laws of hackney carriages. Mr Thomas Errington, a coachman, was brought before the magistrates this morning charged with carrying a child in his cab suffering from typhus fever. The case was outlined by Mr William Whitehead of the Board of Works, who told the court that Mr Errington had carried a person from Vienna Street to the House of Recovery, and he was not aware until he reached Vienna Street what his coach was required for. He at first refused to accept the fare, but the mother and father of the ill child were so distressed that he agreed to take the child to the gates leading to the House of Recovery. Mr Errington told the court that he was sorry for the offence and would not break the bye-laws again. He was asked if he had used the coach since the incident and he told the court that it had been locked up ever since. In view of his seeming contrition it was agreed that he would just be fined for the court costs. (*Leeds Mercury*)

NOVEMBER 5TH

1857: A charge was brought against a keeper of a dancing saloon in Trinity Street for 'knowingly permitting prostitutes to assemble there on the 31st October'. A newly appointed police officer named Mawson had been sent to the saloon that night in plain clothes. Undetected, he remained there until a quarter to eleven, during which time he purchased some cigars and two glasses of brandy. He was then joined by Superintendent Graham, and other officers, also in plain clothing, who found in the room amongst the company, eight known prostitutes. Superintendent Graham told the court that there had been no improper conduct on that night, but nevertheless the defendant, Edward Clarkson, had previously been cautioned for the same offence. Mr Ferns, Clarkson's defence, questioned whether his client's attention had been directed to any of the women present and whether they had been identified to him as prostitutes. The Superintendent told him that he hadn't, and Mr Ferns submitted that there was no proof that Mr Clarkson knew these women were prostitutes. The bench, after retiring for a short time, dismissed the case on lack of evidence and Mr Clarkson was warned that it would be a different tale if he came before the bench on a similar charge once more. (*Leeds Mercury*)

NOVEMBER 6TH

1902: Today, Lt-General Sir John French was presented with the Freedom of the City of Leeds, in accordance with a resolution passed by the Leeds City Corporation on October 1st of this year. General French arrived in Leeds from London at 1.30 p.m. and was accompanied by Captain Stanley Barry. He was met at the Great Northern station by the Mayor, Alderman A.E. Butler, the Town Clerk, and the officers of the local Volunteer regiments. The General was driven through the town, thronged by cheering crowds, and his coach was escorted by the Leeds troop of the Yorkshire Hussars. After lunching with the Lord Mayor, General French – in the presence of an assembly of between 3,000 and 4,000 people – was presented with the certificate of the Freedom by the Mayor, who spoke eulogistically of the General's services. The Mayor made a special mention of his brave escape from Ladysmith, and told the General that 'but for that, the whole course of the war might have been different'. General French thanked the Mayor for the presentation, which included a fine silver casket, engraved and enamelled. After the speeches, certificates recording the thanks of the city for their services were presented to between 300 and 400 Volunteers. (*The Times*)

NOVEMBER 7TH

1846: Today, a case was heard before the Leeds magistrates regarding the ill treatment of a chimney sweep boy. The *Leeds Advertiser* reported that: 'A man named Mr Fenton had been walking along Merrion Street, when he saw a young boy crying in a most dreadful manner. The boy, whose name was John Heath, was only seven years of age and he told Mr Fenton that he had been put up a chimney by his master, chimney sweep John Fawcett. Because of a blockage he could not climb any further and he had subsequently been dragged down by his feet by his employer. Mr Fenton told the court that he went to speak to the parents of the boy at their home on Ebenezer Street and was met with the most gross and insulting behaviour. The boy's parents told him to 'get back to Mr Fawcett and continue with his apprenticeship'. Fawcett denied having laid hands on the boy, but the magistrates castigated him and the parents of the boy and gave them a severe reprimand. Fawcett was fined £5 or two months in the House of Correction in default of payment. On imposing the sentence the magistrates told him that 'had he not been a poor man, the highest penalty of the law would have been imposed'. (*Leeds Advertiser*)

NOVEMBER 8TH

1823: It was reported that the Union Inn, in Briggate, was thrown into the greatest consternation by the sudden appearance of an unwelcome guest. Whilst people were sitting in the bar area, a large black bear walked majestically into the passage from the street outside. The newspaper described how 'the bear was first met by an old woman, who was selling nuts and gingerbread in the public house. The bear then proceeded into the bar, and afterwards into the kitchen, where the confusion might be better conceived than described. The guests were climbing over long settles and tables in their haste to get away and back out into the street. Glasses and pints were upset in their haste to make their escape, one over the other in the best way possible. In a room adjoining the bar men piled chairs and tables at the door, in an attempt to keep out the animal. His master, one of the men belonging to Messrs James and Wombwell circus, happily came to their assistance. When the bear was secured in chains, he was removed temporarily to an empty local stable. Later a cage was secured for him and with the help of four of the circus men he was safely removed back to the circus'. (*Leeds Intelligencer*)

NOVEMBER 9TH

1839: Today's newspaper carried an account of the melancholy history of a young female criminal of Leeds, named Hannah Dixon, alias Henderson. A list of thirty-three charges, which had been found against her, were published in the local newspaper, which included five times imprisoned for vagrancy, twice being charged with assaults, four times for disorderly conduct and eighteen times for pocket picking. For the last case of picking pockets, she was sentenced to seven years' transportation. The girl was only aged sixteen years and the punishment list which was published was taken from the gaoler's book at the Leeds courthouse. The *Leeds Mercury* notes that: 'The list cannot fail to excite painful feelings, as well as to prove the importance of well-conducted institutions for reclaiming unhappy females as soon as possible after their first fall into vice. Had the Town Mission existed when Hannah Dixon began her carer of sin and wretchedness, that instead of this succession of offences, her conduct might have become praiseworthy and she might not have been expelled from this country'. The editor condemned the young girl's history and offered the hope that 'her seven-year exile from the town of her birth might instil in her remorse for her deeds and the virtues of honesty and decency'. (*Leeds Mercury*)

NOVEMBER 10TH

1854: During the last few days, it had been reported that there have been many cases of Scarlet Fever in the town. 'The Medical Officer of Health, Dr Goldie, has been told that "in one district bordering upon Victoria Road, Headingley, the disease may be quite honestly called an epidemic". In one street that Dr Goldie visited yesterday – along with Mr Newhouse, the superintendent of the sanitary department – there were sixteen cases of the fever. The outbreak has been traced with near certainty to a milk supply, as the supplier of that area has been supplementing his own milk with some from Beeston. The milk from there is said to have come from an infected house, where there has been reported several deaths from Scarlet Fever. There have also been deaths reported at Potternewtown and Moortown, which are both affected, and there have been so many reports of families with the disease that the Medical Officer is requesting that the schools be closed for the duration of the epidemic'. The newspaper stated that 'we are aware of how quickly such fevers spread around the town and we request the Medical Officer to do all in his power to prevent the spread of infection'. (*Leeds Mercury*)

NOVEMBER 11TH

1849: The *Leeds Intelligencer* joyfully announced today that a scheme which had recently been tried in Leeds for post office workers to work on Sundays had failed. The editor announced that, 'we rejoice to be able to state that there is good reason for our belief that the Post Master General of Leeds, Mr Rowland Hill's scheme for the desecration of the Sabbath at the post office, has proved suicidal. We believe that before many days it will cease to exist, save in the minds of the masses of individuals, whose earnestness, zeal and complete fidelity to the claims of our religion, have contributed to the downfall of this daring plan. We can inform our readers that on Saturday evening the superintendent President of the Inland Revenue Office announced that yesterday (Sunday) shall be the last Sabbath on which he would perform the duties recently imposed on him. The result, there is every reason to expect, will be a complete abandonment of the whole scheme in the course of a few days; but whilst there is even a shadow of a doubt of success remains, no effort to procure a triumphant issue should be left untried'. (*Leeds Intelligencer*)

November 12th

1859: An adjourned inquiry into a case of alleged neglect by a surgeon, was heard at the Leeds courthouse by the coroner, Mr Blackburn. Rebecca Whittleston, a single woman aged thirty-seven years, had concealed from her parents, with whom she lived in Hunslet, the fact that she was pregnant. Although in great pain she refused to go to a doctor, but in the end, between 10 p.m. and 11 p.m., the parents sent a young nephew to the house of Mr Henry William Pullen, the surgeon. He made up some medicine and sent it back with the nephew. At two o'clock, the following morning, medical aid was once again sought; the nephew told Mr Pullen that the case was one of an emergency. The surgeon stated that he would follow him to the house, but he did not arrive. Later the boy went back again telling him that the patient was much worse, but Mr Pullen told him that he had just got in and did not intend going out again that night. Rebecca Whittleston died at 6.15 a.m. and the post-mortem showed that puerperal convulsions had resulted in her death. The jury brought that in as a verdict, but censored Mr Pullen for his non attendance. (*Leeds Mercury*)

NOVEMBER 13TH

1861: It was reported today that two men, Thomas Smith and Samuel Miller – who were described as 'travelling vagrants' – were charged with passing on (or uttering) base coins. When they were arrested and brought into the police station they were searched, and it was found that between them they had forty base half crowns in their possession. Smith had gone into a shop on Kirkgate, kept by Mrs Gibson, and had tendered one of the coins in exchange for some tobacco. Mrs Gibson recognised it as a forged coin and before the prisoner had left the shop, she took the tobacco away from him. He told her that he had no more money on him and she returned the base coin to him. He was then seen to go to the other prisoner, who later went into another shop owned by Mrs Clifton and used the false coin for some goods. The police, by now, had been notified and the two men were arrested outside Mrs Clifton's shop. Miller told the police that a 'strange man in Hull had given them the coins to give to a strange man in Leeds'. Superintendent Pollard stated that he could prove that the two men were working in tandem and they were remanded for a week. (*Leeds Express*)

NOVEMBER 14TH

1845: A letter was written to the Editor of the *Leeds Mercury*, regarding an accident which had happened on Kirkstall Road the previous Friday. The letter, signed by James A. Cooper, stated that: 'Two gentlemen were going from Leeds in a gig, which was being driven very recklessly with no lamps lit and the night was very dark. Upon passing Messrs York and Sheepshanks mill, the horse knocked down a poor old man and the wheels passed over his thighs. Immediately on seeing what had happened, the two men set the horse to a gallop and left the old man in the road'. Mr Cooper, who was passing, rendered aid to the injured man whose name was Isaac Scholey, aged fifty-five, and who worked at the York and Sheepshanks mill. Mr Cooper states, 'I will say nothing of the cowardice of the parties, but I do say whoever they were, they are bound in honour and in honesty to provide Scholey with the means of medical aid, subsistence during his confinement, and some recompense for his sufferings. I trust they will do this at once (for the man is poor and needy) by remitting something to him, or on his behalf, to Messrs York and Sheepshanks, Leeds'. (*Leeds Mercury*)

November 15th

1828: Today's newspapers contained details of a robbery which had happened at the Commercial Inn, Leeds. The landlord, Mr Cockerham, had put a couple into rooms usually occupied by his family, at a busy period due to a fair which was attracting hundreds of people to the town. The man and woman, who were named Mr and Mrs Wheatley, and who were described as being 'of respectable appearance', took the opportunity to force open three drawers in the room and carried away the contents without being observed. A reward of ten guineas was offered for such information as will lead to the conviction of the couple. An advertisement in the same paper gave a list of the missing articles, which amounted to upwards of £40. (*Leeds Mercury*)

1866. The Leeds Guardians received a glowing report on the state of the workhouse from Frederick Needham of the York Lunatic Asylum. He writes: 'I have this day gone over the Leeds workhouse, imbecile, vagrant and infirmary wards, accompanied by the master, Mr Douglas, and I desire to express my high sense of the excellent arrangements, order and cleanliness pervading all departments. I cannot help expressing my approbation for the various means in the imbecile ward which are used to amuse and interest the patients and to make their rooms as cheerful as possible'. (*Leeds Mercury*)

NOVEMBER 16TH

1866: The continuous rains in Yorkshire caused the River Aire to overflow its banks, resulting in the most disastrous floods to have occurred for a great number of years. At the junction of Hunslet Lane and Meadow Lane, the water was about two feet deep. There was also a great overflow at the Waterloo Ford, near to the Wellington Station, where the water flooded the works connected with the new station and carried away a footbridge. The water swept into the Kings Mill dam, causing a chimney of the corn mill, occupied by the executors of the late Mr Edward Hudson, to collapse. A large piece of masonry from the chimney projected across the dam and struck the roof of a building in School Close, completely demolishing it, and both the wife and son of Mr Thompson were both buried in the ruins. Thankfully, they were both safely rescued and taken to the Infirmary. An empty barge swept away from Howard's wharf and smashed against another, causing it to break into pieces and sink. The other barge, carrying coal, was swept downriver with such force that it was only brought to a stop by the abutments of Leeds Bridge, where part of it remained fixed. (*Leeds Express*)

NOVEMBER 17TH

1942: It was announced in today's newspapers that a special meeting of the Town Council will be convened tomorrow for the purpose of electing the first woman Lady Mayor of the city. The election of a new Mayor was needed due to the sudden death of Alderman Arthur Clarke, who had died a few minutes after his election as Lord Mayor had been announced. 'Although it was a very sad occasion, the Liberal Party felt that under the circumstances they should elect a non-party successor from outside the council. The nomination of Mrs Jessie Beatrice Kitson, which had been received, was heartily and almost unanimously agreed. In Miss Kitson they found an independent woman, with a long and distinguished record of public service. Miss Kitson, who is sixty-six years of age, is a well known social worker, as well as the niece of the first Lord Mayor of Leeds (Sir James Kitson MP). She also is the granddaughter of a former Lord Mayor of Leeds (Mr James Kitson) and the cousin of a former Lord Mayor (Mr F.J. Kitson)'. (*Manchester Guardian*)

NOVEMBER 18TH

1865: The Medical Officer, Mr Beardshaw, brought to the attention of the Leeds Magistrates, the matter of the rapid increase of fever in the lower parts of town. Mr Beardshaw laid the matter before the bench, and stated that his duties brought him daily into contact with such diseases, which resulted from defective sanitary arrangements. The privies and spoil heaps of the lower parts of the town were in a disgusting state and it did not surprise him that the number of cases of fever was on the increase. His daily visits to the area had given him an experience which was of a very painful character. Not only were the dead bodies of fever patients allowed to remain in the confined rooms where they had died, for days and days after their death, but they were permitted to be visited by scores of friends in order to make their last respects. Everywhere in that district the cleanliness of either house or person was almost entirely neglected, and steps needed to be rapidly made before fever attacked the central part of the town. (*Leeds Daily News*)

NOVEMBER 19TH

1857: The local news reported a suspicious death of a young man engaged as a wherryman, who lived with his father in Saxton Lane. The man, Thomas Winn, was aged twenty-one years and had been missing from home for about two weeks. His body was eventually found in the canal, which gave the indication that it had been in the water for all of that time. There were marks on the shoulders and neck, as if pressure had been exerted before death, which initially suggested foul play. On the day in which he disappeared he had been at a house of ill fame owned by Mrs Ann Rundell, and had spent the night with a prostitute called Eliza Wilson, otherwise known as 'Bonfire Nell'. According to the evidence of Mrs Rundell, he left the following morning. There was no evidence before the coroner to show how the man had died, but as Bonfire Nell was presently in Bradford, the inquest was adjourned for a week. At the adjourned inquest there was no further information from Bonfire Nell, and the jury brought in a verdict that the man had drowned under suspicious circumstances and there was no evidence as to how he had died. (*Leeds Mercury*)

NOVEMBER 20TH

1845: Today an article was printed which is very critical of the Guardians of the Poor. The article states: 'The fact is now undisputed that the present Guardians of the Poor, of the Leeds Union, have established the vicious principle that after advertising for estimates, and having them from tradesmen of unquestionable respectability, it is proper for a public board to give the jobs, not to the persons who send in their estimates most favourable to the rate payers, but to those who are of a particular shade of politics. This is "jobbing" in the true sense of the word, and every parishioner who gives his vote to any of the delinquent Guardians in future, is a supporter of a board of jobbers'. (*Leeds Mercury*)

———— ◆ ————

1874. Last night there was held a 'Microscopical Soiree' at the Queen Street Improvement Society, where several valuable and useful instruments were demonstrated. 'Mr Washington Teesdale exhibited the Sciopticon, by means of which he threw various objects on the screen, to the edification of the assembled company. The audience was delighted to see larger versions of ordinary household items which, when held under the Sciopticon, seem to be objects from the imagination'. (*Leeds Mercury*).

NOVEMBER 21ST

1839: In the early hours of this morning, a fire broke out at the Providence Foundry on Hunslet Lane, Leeds, at the premises of Messrs Turner, Ogden and Company, engine builders. 'The fire appears to have originated in the model room, and soon after it was seen by the watchman, flames burst through into the upper windows of the turning shop. Fire engines were rapidly sent for and three arrived on the spot in less than half an hour. Despite their promptness, the fire spread with such rapidity, that the whole of the building was quickly destroyed. Thankfully, due to the tremendous exertions of the fire brigade, the fire was prevented from extending any further. A beautiful and very powerful locomotive engine, which had just been completed, was on the ground floor and although it was seen to be enveloped in flames, it was protected from material injury. Messrs Turner, Ogden and Co. have been spoken to, but cannot account for the cause of the fire. The director, Mr Turner, who had been at the foundry the previous night, left the premises at 8 p.m.. He told one of the fire constables that when the men finished working at 9 p.m., all the gas had been turned off and consequently there was no open fires remaining on the premises'. *(Leeds Mercury)*

NOVEMBER 22ND

1539: On this date, the Abbey at Kirkstall was surrendered to the King's Commissioners as part of the dissolution of the monasteries. The Abbot was John Ripley who, with other members of the community, gathered in the Chapter House and surrendered the property to one of the commissioners, Dr Robert Layton. The Deed of Surrender states: 'John Ripley, abbot of the monastery at Kirkstall and the convent of the same place...by our unanimous assent and consent, have freely and of our own accord given, granted, surrender, deliver and confirm to the most illustrious and invincible prince, Our Lord King Henry VIII by the Grace of God king of England and France...our entire house and monastery, the site, grounds, circuit and enclosure and the church of the same monastery'. Along with all the property at Kirkstall, they also signed over to the King all other emoluments, properties in the counties of York and Lancaster, and in the Kingdom of England, Wales and the Marches. (Mitchell, W.R., *A History of Leeds*, Chichester, Phillimore, 2000)

NOVEMBER 23RD

1709: Today the corporation of Leeds attended divine service at the parish church, on a day set aside for a public festival following the success of the British forces. They agreed to 'meet again att Mrs Owens att five of the clock to Drinck to Her Majesty's health and further good success; the expenses of the evening to be att the corporations charge [*sic*]'. To celebrate, the event bonfires were lit in Briggate, and casks of ale were broached on the grassy slopes of the footways on either side of the street. There were displays and pageants performed, to which crowds of people came into the town and the soldiers paraded and volleys fired. Menageries and other itinerant stalls were arrayed along Briggate in the centre of the street. On market days, the same grassy slopes would be filled with sheep, pigs, horses and carts, and agricultural implements, while auctioneer Thomas Stooks would be mounted on his rostrum, conducting his weekly auction sale, surrounded by a crowd of eager country people. Briggate was indeed the great centre of life and business of the town, and the scene of many interesting events in the history of the town. (Robinson, P., *Leeds Old and New*, Leeds, S.R. Publishers Ltd, 1972)

NOVEMBER 24TH

1837: Today the *Leeds Mercury* noted that, due to the heavy rain on the previous Wednesday, one of the 'highest and most sudden floods ever known in Yorkshire had hit Leeds'. The flood had damaged property, in particular the Victoria Bridge, which was at the time being erected in Water Lane. About 11 a.m. a large iron boiler was washed from the bank of the Monkpits by the force of the current, into Water Lane and carried away the temporary footbridge, which lodged against the new bridge and raised the water to a height of 5ft. Thankfully, the beautiful stone arch of the bridge was not affected and no people were on the temporary bridge at the time. However, much damage was inflicted on flax manufacturers in the area, when the flax was saturated with water. The Union Company suffered also, as the water rushed with tremendous force into the stables where there were several horses. Thankfully all the horses were rescued and sent to stables on higher ground. A great many dwelling houses in the town were deluged, and considerable damage sustained by the poorer inmates. Three gentlemen engaged a donkey cart to get them from Water Lane to Briggate, and when the beast became entangled in a hole, the three gentlemen and the driver were tumbled into the water. (*Leeds Mercury*)

November 25th

1864: A most interesting sight was seen in Leeds today, consisting of a fine new lifeboat and transporting carriage passing in procession throughout the town. The boat, which had been presented by the South Manchester branch of the Royal Lifeboat Society, arrived at noon at the central station. The boat was manned by a crew of ten men wearing cork life belts. The flag of the institute was hoisted, and the boat was drawn through the streets by six fine horses and a band of music. The procession was escorted by police who marched along the route along Queen Street from the Old Bank to the Town Hall, where an immense crowd had congregated, despite the rain which was coming down in torrents. Collections were made along the route and three cheers were given for the Corporation of Leeds. The boat remained on view at the Town Hall for about two hours, so that the people of Leeds could closely examine it and talk to the lifeboat men. At 2 p.m. the boat was taken to the Midland Station to continue on its journey to Bradford, where it was to be publicly exhibited the following day. (*Leeds Express*)

NOVEMBER 26TH

1869: Today a very respectable looking young man was brought into the court charged with embezzling £250 from his employer Messrs Robert Garside & Sons, millers and coal owners of Leeds. The man, William Henry Emmerson, was a traveller for the firm who was found to have not paid his employers some of the money that had been given to him by customers. Superintendent Hunt told the court that Emmerson had left Leeds the previous Friday, with a young girl named Foster. His employers, finding that the money was missing, had alerted the authorities that he had absconded to London. Superintendent Hunt communicated with Scotland Yard and from information received found out that the couple were intending to sail for Australia, as two tickets had been bought. A senior member of the firm, Mr Robert Garside, accompanied by Detective Northcliffe, went to Gravesend and found the young man on board the *Sea Chief* just as it was about to leave. The two young people were brought back to Leeds and most of the money was recovered from them. Mr Garside asked for leniency for Emmerson, who had been of good character up to the offence, and he was sentenced to nine months' imprisonment. (*Leeds Mercury*)

NOVEMBER 27TH

1841: Today's newspapers held a report of a gas explosion which had taken place the previous Wednesday evening. The reporter stated that: 'Considerable alarm was excited by an explosion of gas at No. 1, St James Street. The family had been annoyed all the afternoon from an escape of gas, but neglected to take any steps to have it remedied, until about half past five, when a person applied a light near a sink pipe in a cupboard, and an immediate explosion took place. The Gas Company's men were promptly at the place, and upon examination found the main pipe broken, which had been occasioned by the sinking of the ground after a branch drain from the house into the common sewer had been made by the Water Company. It is understood that the workmen neglected to support the main pipe in its original position. We think the above circumstance is a strong motive for increased *care* and *vigilance* on the part of the Water and Gas Companies, the former by the greatest care to prevent damage to the gas pipes, either from present breakage, or the subsequent settling of the ground; and the latter to use every possible care in having their mains and branches properly repaired and made secure when the trenches are open'. (*Northern Star*)

November 28th

1871: A letter to the Editor was printed in the *Leeds Mercury*, regarding the late closing time for the Market Hall. The letter requests: 'GENTLEMEN – In your last Saturdays' issue you inserted a letter signed "Justice" in which the writer states his opinion that, if the Market Hall was closed at 9 p.m. on Saturday nights instead of at the unreasonable hour of 11 p.m., the early closing of the shops would be sure to follow. This is not only the opinion of "Justice" but of nine tenths, if not all the shopmen of Leeds. If our worthy Mayor only knew with what eagerness they await a move from him in the matter, and with what deliverance from this unfair and cruel custom would mean, he should surely use his influence. There can hardly be anything urged in favour of keeping the Market Hall open after nine o'clock, for as the member of nearly all other tradesmen cease work and are paid early in the afternoon, they have ample time to make their purchases by nine. Hoping the matter will not be permitted to drop, but that those who have influence will see us righted. I remain, yours very truly A SUFFERER'. (*Leeds Mercury*)

NOVEMBER 29TH

1865: A shocking sanitary report, by Dr Hunter, was placed in the hands of the Corporation today. He had been asked by the Board of Health to investigate the state of the privies in the town. He stated that there was thousands of tons of filth filling the receptacles of the middens; scores of tons of it lay about and hundreds of people (long unable to use the middens because of the rising heap) were depositing it on the floors. Even when the filth was removed, it was deposited in immense quantities in a locality not far from the town centre. The drainage system was so defective that populous streets were not connected to the drains, and the midden filth went to outfalls into the River Aire, leaving it nothing better that an open drain. Dr Hunter remarked that 'the River Wharfe, and the place where the water supply for Leeds is drawn from, receives large and constantly increasing quantities of filth so I cannot but think that the water, if at present is wholesome it is of a very precarious wholesomeness, and I should think it greatly to be desired that the town of Leeds, wealthy and populous as it is, should derive its water supply from sources to which no reasonable suspicion of unwholesomeness or uncleanliness is attached'. (*Leeds Mercury*)

NOVEMBER 30TH

1863: A terrible accident occurred at the premises of Mr John Barran, a wholesale clothier of Alfred Street, Boar Lane, yesterday. 'The premises, which are four storeys in height, contain 160 young women as machinists. The top attic floor, due to a sloping roof, had less room for the sewing machines, so Mr Barran had decided to change it from a sloping to a flat roof. A large quantity of bricks and lime had been placed on the floor by workmen, who had started the work about a week ago, and this extra weight bore down on the feeble supports. As a result, the floor fell in on top of about forty young women working beneath. Six females, namely Emma Walker aged seventeen, Sarah Ann Phillips aged nineteen, Ellen Bouskill and Martha Balance both aged sixteen, Margaret Barry aged eighteen, and Mary Kelly aged twenty-four, were buried in the rubble. Emma Walker was the most seriously hurt and is not expected to live. The building has been erected some twenty-five to thirty years ago and had every appearance of being a strong, safe structure. However, the rafters – instead of being supported by joists – were placed on a thin piece of wood not more than an inch thick and three or four inches deep'. (*Leeds Mercury*)

December 1st

1832: It was announced that the recent epidemic of Cholera Morbis had come to an end in Leeds. The *Leeds Mercury* reported: 'The Board of Health sat today in a special meeting and it was expected that they will not have to meet again. The last two cases remaining under treatment at the previous sitting have now been reported as having recovered. The total number of cases of the cholera from the commencement on the 28th May is 1,817, out of which 702 have proved fatal and 1,115 have recovered'. A special meeting of the board was convened to consider the propriety of dissolving the board, now that the epidemic had passed, which was agreed. A resolution was also adopted to the effect that 'the Board of Health respectfully recommend to the inhabitants of Leeds, to observe Wednesday next, the 5th December, as a day of solemn thanksgiving to Almighty God for his merciful interposition in checking the ravages of the fatal disease, by which the town was lately visited and in having at length entirely removed it'. (*Leeds Intelligencer*)

DECEMBER 2ND

1811: It was announced today that the previous evening, the Lady Mayoress, according to the usual custom, gave her annual treat at the Mansion House 'to numerous assemblage of persons of fashion'. It was reported in the local newspapers that 'the tables were decorated with taste and displayed a great profusion of dainties that have ever been recorded before. A most excellent dinner was served up in the State Room consisting of every delicacy the season could afford and the dessert seemed culled from the greatest luxuries the Hot House could produce. We are pleased to announce that each visitor departed highly gratified with the hospitality of their hostess'. (*Leeds Intelligencer*)

1865: It was reported that the naked and unfinished appearance of the entrance to the front of the Town Hall was no longer to remain a matter for public complaint. The article stated that, 'the Corporation, at a special meeting today, granted the sum of £600 for providing four stone lions, to be placed on the vacant pedestals'. Two stone lions were erected on February 15th 1867, which measured 11ft in length, and 5ft 6in in height. The last two lions were erected on June 7th 1867, the total cost amounting to £550. (*Leeds Mercury*)

DECEMBER 3RD

1812: A reward was offered today in the *Leeds Mercury* for bringing the name of the person who committed Highway Robbery of the mail, two months previously, to the authorities. The culprit had not been found and a large reward was offered. The account read: 'About seven o'clock on the evening of Monday 30th October, the Leeds Mail Coach was robbed of sixteen bags of letters for London, between Kettering and Higham Ferrers, by forcing the lock of the Mail Box. Whoever shall apprehend the person or persons who committed the said robbery will be entitled to a reward of £200. One moiety to be paid on commitment for trial, and the other moiety on conviction. If an accomplice in the robbery will surrender himself and make discovery [give evidence], whereby one or more of the persons concerned therein shall be apprehended and brought to justice, such discoverer will be entitled to the said reward and be admitted as evidence for the Crown. By command of the Postmaster-General, F. Freeling, Secretary'. (*Leeds Mercury*)

DECEMBER 4TH

1875: A suspicious death at Armley was reported in the local newspapers. It was reported that last Tuesday, Michael Snee, who lived in Mistress Lane, Armley, was found dead in his own house. The evidence of his wife, sons and daughter-in-law was heard at the inquest held before the Leeds deputy coroner, Mr W. Emsley. All the witnesses in the house reported that on that night everyone was sober, apart from the deceased. They had gone to bed about 11 p.m. and there had been no quarrelling. About 8 a.m. the next day, the body of the dead man was found at the foot of the stairs, naked, apart from a shirt and stockings. Contrary evidence, however, was given by a police constable and one of the neighbours, stating that there had been loud quarrelling at the house around midnight. The surgeon gave evidence that the cause of death was a broken neck and he gave his opinion that it was broken by a fall. Superintendent Greenwood told the jury that the family had a very bad character and several of them were, at present, in custody. The jury was only retired briefly before giving a verdict of accidental death. (*Leeds Express*)

DECEMBER 5TH

1879: A meeting of the Leeds workhouse Guardians was held to discuss the amount of vagrants present in Leeds at the moment. One of the guardians, Mr Joseph Lupton, stated that in the nine weeks of October and November, an average of 410 vagrants were passing through the vagrant wards, and stated that 'in his eyes there must be something wrong'. He had found that the food they gave morning and evening, was a pint of gruel and 6oz of bread. For that they had to break 3 cwts of stones for the first night at the workhouse, and if they stayed a second night the amount was increased. Another guardian, Mr Wilson, stated that the matter had been subject to great scrutiny by the Workhouse Committee, and he felt that there was very little they could do. He remarked that 'it had always been the case that a vagrant that had no home, and no means of paying for a nights lodging, should be permitted to go into the vagrant ward'. He also said that, 'I for one should very strongly object to a tighter line, which would prevent a poor man, who had no place to go to, from entering the workhouse'. (*Leeds Mercury*)

DECEMBER 6TH

1886: At a meeting held tonight, the causes of the present trade depression were discussed by Mr H.T. Lawrence of London. 'The meeting, which was held at the Vegetarian Restaurant on Park Lane, was packed to hear the speaker, who attributed the trade depression to the demonetization of silver in 1874, and the consequent appreciation in the value of gold. Mr Lawrence provided statistics to support this view. He stated that unless some reform were effected in our systems of currency, the price of commodities and produce will fall to such an extent, that it would involve ruin for the majority of farmers, manufacturers and mining proprietors. It would clearly be in the interests of these groups, that silver should be placed on a fixed basis, relative to the gold standard; either through England alone or with a combination of other nations. The lecturer further went on to suggest that a British dollar, or four shilling piece, should be made of silver; the weight of which should be decided by the Government when they had purchased a sufficiency of silver for the purpose of this coinage. Through such action, the value of silver should rise to its normal proportions; its adoption as part of our legalized currency would confer immeasurable benefits upon our country'. (*Leeds Mercury*)

DECEMBER 7TH

1880: Today there was a report of a suspected case of abortion in Leeds. 'An inquiry was opened yesterday into the death of Ann Ingilby, aged twenty-four years, which had occurred last Sunday. The death happened at the house of her mother, Mrs Towler of North Street, and it appears that Mrs Ingilby had given birth to a child, the body of which had been concealed. The coroner, having been given information regarding the woman's death, directed a post-mortem to be held. It was found that the deceased had given birth at only four months gestation, and that the birth of the child was the consequence of an abortion. Mrs Ingilby had been married eight years ago, but was now living apart from her husband. Mrs Towler was too ill yesterday to give evidence and the case was adjourned for a week'. When the case was resumed, several witnesses were questioned, but, despite the fact that many of the witnesses seemed to be 'suppressing the facts', the surgeon stated that death was due to blood poisoning following an abortion, but that there was no evidence to show who was responsible. (*Leeds Daily News*)

DECEMBER 8TH

1862: Today at the Leeds Town Hall, Robert Pearson and James Kirk were charged with being involved in the robbery of the Aire and Calder Company's house, on Dock Street, on the night of November 21st. The agent, Mr McReady, gave evidence that he had locked the money away in the safe and had made sure that the premises were locked and secured when he left. In the morning he found that thieves had broken in and stole a total of £86 5os 2d. A lantern had been left by the thieves, and although the money had been taken, a bottle of gin and three bottles of wine had been left in a cupboard untouched. Pearson, who was a strong suspect, was arrested the same day and a warrant was issued against Samuel Spence and James Kirk. Pearson, who was only seventeen years of age and an ex-clerk at the works, told how he had planned the robbery with Spence and Kirk because he was familiar with where the keys were kept. Pearson was persuaded to turn Queens' Evidence against the other two men and he told how Spence had hidden himself in a closet until the premises were locked up. Both men were sent to take their trial at the assizes, where they were sentenced to six years penal servitude for their part in the robbery. (*Leeds Mercury*)

December 9th

1893: Last night the people of Leeds were invited to attend a lecture by Mr J. Keir Hardie MP, at the Coliseum, on the subject of 'Pensions for Nothing'. Mr Hardie, who had been invited to Leeds by the Leeds Sunday Lecture Society, appeared before an exceptionally large attendance. He stated that: 'Of all our population the poor aged people were treated the worse. In our society they are treated more like beggars than aged veterans of industry. I am aware that there were societies that looked after the aged people such as Trade Unions and Friendly Societies, but not enough was being done for them. The only reason they were unable to work was because of old age, and many became reliant on their sons or daughters for a living'. He referred to Mr Chamberlain's scheme, which proposed that each person who attained the age of twenty-one should deposit £5 with the state and go on paying £1 a year thereafter, until he reached the age of sixty-five, when he would become entitled to 5s a week for the remainder of his life. Loud applause greeted Mr Hardie at the end of his speech. (*Leeds Mercury*)

DECEMBER 10TH

1849: Today the Leeds courthouse heard a seemingly trivial story of two boys – aged fifteen and fourteen – attacking a Sunday school teacher, Mr Walker. The boys were brothers named Charles and Henry Westmoreland, who had gone to the school which was held at St Luke's Church on North Street. About 2.30 a.m. on the day in question, the teacher, Mr Walker, heard shouts coming from the yard and went outside to investigate. It was at this point Charles threw a stone at him and Henry attacked him with a stick. Mr Walker was assisted by a passing gentleman, but he summoned the boys for assault. When the case was heard by the court it seems that another brother, James Westmorland, had been severely beaten for misbehaving by a superintendent at Etches School, on October 14th, and he had died three weeks afterwards; the marks of the beating were still visible at the time of his death. The magistrate, Mr Bruce, defended the boys, and stated that any teacher or superintendent needed to maintain discipline, but not to beat a child to death. The magistrates consulted and then told the court, 'we cannot but regret this case has been brought here. We dismiss the charge'. (*Leeds Mercury*)

DECEMBER 11TH

1847: Today, a case was reported in the *Leeds Mercury* of a young woman aged twenty-one years, who was brought into the courtroom charged with the concealment of an illegitimate birth on November 21st last. The Chief Constable outlined the case for the magistrates. He told them that the woman, Martha Ellis, had given birth in a privy at a house in Kirkstall, which was owned by a woman named Robinson. Despite the fact that the prisoner had lodged at the house for six months previously, Robinson claimed that she did not know that Ellis was pregnant. The following morning, from indications given by a neighbour, the privy was searched and the body of a seven-month-old foetus was found. The surgeon, Mr Bishop, gave evidence that he had completed a post-mortem and gave his opinion that the child was free from any signs of violence, but it had been stillborn. Since the birth, the mother had been very ill and he gave that as the reason why the examination of the girl had been postponed. She was sent to take her trial at the assizes. At the next spring assizes, Ellis was found not guilty and discharged. (*Leeds Mercury*)

December 12th

1857: Mr Charles Thornton, the landlord of the White Swan Inn on Briggate, was brought before the bench, charged with allowing 'improper characters' to assemble in his house on the previous Friday night at midnight. Police officers Griffin and Simpson stated that on the night in question they were on duty in plain clothes and saw, standing at the bar, eight well-known prostitutes and some men who they knew as convicted thieves. Several of the parties were also well known to the landlord and had been pointed out to him on previous occasions. The defendant stated that he had done all in his power to prevent the evil complained of, but that the women rushed into his house when the theatre closed. He apologised for the oversight and promised to assist the police to keep the law in future. The bench remarked that it was their determination to prevent the assembling of bad characters in public houses of the town; but as the defendant had promised to assist the police they would only inflict the mitigating penalty (being a second offence) of 50s and costs. (*Leeds Express*)

DECEMBER 13TH

1859: An application for the protection of property was made at the Town Hall, on behalf of a Mrs Sarah Smith of Bread Street, York Road. Her solicitor, Mr Naylor, claimed that Mrs Smith and her husband had been married for several years, although Mr Smith had deserted her before on several occasions. Two months ago, whilst they were living at Bradford, her husband told her that her mother, who lived in Leeds, was ill and Mrs Smith came to the town, where she found her mother well. On returning back to Bradford she found that her husband had broken up the house and sold all the furniture. A day or two afterwards, he went to America and informed his wife to 'do the best she could as he had no intention of returning to her'. She told the bench that she did not have the letter as she had destroyed it in anger. The magistrates thought that under the circumstances an order could not be made, as the desertion had not been long enough, although Mrs Smith might apply again if her husband did not return. (*Leeds Mercury*)

DECEMBER 14TH

1816: The visit of Grand Duke Nicholas of Russia was reported in the *Leeds Mercury*. He was on a tour of Britain, following the defeat of Napoleon Bonaparte, with his older brother Alexander I, the Emperor of Russia. Breaking free of the royal party, Nicholas was more interested in visiting places of manufacture and industry in Britain. He came to Leeds on the evening of Monday December 9th, and spent the day accompanied by Sir William Congreave, after having spent some days with the Duke of Devonshire at Chatsworth. Early on Tuesday morning, he walked through the Cloth Hall, and from there proceeded to inspect several manufactories and foundries of the city before seeing the 'steam-impelled machine' on the railway of the collieries of J.C. Brandling Esq. The Grand Duke appeared to be much gratified and frequently expressed himself in terms of admiration for the industries which he visited. His Royal Highness was described as 'being between 20 and 30 years of age, of good figure and with a handsome prepossessing countenance and extremely affable in his deportment'. In his suite were several Russians of distinction, including Baron Nicolay, General Koutousoff, and General Sarnatoff with their Aides de Camp etc. At 4 p.m. he left Leeds to visit Harewood House for dinner with the venerable Earl. (*Leeds Mercury*)

DECEMBER 15TH

1934: After a retirement of only two hours today, the jury at the West Riding Assizes at Leeds found David Maskill Blake, an unemployed steel erector of Lady Pit Lane, Leeds, guilty of the wilful murder of Emily Yeomans. The girl had been found strangled with her own scarf in Middleton Woods on October 16th; Blake was sentenced to death. It was alleged that Blake had met the girl on the night when she was last seen alive, and killed her. He was married the next day to a girl employed as a waitress at another café. In passing sentence, Mr Justice Goddard said that Blake, 'after a long and patient trial, had been found guilty of a cruel, treacherous and brutal a murder as any in many years experience of law I had ever come across. I have nothing to say except that in my judgement the verdict is most aptly warranted by the evidence, and I fully agree with it'. The judge went on to praise the detective department of the City of Leeds police force, who, with little to work on, succeeded in bringing the culprit to justice. (*The Times*)

DECEMBER 16TH

1688: Rumours were heard in Leeds last night, that the many thousands of Irish troops who had been brought over by King James and since been disbanded, were 'ravaging the country and slaying and burning all before them'. The Mayor's account of this day states that: 'Watch and ward are kept every night by the principal inhabitants in their own persons and dispatches are sent to bring intelligence from diver's places. So that on Monday there were assembled at Leeds, about seven thousand horse and foot in defence of their lives and liberties, religion and property, against those barbarous and inhuman wretches… Our fears were realised when last night all upon the sudden the most dreadful alarm was heard and shouts of "the enemy is upon us". The drum began to beat and the bells rang, whilst men left all behind them (even monies and plate upon the table) and wives who ran for shelter to the barns and haystacks in the field'. Thousands of men were mustered in the town with their horses prepared to fight the invader, but, thankfully, it was later proved to be a false alarm. (Robinson, P., *Leeds Old and New*, Leeds, S.R. Publishers Ltd, 1972)

December 17th

1865: The Bishop of Ripon presided over the first annual meeting of the Leeds Ladies' Sanitary Association. The chief object of the society, as explained in the Committee's report, was to endeavour to improve the dwellings and the condition of the poor, by spreading amongst them knowledge of sanitary matters. During the year they had distributed 3,000 tracts upon topics such as; the use of sunlight, fresh air and regular exercise ,and cleanliness. In order to achieve the latter, the ladies of the Committee had supplied to the poor soap, lime, brushes, etc. for cleansing their dwellings. The Bishop of Ripon said that he was delighted to hear that the Committee had contemplated the organisation of a course of lectures next year, on subjects coming within the scope of the object for which the society was formed. They thanked the people of Leeds who had offered their support to this cause, and they appealed to the inhabitants for increased support over the next few years. They further urged that the town council provide improved dwellings, which should be erected for the working classes, and that a medical officer of health should be appointed. Resolutions were adopted approving of the objects of the association, and commending it to the more enlarged sympathy of the public. (*Leeds Express*)

DECEMBER 18TH

1673: It was ordered on this date that, 'the commission appointed to enquire into the administration of the several charities within the borough of Leeds, should appoint trustees for the management thereof'. It was also ordered that 'all deeds and writings relating thereto, should be safely laid up in a strong chest, to be provided for that purpose, in the registry of the Parish Church of Leeds, which chest shall be locked with three keys. These documents, with others collected by the corporation, and many of a later date, are deposited in an iron safe in the vestry of St Peter's Church, secured by three separate locks, of which one key is kept by the mayor, another by the vicar and a third by the churchwardens'. (Mitchell, W.R., *A History of Leeds*, Chichester, Phillimore, 2000)

───── • ◆ • ─────

1858. 'A dinner was given tonight at Mr James Long's Red Lion Inn, by the sergeants recruiting in Leeds at the moment, to Sergeant Joseph Oates on his retirement from the 68th Light Infantry. Sergeant Oates is intending to join the recruiting staff of Her Majesty's Indian Force. He filled the position of Sergeant Major of the recruiting party for about four years and has gained the good will of all who knew him'. (*Leeds Mercury*)

December 19th

1913: It was reported that 'the municipal strike of the trams have become distinctly graver'. *The Observer* reported that: 'So many attacks have been made on trams that mounted police were called out this afternoon. By design they came from different routes, but such crowds collected as they went along the road that poured together in one mass. One or two of the mounted men took their horses onto the pavements in an attempt to clear the crowd and they were roundly booed and hissed at. Policemen are very many in the town, as they have been drafted in from other forces such as Hull, Bradford and Huddersfield. The men who are running an emergency tram service are made up of clerks, tram inspectors, a few regular men and lads who look like they have just come from a farm. Clerks are also carrying out lamplighters duties at dusk'. It was also reported that 1,500 men went to Victoria Square for a meeting this morning, and then walked to Woodhouse Moor. A resolution was called for the civic authorities to enter into negotiations to end the strike and to arrive at a satisfactory settlement. (*The Observer*)

DECEMBER 20TH

1876: The local papers reported on a case of adulterated milk by a Leeds woman named Jane Forbert. She was accused of selling a quart of milk, which had been diluted, in direct contravention of the Adulteration of Food Act. The woman was a milk dealer of Greenfield Road, Bank, and she was summoned before the magistrate Mr Bruce. The certificate of the Borough analyst showed that the milk, which had been purchased from her, was adulterated with water to the extent of 10 per cent, together with a small amount of sugar and other ingredients. Mrs Forbert denied the charge, saying that she had bought the milk from the wholesalers in good faith, and in that same condition. Mr Bruce considered that, although the case was a bad one for poor people, on the other hand, small dealers ought not to be made responsible at all times for the probable act of wholesale dealers. The defendant was convicted of the charge, but judgement was reserved for a month. Mr Bruce warned her that if such a case was brought before him again, committed by her, he would have no choice but to deal with it very severely. (*Leeds Mercury*)

DECEMBER 21ST

1867: It was reported that the overseers of Holbeck workhouse distributed thirty-six pairs of blankets, twenty cotton quilts, twenty pairs of sheets, fifty petticoats and 900 yards of calico, to poor families of the parish, at a cost of around £51. It was reported that the funds, which paid for these donations to the deserving poor, was discovered when the overseers found that a man named Henry Metcalf of Holbeck, had left two fields of about four acres in extent in Oldfield Lane, for the benefit of the poor many years previously. Henry Metcalf had stated that the gift was to be given to the poor in the form of warm clothing, to be distributed at Christmas time. The overseers found that soil in the four acres of land had contained valuable minerals, and in order to make more money out of the estate, applied to the Charity Commission to sell the land, which was granted. The sale of the land had brought in £1,127 10s 6d and it was agreed that they would invest this in Consols, which that year had made a total of £44. The overseers added £10 in order to give warm clothing to 120 of the poor of the township. (*Leeds Express*)

DECEMBER 22ND

1874: A tragic case of death by starvation was heard in Leeds. The inquest on the body of Rose Reynolds, aged sixty-one, was heard before Mr W. Emsley, the Leeds deputy coroner, at the Blue Bell Inn, Warwick Street. The daughter of the deceased stated that her mother, Mrs Reynolds, had lived with her on Millwright Street, Leyland, Leeds. She told the coroner that she had been forced to support herself, her mother, and her child on an income of 9s a week. Out of that she had to pay 3s 2d a week for rent and this left very little for food. The deceased, who had been ill for some time, had had no other food apart from bread and tea during the past three months. Mrs Reynolds appeared to be in no pain, but she was found dead in bed on Saturday morning. The jury were of the opinion that she had died from the want of proper support, and returned a verdict accordingly. It appeared that the deceased had a son, who had been in the army, but who had done nothing towards supporting his mother. The coroner castigated him for his callous behaviour towards his mother. (*Leeds Mercury*)

DECEMBER 23RD

1871: Mr Wetherall, the Chief Constable of Leeds, read out his annual report today to the Watch Committee, and it was reported in the local newspaper. He stated that: 'There is a general decrease in crime in the borough and the number of bad characters of various sorts in Leeds has decreased from 804 in 1870, to 520 in 1871. Of 90 persons who were sentenced to police supervision and who came out of prison last September, only 31 have relapsed into crime. As regards the proportion of more serious offences, Leeds still compares favourably with other large towns. The proportion of committals to offences is lower than last year, but the percentage of convictions on committals is much higher'. Mr Wetherall likewise notes, 'a decrease of 20.3 per cent in the number of offences disposed of summarily and notes that the number of charges of drunkenness has fallen from 1,940 to 1,612'. He told the members of the Watch Committee that he believed the reduction of the criminal convictions had much to do with the improvement in the conduct of public houses and beerhouse; it was thought that they had greatly reduced and regulated the incidents of drunkenness. (*Leeds Mercury*)

DECEMBER 24TH

1853: A blind man named Michael Cook, who said he was a native of America but had lived many years in England, was charged at the Leeds Town Hall with vagrancy today. It was alleged that he had stood in the market place with a begging petition before him, and that he had with him a lame wife who walked upon crutches. The magistrate, Mr Armitage, told the court that he had seen the parties in the street and had ordered them to be brought to the courthouse, and for the case to be investigated. Another magistrate, Mr Bruce, stated that he thought that as paupers they ought to be maintained by their parish, rather than to be allowed to beg in the streets. The prisoner said that he had walked to Leeds from Bradford, and if the magistrate would dismiss the charge, he would leave the town at once. The justices sent him to prison for seven days and intimated that if other parties were brought up for similar offences, they should inflict a much heavier punishment. Mr Armitage told the court that 'he was determined to stamp out mendicancy in the streets of the town'. *(Leeds Mercury)*

DECEMBER 25TH

1887: It was reported that last evening the people of Leeds were treated to a concert by Mr Sam Hague's minstrels from Liverpool. The engagement, which was expected to extend over the Christmas holidays, were appearing at the Coliseum and it was thought that there was little doubt that Mr Hague would make a favourable impression, as he did on his previous visit to Leeds. Although the programme was reported to be 'an old one', nevertheless, it was very effectively rendered. 'There is the usual variety of Christy minstrels consisting of pretty ballads, rousing comic songs, dancing and an abundance of humour and fun. One may detect a weak member among the vocalists, but the efforts of Mr Billy Richardson, and his oration of Mr Tom Beet in his banjo eccentricities, would cover a multitude of defects. The medley closed last night with "Plantation Pastimes", or "Massa Georges Birthday" which affords the whole company much amusement'. Mr Sam Hague was applauded loudly, and at the close of the performance the audience shouted encore several times before the show ended. (*Leeds Express*)

DECEMBER 26TH

1864: This evening a Frenchman of extraordinary height and bulk exhibited himself at the Music Hall, Leeds. Monsieur Joseph Brice, known as 'the modern Goliath', was described thus: 'His deportment is at once affable and kind, and be has an agreeable expression of countenance, indicative of goodness of disposition and an average amount of intelligence. As to his size, he is a giant in every sense of the word, being, though only 24 years of age, eight feet high, and 30 stones weight. He is a remarkably well-built man. His proportions are good; his features agreeable and his manner gentlemanly and pleasing. The tallest gentleman in the room passed under his arm, when extended horizontally, without touching it and the largest hand in the room bore about the same relation to the giant's that a child's hand would bear to that of a full-grown man. His parents, who are still living, are respectable hard-working normal sized farmers, and there was nothing in their constitution that they would have a giant son. He also has three brothers and two sisters, who are slightly less than the average size'. (*Leeds Express*)

DECEMBER 27TH

1876: In connection with a series of lectures at the Leeds Church Institute, Archdeacon Wright gave an address on Church Missions in North America, this evening. The lecturer spoke mainly about the early work of the Church in America, who had been assailed by the Puritans and all who differed from them. Even worse, he told them, 'they had murdered the Indians, who they pretended to trade with, as well as many of their chiefs. But the main cause of the Church languishing in North America, at that time, was attributable to the lack of Episcopal care and the isolated position of many of the missionaries. They were, in many cases, the representatives of a body of foreigners across the ocean, who offered support and direction and it had been found that in America it was a dismal failure. Again and again appeals were made to the Mother Church to consecrate bishops, but nothing was done. At length came the revolt of the American colonies, out of which arose better days for the Church; for soon after the close of the war, the first Bishop of America was consecrated at Aberdeen, by the Bishops of the Scotch Episcopal Church.' Archdeacon Wright was warmly applauded for the success of his lecture. (*Leeds Mercury*)

DECEMBER 28TH

1856: Today, a melancholy suicide was heard about in Leeds, in consequence of the body of a young man being found in a field at Lofthouse. The man was an assistant to Messrs Bilbrough, druggists of Briggate, and he was twenty years of age. The day before, he had omitted to send a parcel to Beech Grove Terrace, and his employer asked him to deliver it in person on Friday night. Near to the body was an empty phial which had contained prussic acid. It seems that the man had been in low spirits for a fortnight, following a female making a disgraceful accusation against him. Despite this, he had been a steady and industrious young man, who had lodged for the past two and a half years at Mr Manns, of Guildford Street. A letter was found in his warehouse coat which read: 'My mind is affected with things to no good that I am disposed to destroy myself. What a thing it is to be steady and industrious. I am ruined for life. May the Lord have mercy on my poor soul. I am afraid of the things of this world'. A later inquest held on the body returned a verdict of 'poisoned himself during temporary insanity'.
(*Leeds Intelligencer*)

DECEMBER 29TH

1876: The traditional Christmas gathering for the boys at the Leeds Industrial School took place. 'The schoolboys and old scholars – who have been discharged from the school in Great Garden Street over the last four years, and who are now in situations in and around the town, were also present. The headmaster told them that he was delighted to see some of his old scholars once again. There was a tea provided and afterwards a highly entertaining concert was performed. The schoolchildren, under the direction of Mr John Humphreys, the principle tenor at York Minster, gave a powerful rendition of "Men of Harlech". This was followed by the "Shoeblack Song" which was received with a storm of applause. Recitations were given by some of the boys, which showed considerable power of memory. During the course of the evening, thanks were given by the ex-Mayor, Alderman Croft, who told the assembled crowd that the school had been started by the munificence of Mr Glover Joy, and since its foundation, between 2,000 and 3,000 boys had passed through it, many going on to a successful and useful career in life'. (*Leeds Mercury*)

DECEMBER 30TH

1839: Today, two men were brought before the Leeds magistrate charged with committing a brutal and unprovoked attack upon Joshua Hainsworth – a watchman. 'The assault had been inflicted on this poor man in the early hours of Christmas morning, by James Brewer and Samuel Harrison. The prisoners, who were disturbing the neighbourhood of Lady Lane, were requested by Hainsworth to go peaceably home. Instead of doing as he requested, they took his stick and his staff and knocked him to the floor. They then proceeded to kick and beat him so severely that he has since been an in-patient at the Leeds Infirmary. The magistrates censured the men for their behaviour on that special day, and deplored the violence which had been inflicted on a man who was simply doing his duty. He fined the delinquents £4 10s each and costs; in default of payment they were committed to the Wakefield House of Correction for two months'. (*Leeds Mercury*)

DECEMBER 31ST

1872: It was recorded that John Masterman, one of the few remaining Waterloo veterans, had died, aged seventy-five, at his residence in Headingley, Leeds. The deceased had been a sergeant in the Royal Horse Artillery, and had been in receipt of a service pension since 1815. He had been an orderly sergeant to His Grace the Duke of Wellington, and had been wounded in four places at the Battle of Waterloo. It was reported that 'so serious were his injuries that on that memorable occasion, he was supposed to have been killed. Some fellow soldiers were indeed in the act of carrying him away to be buried with the dead, when a spent shot smashed the board on which he was being carried. As he fell to the ground, the shock so caused, revived to some extent his vital powers, and a bugler, who happened to pass at that very moment, saw the wounded sergeant was still in life, and secured for him the benefit of medical assistance, after which he recovered'. Mr Masterman returned back to his home town in triumph, along with other soldiers from Leeds, to receive a civic welcome. Gradually his fellow soldiers of that great battle had died as the memory of the battle disappeared. (*Leeds Express*)

BIBLIOGRAPHY

BOOKS

Feather, J.W., *Leeds: The Heart of Yorkshire*, Leeds, Basil
 Jackson Publications, 1967
Milner, L., *Leeds Pals*, Leeds, Pen and Sword Books Ltd, 1998
Mitchell, W.R., *A History of Leeds*, Chichester, Phillimore, 2000
Read, D., *Press and People 1790–1850 Opinion in Three
 English Cities*, London, Edward Arnold, 1961
Robinson, P., *Leeds Old and New*, Leeds, Wakefield, S.R.
 Publishers Ltd, 1972
Thornton, D., *Leeds: The Story of a City*, Ayr, Fort, 2002

NEWSPAPERS

Leeds Daily News
Leeds Express
Leeds Intelligencer
Leeds Mercury
Leeds Times
Manchester Guardian
Northern Star
The Guardian
The Observer
The Times
York Herald